LAS VEGAS

Not surprisingly, Las Vegas can be seen from space. Las Vegas News Bureau

FIRST EDITION

LAS VEGAS

Crystal Wood
and Leah Koepp

The Courtryman Press
Woodstock, Vermont

Las Vegas: Great Destinations
ISBN 978-1-58157-075-5

Interior photographs by the authors unless otherwise specified
Maps by Erin Greb Cartography © The Countryman Press
Monorail map courtesy of Las Vegas Monorail
Book design by Bodenweber Design
Composition by Christine Cantera Design

Published by The Countryman Press, P.O. Box 748, Woodstock, VT 05091

Distributed by W. W. Norton & Company, Inc., 500 Fifth Avenue, New York, NY 10110

Printed in the United States of America

10 9 8 7 6 5 4 3 2 1

GREAT DESTINATIONS TRAVEL GUIDEBOOK SERIES

Recommended by *National Geographic Traveler* and *Travel + Leisure* magazines

A crisp and critical approach, for travelers who want to live like locals.
—*USA Today*

Great Destinations™ guidebooks are known for their comprehensive. critical coverage of regions of extraordinary cultural interest and natural beauty. Each title in this series is continuously updated with each printing to ensure accurate and timely information. All the books contain more than one hundred photographs and maps.

Current titles available:

The authors in this series are professional travel writers who have lived for many years in the regions they describe. Honest and painstakingly critical, full of information only a local can provide, Great Destinations guidebooks give you all the practical knowledge you need to enjoy the best of each region.

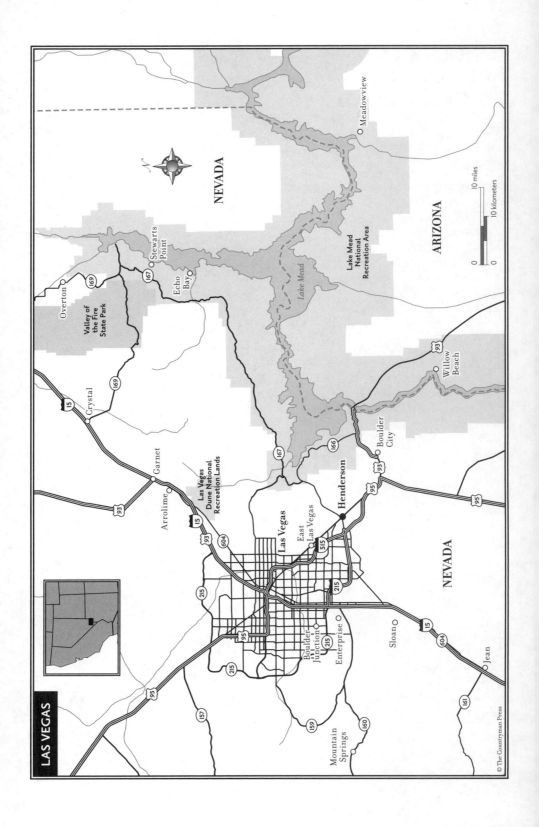

Contents

ACKNOWLEDGMENTS

No matter how well we know and love Las Vegas, we couldn't have researched and visited it and written this book without the help and support of so many folks. A tidal wave of media requests on Las Vegas hits public relations and marketing folks each and every day. Thanks to every public relations individual and firm that helped us get the details we needed. Special thanks to Ginny Poehing and Alicia Malone at the Las Vegas Convention and Visitors Authority.

We would also like to express eternal gratitude to Kim Grant of The Countryman Press. Thanks to her, we got to do something we'd always wanted to do—speak well of our beloved and often misunderstood hometown.

—CW & LK

It is a true test of love and friendship when people help you to work on and finish a book without any regard for what they will get out of it. Without these selfless family and friends, this book may have never made it. Thanks to my husband, Ricky, for allowing me to put other needs on a back burner and push me when I needed it. Thanks to my mom, Bonnie, for taking over as Nana on each trip. Thanks to Cliff for graciously opening up his home to us. Thanks to Monica for jumping in when we needed her to. To Bryce and Sylvia, thanks for your expert advice. And to our dearest friend, Charo, who answered the call to duty more times than can be counted, thanks, Lady.

—CW

Many loving thanks to my husband, Rod, and my son, Nick, for putting up with long hours of writing and research. I appreciate their understanding on those nights when I had a late show or dinner to attend, and for supporting Crystal and me in seeing this book through. Words can't express my thanks to my oldest and dearest friend and coauthor, Crystal Wood, for bring me on board in the writing of this book, and then for taking on, without hesitation or complaint, so much of the work of completing it in the face of an unexpected, life-changing event that severely curtailed my contribution to and participation in this project. Extra-special thanks to our great friend Charo Burke and her son, Riley Molina, for their willingness to help with research at a moment's notice. They lent many hours of their time and offered awesome observation and reporting skills to our project; their contributions were invaluable and very much appreciated.

—LK

How to Use This Book

Las Vegas changes more rapidly than any other city in the United States. The new shows, restaurants, attractions, and properties that constantly join the landscape make it impossible for a book to be absolutely up to date. Should there be an attraction you're interested in that isn't listed in the book, it's best to ask the Las Vegans you meet. Any individual that you make a connection with is going to give you an unsolicited opinion. Las Vegans have seen and been to it all, and they know their stuff.

Dining Prices
(per person including appetizer or dessert, and entree, but excluding drinks, tax and tip)

Inexpensive:	Up to $20
Moderate:	$20 to $35
Expensive:	$35 to $75
Very Expensive:	$75 and up

Lodging Prices

Inexpensive:	Under $50 per night
Moderate:	$50 to $100 per night
Expensive:	$100 to $150 per night
Very Expensive:	$150 and above per night.

ORGANIZATION

The ten chapters of this book are fairly straightforward, but as each travel destination has its own quirks and personality, a bit of explanation may be helpful. Chapter 1 is a speedy history of Las Vegas, a very young city. Due to the city's fondness for literally blowing up its past and reinventing itself, most visitors won't get to see much surviving history. Chapter 2 focuses on the few ways of getting from one end of the Strip to the other, and of getting out of town, too.

Lodging is the concentration of Chapter 3, but don't expect details about hair dryers and cable channels. Most Vegas vacations aren't spent in one's room. And because the Strip's most frequented and largest properties are owned by the same few companies, there isn't much difference in basic amenities offered at many resorts. What we have included is information on each resort's location and details that will help you to make informed decisions about your stay in Las Vegas.

Chapters 4 and 5 are about what to do in Las Vegas, both on and off the Strip, respectively. This way those with or without a car don't have to wade through what isn't needed. Also, pay close attention to the locales of your interests. This way is there is less time spent going back to the Bellagio to see their decorated conservatory even though you were just there last night to view the fountains.

The shows described in Chapter 6 are not intended to be reviews or personal opinions. The descriptions are given so that you can make your own judgment before purchasing the ticket. If there is a show that isn't included here that you're thinking about seeing and on which you'd like someone's opinion, ask the locals. Your waiter, bellman, or dealer can be a wealth of information, and they're happy to help. One thing you'll find—most Las Vegans' favorite topic of discussion is Las Vegas itself.

The restaurants in Chapter 7, as well as the stores and malls in Chapter 9, are organized by On the Strip and Off the Strip. Restaurants around the city are grouped by the area of the town in which they lie.

You'll notice that there's one aspect of a Vegas vacation we haven't covered in this book, and that's gaming. We feel that this is one subject that is best left to the experts, of which there are many, and each expert has their own opinions and methods. Detailed writing on all forms of gambling can be found at the Gambler's Book Shop (Chapter 9). Or if basic rules are all you need to hit the tables, ask at your hotel. Many offer free demonstrations on 21, craps, and roulette. If you're new to gambling, consider heading downtown or out to one of the "locals" casinos found around town, such as the Gold Coast, the Orleans, or any of the Station casinos. Here dealers are likely to be more helpful and the minimum bet is lower. Most importantly, remember that gambling is supposed to be entertaining. If it stops being fun, it's time to walk away. If you or anyone you're with needs help with a gambling problem, please contact Gamblers Anonymous at 888-442-2110.

INTRODUCTION

In August of 1973, I was too young to have any say about our move from Los Angeles to Las Vegas. It was all my father's idea. Being the drummer for pop idol Tony Orlando and Dawn meant spending a lot of time in Las Vegas. His idea was if we lived where he so often performed, it would be better for all three of us. Less than three months later, he left us. Luckily, we were in a town where a single mom could support herself and her daughter. So began my unusual Las Vegas childhood.

I didn't realize how odd growing up there was until many years later. Although throughout my childhood, countless silly questions and assumptions were made.

"No, my mom is not a showgirl."

"No, we don't live in a hotel or casino."

"Yes, people actually live in Las Vegas."

I also fielded questions about the mob and was told that I seemed pretty normal for being from such a mysterious place. As the years would pass and the city grew and grew, the Las Vegas veil of intrigue began to lift. But never entirely.

In time, I came to enjoy the incredulous looks and raised eyebrows that my childhood yarns elicited. At 23, my mom started as a keno runner at the Flamingo. Her bosses offered to "find your husband and bring him back" to keep her from crying. She promptly declined. The same bosses threw a Christmas party exclusively for the children of their employees complete with a sit-down meal and live entertainment. I was thrilled to see the Candyman, Sammy Davis Jr., on the stage. When I was 9 years old, I "played" keno in the Riviera coffee shop to keep entertained. That is, I marked the numbers and my mom gave the card and money to the runner. A few times, I got enough numbers right and won another game. Then, I got enough right numbers to win over $100. It was the first and last time I ever won at gambling.

The idea that all Las Vegas residents must partake in at least one of its vices isn't at all true. If it was so, then no one would have ever had the rent on time. Even though my mom was in the first wave of female blackjack dealers hired on The Strip, I don't enjoy or care about the tables. There are many who move to Las Vegas and can't handle the 24-hour bars or the easily accessible live gaming. Most of them had these tendencies in their hometown as well.

I often have to defend Las Vegas and do so vehemently. To me, it was truly a democratic city where a quick-learning hard worker could realistically achieve the American Dream, no matter their bloodline or education. Sadly, the corporatization of the Las Vegas casinos and the bank/mortgage fiasco have changed this somewhat, but this town, having finally fully come into its own in recent years despite having been born out of dust, rock, and hardpan, will always draw those seeking a better way of life. Las Vegas is as much a fighter as the people who settled it, and who continue to build it.

There is nothing more grating than to hear your home state pronounced incorrectly. Nevada is consistently pronounced the wrong way. In fact, it's the most mispronounced state in the nation. The word "nevada" is Spanish for snow-capped and pronounced "neh-va (like "cat") dah." Valerie Fridland, a linguistics professor at University Nevada Reno (UNR), has been on radio and television news talking about this very subject. This was

The now-iconic sign may be dwarfed by its neighbors, but it's more popular than ever. Las Vegas News Bureau.

after George Bush Jr., Joe Lieberman, Howard Dean, and George Stephanopoulos all pro-nounced it incorrectly while speaking from Nevada.

Some people think they know Las Vegas from watching television and movies. But since when does Hollywood get anything right? Besides, most of what's shown is what we portray, not who we are. The cocktail waitress is married, has a family, and shows dogs. The craps dealer has a college degree in an elite discipline that he detested. Visitors believing the hype and not knowing about the normal, mundane lives Las Vegans lead is how it's supposed to work. You've come to escape your everyday existence in the same place we eke out ours. It's okay. Treat us nicely and we're happy to say it with you: "It's Vegas, baby!"

Las Vegas's Welcome Sign in its original location and with an empty backdrop. Las Vegas News Bureau

1

HISTORY

Overview

Las Vegas, Spanish for "the meadows," is located in the most southern county in Nevada. The city is located in the Mojave Desert, an arid region of the United States that spans multiple states and is encircled by mountain ranges on all sides. The name "the meadows," though a bit incongruous now, accurately described the city's early beginnings, as the area that is Las Vegas was once known and sought out by travelers for its lush, verdant landscape and abundant water sources.

Beginning thousands of years ago, the Las Vegas area became a home to various native peoples, but they each quickly vanished and all that remains of their cultures are relics and many unanswered questions. As time progressed into the modern era, the Las Vegas Valley became an oasis for travelers and a whistle-stop for the railroads. It was settled by Mormons. The city was finally established, and it was, as it is even now, one of the most isolated large cities in the lower 48 states.

Despite its distance from its closest neighbor, Los Angeles, which is about 270 miles away, people came to live in Las Vegas, and the area began to grow. Homes, churches, and schools were built in the city, and the Valley's precious water was drained by its unprecedented growth. Las Vegas prospered thanks to its controversial industry—gambling. Many colorful but historically significant characters moved to Las Vegas, taking advantage of its legalized gambling to make their fortunes, and, in a few instances, hide from their criminal pasts. The city continued to grow, and its status as an adult playground became legendary. Las Vegas is a resort town with a rich, colorful history that attracts visitors from around the world and is now home to a local population of more than 2 million residents.

THE NATIVE PEOPLES
The Clovis Lead the Way

About 11,000 years ago, at the close of the Ice Age, the Las Vegas Valley was first inhabited by the Clovis peoples. Though they were nomads who lodged at different sites throughout North and South America, the Clovis peoples lived, albeit temporarily, in the northern area of Las Vegas now known as Floyd Lamb Park at Tule Springs. They hunted the local animals and foraged for plants that lined the numerous springs, streams, and lakes of the then-fertile region. In the 1920s, the archaeologist Mark Harrington described the area at the time of the Clovis as "green and well-watered." When the Clovis moved on, they left behind

Petroglyphs from 3,000 years ago found at Valley of Fire. Las Vegas News Bureau

crude stone tools and charred bones of mammoths, native horses, large buffalo, giant sloths, and other creatures now extinct.

The Lake Mojave People Move In and Adapt

The people who next took up residence in the Las Vegas Valley were the Lake Mojave (pronounced Mo-ha-vee) people about 9,000 years ago. They, too, sustained themselves on the meats of the local animals and gathered the seeds of natural vegetation as food sources for many years, but the area became increasingly arid. As the water sources dried up, the Lake Mojave culture is believed to have evolved into what experts call the Pinto Basin culture, about 7,500 to 4,000 years ago, and the people moved to sites with more water, successfully adapting their lives to the transforming region.

The Gypsum People, the Sophisticates

The Gypsum people, who next moved into the area, lasted until approximately 1,500 years ago, and lived during a time of high precipitation and plentiful plant life. Their residence in the region marked a time of great cultural and human evolvement; the Gypsums are known for the sophisticated stone tools they used for milling seeds and their refined weaponry for hunting. Like the cultures that came before them, they, too, left behind clues about their lives in the Las Vegas Valley. Using sharp stones or tools, they etched images into the walls of caves in the nearby Overton area. These petroglyphs record their history, including their transition from throwing spears to using the more effective bow and arrow for hunting small game.

Moving In—The Virgin Anasazi Make Their Way

The Gypsum people were no longer alone when the Virgin Anasazi moved into the territory along the Muddy and Virgin River Valleys near current-day Overton, a town 65 miles north of Las Vegas in the northern Las Vegas Valley. Related to the Anasazi tribe of the Four Corners area, the Virgin Anasazi built small permanent pueblos. Unlike any other known native peoples before them, they also made pottery and practiced agriculture; grew beans, corn, and squash; and even began salt and turquoise mining operations. The Anasazi successfully participated in a larger trading network with their Four Corners counterparts for many years. However, they abandoned the area in the 12th century, creating what is now known as the "Lost City." Some experts speculate that their trading networks collapsed or that a drought set in, but the exact reasons for their departure remain unknown.

The Southern Paiutes Find a Permanent Home

One of sixteen bands of the larger Paiute tribe that spread through Southern Nevada, southwestern Utah, northwestern Arizona, and southeastern California, the Las Vegas Paiutes were a largely independent band comprised of several families. The Nipakanticimi or the "people of Charleston Peak," as they called themselves, the Southern Paiutes resided in the Las Vegas Valley for centuries and were the first native peoples encountered by European explorers when they first arrived in the area in the 1820s. Initially hunters and gatherers, they rotated through camps in Las Vegas, Indian Springs, Ash Meadows, and Cotton Island along the Colorado River as they followed the harvesting cycles of the various edible plants. The Southern Paiutes were known for their basket-making skills and used

Enuintsigaip—whose name means "one of the ancients"—was a Paiute guide from the Las Vegas area on a Colorado River survey expedition (1873). Library of Congress

their handiwork to store water and food, aid in food preparation, and assist in the trans-porting of goods. The Southern Paiute culture and the European settlers who eventually established themselves in their area did not always live peacefully, and the Southern Paiutes eventually settled on 10 acres of land off Main Street, now known as the Las Vegas Indian Colony. The Southern Paiute people were well suited to survive in the in the arid desert, and they still live and work in the Las Vegas Valley today.

THE EUROPEANS ARRIVE

On the Map

Explorers generally avoided the Southern Nevada, Southwestern Utah, and Southern California region because of its hot desert climate, which proved inhospitable to travelers. The area remained largely unexplored by Europeans until 1829, when Antonio Armijo, a New Mexico merchant, and his party embarked upon a journey to reach California from New Mexico on a route now known as the Spanish Trail. Rafael Rivera, a young scout sent ahead of Armijo's party in search of water, guided the group as they traveled along the Colorado River, into the Las Vegas Valley, then south to nearby Jean, on to Goodsprings, crossing the Pahrump Valley, and through the Mojave Desert to Los Angeles. Rafael's dis-covery of the unlikely oasis, with its wild grasses and fresh, abundant water, as provided by two natural springs in a dry region, inspired him to name the area Las Vegas, translated from Spanish as "the meadows."

The area was the perfect location for a much-needed respite on their long journey, and the explorers added Las Vegas to their maps before moving onward. This new revelation would soon be shared with other would-be travelers. They, like those who soon followed, visited one Paiute watering locale after another, often to the dismay of the Southern Paiutes, who began to retreat farther away from the visitors.

Renowned explorer John C. Fremont, the famed adventurer who explored and mapped much of the American West, camped in the area in May 1844 and made notes of the oasis in the desert. His journal, which was eventually published, brought westbound travelers following his path to the area.

THE MORMONS ARRIVE

Missionaries, Mining, and Abandonment

Members of the Church of Jesus Christ of Latter-Day Saints (Mormons) settled in Salt Lake City in 1847 and eventually moved south to settle in the Las Vegas area. The Mormons first arrived in 1849 and finally settled in 1855 on Paiute lands. Las Vegas proved to be an inte-gral spot along the Mormon Trail that terminated in the group's settlement in San Bernardino, California, and the Paiutes, who disliked contact with others outside their tribe, adjusted their food gathering and housing efforts to avoid contact and, ultimately, confrontation with the Mormons. However, the missionaries were tasked with establishing good ties with the Southern Paiutes and attempted to convert them, as well as establish a stronghold within the area. The Mormons built a fort, planted gardens, and monitored the mail route. Unprepared for the climate and terrain, the Mormons found farming difficult in the desert soil, and they turned to mining to save their struggling settlement. In the end, the Mormons abandoned Las Vegas because of internal disputes about mining rights.

In 1849, the eastern portion of the Spanish Trail from New Mexico to Las Vegas was abandoned, and the remaining path from Las Vegas to California merged with another trail that connected to Salt Lake City. This new passage came to be known as the Mormon Trail. Because Las Vegas was the halfway point between Los Angeles and Salt Lake City, the area was settled again. The Gold Rush migration to California also took place in 1849, and this new passageway provided a path for the would-be fortune seekers to get to their destinations. The Mormon Trail became essential to the development and inhabitation of the Las Vegas Valley.

The Mormon settlement was eventually abandoned in 1858, but news of gold and silver in the area rippled throughout the territory. Mining prospectors who had heard about the Mormons' earlier mining discoveries attempted to resettle the area, and by the early 1860s, between 300 and 500 people worked in the El Dorado Canyon at their staked claims near the Colorado River, hoping to find riches embedded in the land.

LAS VEGAS ON PURPOSE: A DESTINATION LOCATION
The Railroad Rolls in and a Star is Born

Salt Lake City was an important stop along the railroad line between New York and San Francisco, but it wasn't an effective way of routing goods to the southern portions of California. Rumors of a Los Angeles–bound train route through the Las Vegas Valley circulated, and people were drawn to the area, establishing a collection of tents, miners, and opportunists looking to profit from the eventual creation of a town. The San Pedro, Los Angeles, and Salt Lake Railroad rolled onto the scene, and by 1899, trains ran between Salt Lake City and Nevada. Approximately 110 acres of land that surrounded the rail lines were sold at an auction on May 15, 1905, and the city of Las Vegas was born. The demand for land in this new town was so great that lots on Fremont Street between Main and First Streets sold for between $750 and $850, exorbitant sums for the time. Building had begun on many of the sold lots before the end of that first day, and by morning, many new establishments were open for business. Las Vegas was the perfect place for trains to stop and refuel and for travelers to rest.

Room, Please!

The first hotel, known as Ladd's Hotel, opened in February 1905. It was a tent only 12 feet by 20 feet, and it housed only four double beds. Captain James H. Ladd, owner and operator of the hotel, imposed one rule about his hotel patrons—if they scratched themselves in any way, they were not worthy of a bed. In 1906 longtime Las Vegan C. P. Squires followed suit and opened the Hotel Nevada three doors down. Like its neighbor, Hotel Nevada was a tent, but it boasted luxuries such as a plank floor, canvas partitions, a lobby, and a front porch. Each room also had a washbowl, a chamber pot, and even a bracket that could hold each guest's drinking glass. The tent structures, in time, evolved into framed and concrete-block construction, making the Hotel Nevada known as the ultimate place to stay. Hotel Nevada even had the first telephone in town, and the owners continued to make improvements, offering such amenities as 100-square-foot rooms, electric lighting, ventilation, and steam heat radiators. The Hotel Nevada eventually changed its name to the Golden Gate Hotel and Casino, and it is a lively downtown resort still operating today.

PUTTING THE WILD IN THE WEST

A Legislative Ban on Gambling

The Nevada Legislature instituted a ban on gambling in 1909. Many Las Vegas locals, who preferred to live by their own rules and enjoyed the isolation that life in the desert afforded them, chose to not to adhere to the legislative ruling. As a result, widespread illegal gambling took place and was largely accepted by the locals until 1931, when the ban was repealed.

Undoing the "I Do"

Divorce laws for the state of Nevada were drafted in 1911, and the residency requirements for both current residents and potential residents became shockingly easy to fulfill. The "quickie divorce" was invented— anyone who lived in Nevada could apply for a divorce after only six weeks of residency. Unsurprisingly, short-term residencies increased, and visitors stayed at dude ranches to obtain legal Nevada residency. The ranch house residencies were precursors to the Strip hotels.

The Desert Goes Dry, But All Is Not Boring

In 1919, the 18th Amendment and the Volstead Act were enacted, prohibiting all consumption, manufacturing and distribution of alcohol in the United States. Las Vegas, like every other community, was required to follow the law, and efforts were made to prosecute the alcohol producers that filled the town. The law, however, proved extremely unpopular with the locals, who enjoyed their freedom and had a history of defying laws that were deemed bothersome. Almost half of the initial lots purchased in the 1905 land auction were sold to bootleggers who built their homes over distillery-filled basements, and the independent spirit of these westerners resisted Prohibition. Many of the violators moved north to avoid prosecution, but speakeasies flourished within the small town.

Some of the businesses responded to Prohibition differently, often through creative maneuvering. To evade the "no-liquor" clause, many businesses added a few rooms for rent, asserting that they were hotels and could, therefore, serve alcohol legally. Purveyors almost always received an early warning of pending visits from the authorities, and an occasional arrest was made for the sake of appearances. Small fines were assigned to the offenders, and they were usually back to their old antics within a few days.

Prostitution was also plentiful in Las Vegas. It was legal, and brothels were licensed and regulated by the city's officials. Las Vegas was gaining its early reputation as Sin City.

The Great War Ends

In November 1918, World War I ended. While the nation cheered the end of the war, the country's need for metal significantly decreased, harming Nevada's growing mining industry. As a result, many businesses in the town closed or went bankrupt. Las Vegas shriveled from a thriving town to a mere railroad maintenance stop. Without the lure of gambling and a dwindling mining market, there was little to draw visitors to the area, and money was scarce.

Las Vegans, still optimistic about their growing town, continued to depend on the railroad for survival, but in 1921, officials dismissed 60 workers from the Las Vegas–based train repair facility without any explanation. Angered, the remaining Las Vegas workers joined a nationwide strike in 1922, much to the dismay of Union Pacific, the company that had recently taken over the railroad holdings. Scabs were brought in as replacements, and bouts of violence erupted. The tracks were closed for several weeks while negotiations continued, and the city's fragile economy was further injured. The final blow came when the strike ended; resentful over the workers' willingness to participate in the strike, Union Pacific moved the repair facility to Caliente, a town about 100 miles north of Las Vegas. The move meant the loss of 300 jobs and continued resentment toward Union Pacific. Caliente, even today, remains an essential locale to the railroad.

Gambling Reinstated

The 1931 Nevada Legislature, tired of the tight Nevada economy, loosened its marriage and divorce laws and repealed its gambling ban. Las Vegas revived itself from the brink of death and was well on the way to becoming a gaming hotspot.

A Dam Good Project: Boulder Canyon Is Approved

Luck for Las Vegas began to change. The Boulder Canyon Project Act, which called for the construction of a dam on the nearby Colorado River, was approved in 1928 and started an economic boom for Southern Nevada. Henry C. Schmidt, a central Nevada businessman, filed an application with the U.S. Department of the Interior, as well as the states of Arizona and Nevada to initiate the irrigation project. The government approved the project immediately. California utility and agricultural companies also took an interest in the project, which evolved from a mere irrigation arrangement to the creation of a power plant. Investors were found for the project, and the Colorado River Power Company began work.

The project brought employment to the area and the demand for construction workers prompted thousands from all over the country, many of whom had been suffering from hardship during the Great Depression, to migrate to Southern Nevada. The population spiked, and the area was soon overwhelmed with people. Shantytowns—also known as tent cities or Hoovervilles—were erected north of the Las Vegas business district and near the Colorado River to shelter workers. To solve the unanticipated housing issue, the Department of Interior declared that a model community would be built near the dam site, fearful that its workers would fall prey to the evils of nightlife: drinking, gambling, and prostitution. The scandalous Block 16 in Las Vegas, the wildest area of town, they contended, was full of bootleggers and other outlaws who would tempt the workers. Las Vegas shopkeepers, eager to see that the workers had plenty of ways to spend their paychecks, guaranteed workers a good time in exchange for their hard-earned dollars.

Boulder City, the new residential community built for the dam's influx of workers, was initially designed to house 5,000

The construction of Hoover Dam was treacherous and 96 workers lost their lives. Library of Congress

people. Its completion was expected before the project began, but the dam's start date was moved up because of the Depression and the urgent need for jobs. As a result, the dam and the town's construction efforts began at the same time. Initially, dormitories were built, housing 172 men. Cottages from the 1931 Los Angeles Olympics were trucked in for workers with families, and rents for these abodes ranged from $15 per month for efficiencies to $30 for three-bedroom units. Plans also called for a hospital, police station, post office, cemetery, train station, school, recreation hall, and commissary. Upon completion of the homes, workers were permitted to move in, pending approval from Sims Ely, Boulder City's manager. If he deemed that the workers were suitable, they were allowed to move in; however, drunks and other undesirables were banned and had to make their homes else-where—most likely in nearby Las Vegas.

The keystone of the Boulder Canyon irrigation effort was Boulder Dam (later known as Hoover Dam). Tunnels were built to temporarily redirect the river around the work site, and more than fifty miles of rail lines were built to supply materials to the dam as it was under construction. Tourists flocked to see this construction marvel—nearly 100,000 in 1932 and 265,000 in 1934. Las Vegas called itself "The Gateway to Hoover Dam" and took advantage of the Hoover Dam tourists, who also stopped in Las Vegas to gamble.

Gamblers' Exodus to Las Vegas, 1938

California authorities cracked down on illegal gambling, and many gamblers fled to Las Vegas not only to escape persecution but also to thrive in a pro-gambling environment.

Happy Endings for Everyone

Weddings and divorces were always easy to obtain in Las Vegas. Las Vegas weddings were made even more attractive when many of Nevada's neighboring states initiated laws that required engaged couples to obtain blood tests in an effort to reduce the spread of venereal disease. Numerous chapels—including Little Church of the West in 1942 and Wee Kirk of the Heather in 1949—opened to accommodate the new, booming wedding industry.

Like the wedding industry, the divorce industry served as a great source of revenue for Las Vegas. Even the local Chamber of Commerce got into the action and began actively promoting Las Vegas as the place to come to get a divorce. The divorce game received an even bigger boost when Ria Langham Gable temporarily moved to Las Vegas in 1939, seeking to complete the six-week divorce residency, and made headlines around the world. While she eagerly awaited her new freedom and enjoyed her time in the town, Hollywood actor Clark Gable and his superstar mistress Carole Lombard were seen gallivanting around together in nearby Los Angeles. Las Vegas reveled in the free publicity and the perception that it was the premier place to get a divorce, and many followed in Mrs. Gable's footsteps. The town also profited greatly from unhappy couples wanting to break ties during World War II.

The Rise of the Military

In the wake of World War II, the U.S. Army noted the isolation of the Las Vegas Valley within the vast Mojave Desert. It also noted its plentiful water and inexpensive energy supplies, as well as its continuously clear weather and year-round flying location. Under the supervision of Major David M. Schlatter, the Army Air Corps created a gunnery school in October 1940. The military had examined various sites for an air base in the Southwest, and the city was eager to attract a military base. In January 1941, the city of Las Vegas purchased an airstrip run by Western Air Express, a U.S. Post Office subcontractor, and immediately leased it to the Air Corps; it was also used for both military and civilian aircraft. Construction of the nearby Las Vegas Army Air Field began later that year, and the gunnery school immediately expanded.

The school reached its height in 1943 and 1944, but the war's needs began to change. The gunnery school closed in September 1945 after the end of World War II, but not before more than 55,000 gunners had been trained at the site. The base was officially closed in 1947, but was soon reactivated by the newly created United States Air Force in March 1948.

Two years later, the need for training resumed with the United States' entry into the Korean War. Soldiers trained first with P-51 Mustangs and then with F-80s and F-86 Sabres, and soon the site became a prime location for testing new aircraft. That same year, the base was renamed for William Harrell Nellis, an Army Air Force P-47 pilot and Las Vegas resident who died in the Battle of the Bulge.

In 1956, the Air Force brought the Thunderbirds, an air demonstration squadron, to Nellis, and they can still be seen at air shows and practicing on clear, cool mornings. Today, Nellis is a major training location for both U.S. and foreign military aircrews and is home to more squadrons than any other Air Force base. The base, however, has potential for even more uses, as it takes up approximately 11,300 acres of land, 63 percent of which remains undeveloped.

THE SHADY SIDE OF A SUNNY TOWN

Bugsy Siegel Ushers in the Mob Era

The gambler and noted mobster Benjamin "Bugsy" Siegel opened the Flamingo Hotel on December 26, 1946. The project cost a whopping $6 million and had many fiscal, political, and organizational pitfalls throughout its construction. The casino flopped, and it lost money because there were no hotel rooms to keep guests gambling into the night.

Gamblers ultimately took their winnings elsewhere, and the casino was in debt. After two weeks, the mob shut down the Flamingo in late January 1947. Siegel was removed from the helm by his angry mobster colleagues, and the Flamingo reopened in March, despite the hotel portion still not being complete. This time, however, the casino was a hit, and the hotel was profitable, but not before Siegel was brutally murdered by "unknown" assailants, assumed to be his former mobster ties.

Bugsy Seigel's Flamingo Hotel in the early days, not long after its 1946 opening. Courtesy Harrah's

Kefauver Investigations, 1950

In 1950 the United States Senate began an investigation into the netherworld of organized crime. Senator Estes Kefauver, a Tennessee Democrat, chaired the committee. The Kefauver Committee interviewed hundreds of witnesses in an effort to expose the vastness of organized crime in America.

Years later, the Flamingo Hotel had yet another new look. Courtesy Harrah's

Kefauver, who was a political opportunist, hoped to gain national publicity and support for the upcoming 1952 presidential election. Permission was granted to broadcast the hearings live, and more than 30 million Americans tuned in to watch Kefauver interrogate some of the most notorious mobsters in the country. Kefauver and his partners gathered public support for his investigation into the underbelly of organized crime, and casino management expected the arrival of the committee in Las Vegas. They knew they were politically vulnerable, despite any protection their connections could provide.

The committee members had already been conducting hearings for five months, and by the time they arrived in Las Vegas in November of 1950, they were tired. Moe Dalitz, along with many of the other notable casino owners who had received subpoenas for the committee, had left town to avoid the hearings. The committee, however, managed to interview six witnesses, and these few interviews did not prove to be helpful. After just two hours of questioning, the committee took a break to visit Boulder Dam and then briefly continued the hearings before calling for a press conference. They announced that the Las Vegas segment of their investigation was complete.

To the locals, the end of the investigation was a relief and a strange ending to a much-anticipated battle. A local newspaper reported, "The United States Senate's crime investi-

As the years progress, the Flamingo Hotel gets many new neighbors. Las Vegas News Bureau

gating committee blew into town yesterday like a desert whirlwind, and after stirring up a lot of dust, it vanished, leaving only the rustling among prominent local citizens as evidence that it had paid its much publicized visit here."

THE MODERN ERA

The Atomic Bomb

The Nevada Test Site in Mercury, Nevada, located about 65 miles northwest of Las Vegas, conducted its first round of nuclear weapons tests in 1951 at its aboveground testing site. Locals and tourists gathered at the downtown hotels to watch. The resulting mushroom clouds were visible as far away as 100 miles from ground zero and onlookers watched each spectacle with awe until the Limited Test Ban Treaty of 1963 directed the testing to move underground. The Nevada Test Site also became a locale for the federal government's scientific research efforts and served as home to the famed Area 51, which is believed to house many strange and secretive activities. Also at the Nevada Test Site is the highly controversial Yucca Mountain Project, the proposed repository for the nation's nuclear waste byproducts.

The Rebels

In 1951, Las Vegas's population rose to more than 50,000, and the University of Nevada, Reno (UNR), about 500 miles north of Las Vegas, established an extension program to cater to the growing need for higher education. Meeting in the dressing room of the Las Vegas High School auditorium, 28 students attended their first college class. Three years later, the Board of Regents formally founded a southern branch of UNR, known as Nevada Southern. The students, glad for the growth but wanting a university of their own, adopted the Rebel mascot, reflecting their desire to break free from UNR. After much pressure from the locals, the regents acquired an 80-acre parcel along a lonely dirt road, Maryland Parkway. The first classes were held on the new campus in 1957, but the school didn't win its autonomy and equal billing as the University of Nevada, Las Vegas (UNLV) until 1968. The 1977–1978 academic year saw UNLV surpass UNR in total student enrollment, and the school boasts a 28,000-plus student population each year.

The Moulin Rouge, Kicking Up Its Heels and Kicking Down Doors

Moulin Rouge, Las Vegas's first racially integrated hotel, opened its doors in 1955 to much fanfare and celebration by many celebrities such as Frank Sinatra, Sammy Davis Jr., Dean Martin, Nat King Cole, George Burns, Gracie Allen, and Jack Benny. All of the casinos on the Strip were completely segregated at the time, and the Moulin Rouge broke new ground within the budding civil rights movement by allowing, even encouraging, blacks and whites to gather together in a friendly environment. Within six months of its opening, the Moulin Rouge closed for financial reasons. Several unsuccessful attempts to reinvigorate the hotel have been made.

Welcome to Fabulous Las Vegas

The famous "Welcome to Fabulous Las Vegas" sign on the south end of the Strip, an icon on the ever-changing resort landscape, was created by Betty Willis in 1959.

Howard Hughes and the Legitimizing of Gaming

The billionaire investor and eccentric entrepreneur Howard Hughes decided to visit Las Vegas and checked into the Desert Inn Hotel on Thanksgiving Day in 1966. Hughes and his entourage rented the top two floors of the hotel and ended up staying well past his original 10-day reservation. The hotel owners, eager to rent out the already-reserved rooms to incoming high rollers who were ready to drop plenty of cash at the highly profitable gaming tables, asked Hughes to leave in December. He refused to leave. Eventually, an eviction notice was served to the billionaire. But instead of complying with the mandate and moving out, he began negotiations to acquire the property, and Hughes assumed ownership of the Desert Inn on March 1, 1967.

His new acquisition drew him at age 61 into a new arena of business—one far removed from his past innovations in aviation and film. He acquired several other properties along the Strip and near both the McCarran Airport and the North Las Vegas Airport. His purchases saved Las Vegas, which was experiencing a steep economic downturn, from destruction and even spurred further growth in the city. Hughes also transitioned the casino industry to one of sinful "gambling," a result of the developments made in the mobster era, to "gaming," a legitimate industry of real corporations with integrity and transparency. Hughes's takeover of the Desert Inn encouraged other corporations, particularly ones with a lot of capital, to enter the gaming industry.

Hughes also began buying other Las Vegas properties, purchasing nearly all of the unimproved real estate available within the local market, including a 25,000-acre parcel in the western area of the city. Hughes became one of the largest landowners in the United States as a result of his new Las Vegas holdings and formed the Summa Corporation. His company, though it has evolved and changed names several times over the years, developed many of the properties around Las Vegas, including Summerlin, a master-planned residential and mixed-use community within Las Vegas; the Hughes Center, a professional and financial complex near the Strip; KLAS, the local CBS affiliate; and Spring Mountain Ranch, an outdoor amphitheater; as well as land ownership for what is now the Red Rock Canyon National Conservation Area, Red Rock Station Casino, the Fashion Show Mall, Nevada Ballet Theater, several school sites within the Clark County School District, and for many institutions for the University and Community College System of Nevada, including the University of Nevada, Las Vegas, the University of Nevada, Reno, and the College of Southern Nevada.

Elvis Has Entered the Building

Elvis Presley performed at the grand opening of the International Hotel in 1969, staging the comeback of his career and establishing himself as a Las Vegas icon. The International Hotel ownership changed hands over the years, but is in operation today as the Las Vegas Hilton.

Legitimate Gaming: The 1970s–1980s

Corporations continued to invest in the hotel and casino industry, and the mob, which had a significant political influence and financial stake in many of the local hotel properties, began to phase itself out. Gaming in Las Vegas became a fully legitimate and respectable business. As a result, some gaming properties become publicly traded companies on the stock market.

A Left Jab by the Mob

In 1982, Frank "Lefty" Rosenthal, a sports handicapper who secretly ran the mob-controlled Stardust, Fremont, Marina, and Hacienda casinos survived an assassination attempt. His Cadillac was wired with explosives, and his life was spared only because of the protective metal plate installed under the driver's seat, a correction installed by GM to resolve a balancing problem. Not long after, Rosenthal was added to the "Black Book," or the *Nevada Gaming Control Board's List of Excluded Persons,* and deemed unwelcome and unable to be hired by any gaming organization within the state of Nevada. In other words, he was forced out of Las Vegas. Rosenthal's story, as well as that of notorious mob hit man Tony "The Ant" Spilotro, who was killed in an Indiana cornfield in June 1986, was the inspiration for the book Casino by Nicholas Pileggi and eventually a film of the same name directed by Martin Scorsese in 1995.

Growing Like a Weed in the Desert

Las Vegas saw a period of unprecedented growth in the mid-1980s that lasted through the mid-1990s. The population doubled between 1985 and 1995, increasing from 186,380 to 368,360, showing an impressive 97.6 percent boom in residency. The city's pace did not slow down; an estimated 5,000 people moved to Las Vegas every month throughout the 1990s and well into the 2000s. The population reached 2 million people in 2008, and the city is still growing.

Fremont Street in downtown Las Vegas in 1954.
Las Vegas News Bureau

The Fremont Street Experience and the Downtown Revitalization Effort

The Fremont Street Experience, a shopping mall and downtown casino walkway, was opened in 1995 as an effort to return the area to its early glamour and appeal. The $70-million canopy above Fremont Street provides visitors with a free spectacular light and music show, complete with a 12.5-million-LED display and 220 speakers capable of producing 550,000 watts of sound. The area has two stages usually reserved for free concerts and hosts an array of downtown parties. This is the only place to see the famous Vegas Vic sign, the waving cowboy offering a friendly "Howdy Pardner!" to tourists and to his girlfriend across the street, Sassy Sally, sometimes referred to as "Vegas Vicky" by those who don't know local history.

Four since-imploded casinos can be seen here—Frontier, Stardust, Desert Inn, and Sands. Las Vegas News Bureau

Some of the mega-resorts found on Las Vegas Boulevard today. Las Vegas News Bureau

Happy Birthday, Sin City!

The city of Las Vegas celebrated its 100th birthday on May 15, 2005. The centennial event highlighted the May 15, 1905 auction in which the sale of 110 acres of desert land laid the foundation for the desert oasis known as Las Vegas. The celebration was marked by the creation and burial of a time capsule at the historic Las Vegas Grammar School on 4th Street near Lewis Avenue, to be opened in another 100 years, as well as the baking and eating of a 130,000-pound birthday cake, free concerts, a large fireworks display, and a drop-in visit from the Flying Elvi (a fleet of Elvis impersonators/sky divers).

A Thoughtful Look at the City's Own Past

The Las Vegas Springs Preserve, a cultural and historic center celebrating the origins and evolution of Las Vegas, is located at the site of the bubbling springs that once served as a water source for the Native Americans and the travelers that visited the area long ago. The massive 180-acre, nongaming, historic site opened in 2007 only a few miles from downtown and offers colorful desert botanical gardens, museum galleries, outdoor concerts and events, an indoor theater, a historic photo gallery, and walking trails through a wetland habitat. The opening of the preserve is a significant event in Las Vegas history, as the town's evolution has been one of constant growth and change and rarely one of thoughtful rumination on its own existence and the acknowledgment of local history prior to the mob era.

The Dealer Wishes You Good Luck

There is no other town in the world like Las Vegas. It does not blink or feign shyness at its colorful, almost mythological past nor does it regret it; instead Las Vegas embraces it. And perhaps it is this very boldness and willingness to defy conventional norms that inspires

The Neon Museum, the graveyard where yesterday's glamour and sparkle now reside. Courtesy Neon Museum

40 million people to visit it each year. Las Vegas encourages the free spirit in its visitors because this same free spirit built this city from a small watering hole to a shining, bustling oasis in the desert. Welcome to our town. May Lady Luck smile upon you.

Sources

Bowers, Michael W. *The Sagebrush State*. Reno: University of Nevada Press, 2000.

City of Las Vegas, www.lasvegasnevada.gov/FactsStatistics/history.htm.

Egan, Ferol, and Richard Dillon, *Fremont: Explorer for a Restless Nation*. Nevada: University of Nevada Press, 1985.

Elvis In Person—At The International Hotel, Las Vegas, Nevada, RCA, 1992.

Golden Gate Hotel & Casino: Our History Defines our Past, www.goldengatecasino.com/timeline.html.

The Howard Hughes Story, www.howardhughes.com/pdfs_hh/allText4.pdf.

Hulse, James W. *The Silver State*. Reno: University of Nevada Press, 2004.

Ivanpah Valley, www.ivanpahvalley.com/id1.html.

Land, Barbara and Myrick. *A Short History of Las Vegas*. Reno: University of Nevada Press, 1999

Las Vegas, an Unconventional History: Timeline: Las Vegas 1829–1945. www.pbs.org/wgbh/amex/lasvegas/timeline/index.html.

Las Vegas, an Unconventional History: Timeline: Las Vegas 1946–2005, http://www.pbs.org/wgbh/amex/lasvegas/timeline/timeline2.html.

Las Vegas Sun, www.lasvegassun.com/history/

Little Church of the West, www.littlechurchlv.com/?sec=history.

Marjorie Barrick Museum, hrc.nevada.edu/museum/Education/paiuteeducation/paiute.html.

McCracken, Robert D. Las Vegas: *The Great American Playground*. Reno: University of Nevada Press, 1996.

Springs Preserve, www.springspreserve.org/html/about.html.

Using the monorail cuts down on taxicab rides. Courtesy Las Vegas Monorail

2

Transportation

Everywhere and There from Here

Getting to Las vegas

By Air

McCarran International Airport (abbreviated LAS; 702-261-5211) is the central airport serving Las Vegas and fortunately it is located right next to the Strip and therefore many of the major hotels. There are two separate terminal buildings and 96 gates. If you just can't wait, there are slot machines located throughout, as well as more than 50 retail shops and almost 30 restaurants and lounges. In 2008, there were over 7.1 million arriving and departing passengers. While this may seem small compared to larger airports around the nation, keep in mind that those airports have been in operation much longer and are located in much larger metro areas. Taxicabs are available on the east side of baggage claim, through doors 1–4. The maximum number of passengers allowed in a cab is five, including children. Depending on which hotel you need, the fare runs from $8 to $20. Check with your hotel to see if they offer an airport shuttle before leaving home. These are usually available for a small fee and require reservations ahead of time.

McCarran International Airport is just so Las Vegas. Charo Burke

> INSIDER TIP: Airport SpeedCheck Advance may be able to save you some traveling hassle. These five centrally located kiosks allow you to check in your luggage and print your boarding pass for certain airlines. They take your baggage to the airport and have it TSA screened and loaded on your plane for a $20 fee per customer. You then bypass the ticket counter and skycaps and head straight to security. Kiosks can be found at The Venetian, Luxor, Las Vegas Convention Center, Sands Expo Center, and McCarran Rent-A-Car Center. Check www.mccarran.com for more information, including each participating airline's advance check-in time.

Rental Cars

The **McCarran Rent-A-Car Center** (702-261-6001; 7135 Gilespie Street) houses rental car company airport locations (Advantage, Hertz, Alamo, National, Avis, Payless, Budget, Savmor, Dollar, Thrifty, and Enterprise). The free shuttles can be found through exit door 10 and 11 at Terminal 1 baggage claim and through the sliding glass doors to the center median at Terminal 2. The center is three miles from the airport, with shuttles leaving every five minutes or so. When you return your car, enter at the north entrance and follow the signs to your rental company. The shuttles to the airport are located in front of the center.

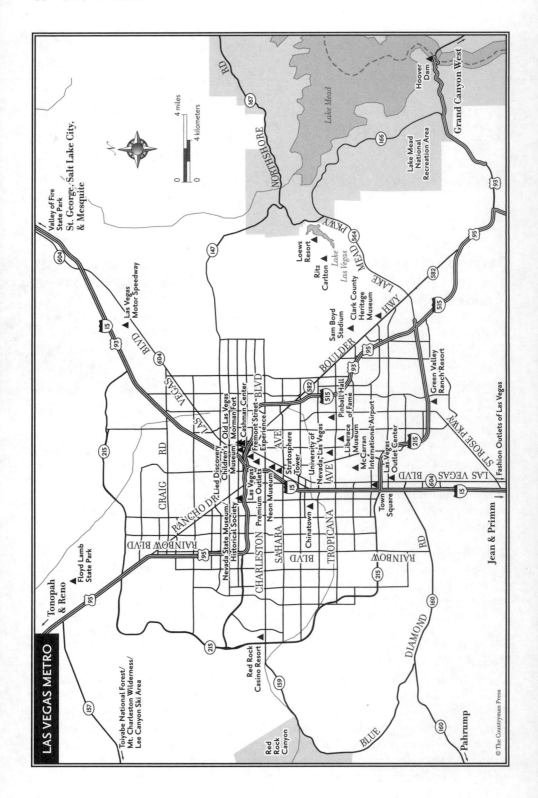

LAS VEGAS METRO

© The Countryman Press

All the car rental companies can be found in one building accessed by shuttles from the airport. Charo Burke

By Car

Getting to Las Vegas via car is pretty direct. I-15, the major thoroughfare from Los Angeles and southern Utah, runs parallel with the Strip. The exit you need depends on your hotel. Those coming from the direction of Phoenix, San Francisco, or Reno will come into town on US 95. If your final destination is the Strip, head south on I-15. If you're heading for downtown, US 95 goes right past it.

GETTING AROUND THE LAS VEGAS VALLEY

By Car

When driving in Las Vegas, it's fairly simple to find your way around since most major thoroughfares are laid out in a north-south or east-west grid, with Las Vegas Boulevard (north-south) demarcating the east and west sides of town. The major freeways running through the valley are I-15, which runs roughly northeast-southwest from Utah and points north down through Vegas and on through to Southern California; and US 95, which comes through town from northwestern Nevada and continues into Arizona. I-215, also known as "The Beltway," circles about two-thirds of the valley and provides easy access to the far southern, western, and northern reaches of the Las Vegas area, including Henderson and Summerlin.

Traffic is at its heaviest during the morning and evening rush hours on major surface streets and freeways, with the southern leg of I-215 and the part of I-15 that runs right through the center of town being particularly congested with commuter traffic on weekdays; weekend traffic on both roadways is usually much lighter. The radical growth of Las Vegas has drastically changed the face of local traffic: so many people moving in from so many different places bringing driving styles and skills unique to their areas of origin have created a traffic "melting pot" of sorts that can be a source of irritation while on the road. Also, many heavily traveled roads and freeways are often either under construction or in the process of being widened; roadwork is rampant throughout the valley, which of course leads to delays and detours. A common complaint of Las Vegas drivers is the poorly timed traffic light system, which often results in cars having to stop at every light instead of enjoying a smooth traffic flow. Traffic on the Strip is always heavy, and on weekend evenings it slows to a crawl. From about 6 PM on, every Friday and Saturday night (but especially at times when the town is busy, such as holiday weekends), it can take over an hour just to get from the southern end of Las Vegas Boulevard, around the Mandalay Bay Hotel, to Fremont Street in the north. If you're sightseeing and enjoying the lights and people, it's worth it; traffic will be moving so slow that you'll have a great view of everything with lots of photo opportunities. If, however, you're trying to get to a show or dinner reservation on the Strip, build plenty of time into your schedule to get there. There are alternatives to Las Vegas Boulevard; Frank Sinatra Drive is just a block west of the Strip and runs parallel to it behind several properties; you can use it to access hotels and resorts from Mandalay Bay north to the Mirage and Treasure Island. Koval Lane is a block east of the Strip and runs behind the Venetian, the Palazzo, Harrah's, the Flamingo, Bally's, Paris, Planet Hollywood, and the MGM Grand.

INSIDER TIP: If you're trying to get west from the center of town and would like to avoid traffic crossing Las Vegas Boulevard, you can use the Desert Inn Road Super Arterial. It runs nonstop with no intersecting traffic from Paradise Road on the east side of the Strip to Valley View Boulevard on the west.

A Note on Parking

You may not think you can get much for free when visiting Las Vegas, but one thing you can almost always count on is free parking. Downtown properties and attractions are the exception—most of the street and garage parking is either metered or by the hour, although many downtown casinos offer parking validation at their cashiers' cages, which can lower the hourly parking rate significantly or give you a few free hours. Along the Strip and at all the outlying properties, however, parking is free and in abundant supply. Of course, at times when properties are at their highest occupancy, parking can prove more difficult, and sometimes the distances from parking lots and garages to the hotel or casino are absurd. At these times, allowing the valet to park your car is a beautiful thing. Valet parking is offered at all properties, and it's free—a couple bucks' tip, or more if you feel the valet has gone above and beyond, and you are out of your car and on your way to your dinner, a show, or the tables. Sometimes it's a bit of a wait when picking up your car, especially at times when shows are letting out, but it can save you some time and energy.

Valet parking is worth the tip. Leah Koepp

By Taxi

Cabs are a mainstay of any major city, but especially Las Vegas. Here, it is illegal to hail a cab on the street; the best way to get a cab if you're walking the Strip on foot is to walk up to any hotel's porte cochere and get in the taxi line. Cabs are constantly picking up and dropping off fares in front of hotels, and are usually waiting in line for new fares. A very important rule, though, not to be broken: It is bad form to walk up and try to hire a cab in the middle of the line; always wait your turn in the taxi line when getting a cab at a hotel, and take the first one in line. Another way to get a cab is to call one of the local taxi companies for a pickup—the bell desk or concierge at your hotel can provide you with the names and numbers of all local cab companies. Be aware that most taxis in the Las Vegas area do

Taxi lines can get long during large conventions and after concerts and events. Charo Burke

not accept credit cards, and that some cabbies may not be willing to take fares to or from areas away from the Strip, Downtown, or airport, because that's where the money is.

INSIDER TIP: Limos may be a good alternative when cabs are scarce, and depending on the size of your group, may not cost you much more than a taxi ride would. It's also a whole lot classier. If you're waiting in a cab line and see a limo idling nearby with the name of a transportation company or it, it may be for hire, and it doesn't hurt to ask.

By Limousine or Shuttle

You just hit Vegas, and you want to go deluxe. What better way than by limo or shuttle? Below is a list of companies offering a variety of transportation services for groups, or for those looking to ride in style.

A limo driver who's not busy may offer a good deal. Leah Koepp

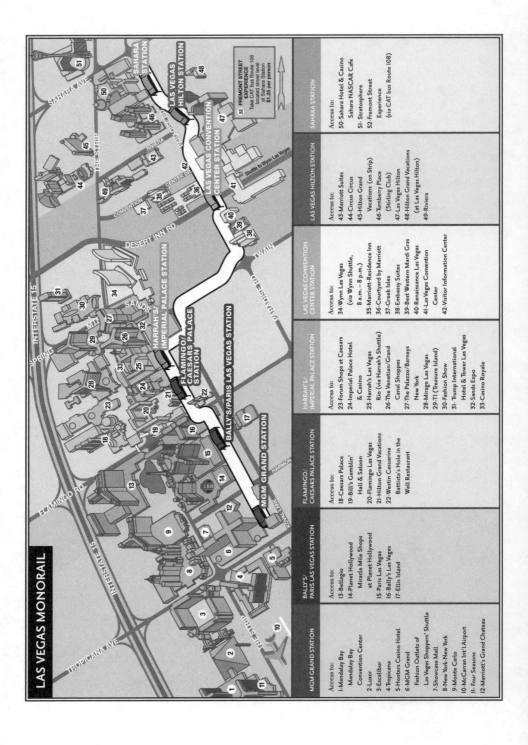

LAS VEGAS MONORAIL

MGM GRAND STATION

Access to:
1- Mandalay Bay
   Mandalay Bay
   Convention Center
2- Luxor
3- Excalibur
4- Tropicana
5- Hooters Casino Hotel
6- MGM Grand
   Fashion Outlets of
   Las Vegas Shoppers' Shuttle
7- Showcase Mall
8- New York-New York
9- Monte Carlo
10- McCarran Int'l Airport
11- Four Seasons
12- Marriott's Grand Chateau

BALLY'S/ PARIS LAS VEGAS STATION

Access to:
13- Bellagio
14- Planet Hollywood
   Miracle Mile Shops
   at Planet Hollywood
15- Paris Las Vegas
16- Bally's Las Vegas
17- Ellis Island

FLAMINGO/ CAESARS PALACE STATION

Access to:
18- Caesars Palace
19- Bill's Gamblin'
   Hall & Saloon
20- Flamingo Las Vegas
21- Hilton Grand Vacations
22- Westin Casuarina
   Battista's Hole in the
   Wall Restaurant

HARRAH'S/ IMPERIAL PALACE STATION

Access to:
23- Forum Shops at Caesars
24- Imperial Palace Hotel
   & Casino
25- Harrah's Las Vegas
   Rio (via Harrah's Shuttle)
26- The Venetian/Grand
   Canal Shoppes
27- The Palazzo/Barneys
   New York
28- Mirage Las Vegas
29- TI (Treasure Island)
30- Fashion Show
31- Trump International
   Hotel & Tower Las Vegas
32- Sands Expo
33- Casino Royale

LAS VEGAS CONVENTION CENTER STATION

Access to:
34- Wynn Las Vegas
   (via Wynn Shuttle,
   8 a.m. – 8 p.m.)
35- Marriott-Residence Inn
36- Courtyard by Marriott
37- Greek Isles
38- Embassy Suites
39- Best Western Mardi Gras
40- Renaissance Las Vegas
41- Las Vegas Convention
   Center
42- Visitor Information Center

LAS VEGAS HILTON STATION

Access to:
43- Marriott Suites
44- Circus Circus
45- Hilton Grand
   Vacations (on Strip)
46- Turnberry Place
   (Stirling Club)
47- Las Vegas Hilton
48- Hilton Grand Vacations
   (at Las Vegas Hilton)
49- Riviera

SAHARA STATION

Access to:
50- Sahara Hotel & Casino
   Sahara NASCAR Cafe
51- Stratosphere
52- Fremont Street
   Experience
   (via CAT bus Route 108)

52 FREMONT STREET
EXPERIENCE
Take CAT bus Route 108
located street level
at Sahara Station
$1.25 per person

Limos:

Ambassador Limousine 888-519-5466; www.ambassadorlasvegas.com

Bell Trans 800-274-7433; www.bell-trans.com

CLS Las Vegas 702-740-4545; www.clsnevada.com

Executive Las Vegas 866-367-7774; www.executivelasvegas.com

Presidential Limousine 800-423-1420; www.presidentiallimolv.com

Shuttle Services:

Gray Line Las Vegas 800-634-6579; www.graylinelasvegas.com

Showtime Tours 888-827-3858; www.showtimetourslasvegas.com

Shuttle Las Vegas/Ritz Transportation 888-519-5466; www.shuttlelasvegas.com

By Bus

Citizens Area Transit, or **CAT**, is a bus line operated by the Regional Transportation Commission of Southern Nevada and that services the entire Las Vegas Valley, including the Strip and downtown. As is the rule in most large cities, the buses are most crowded in the mornings and afternoons and at peak hours and when traffic is heavy, there may be delays. Non-Strip buses run from 5 AM until 1 AM daily with a fare of $1.75. Las Vegas Boulevard north to downtown is serviced by buses called "the Deuce," so named because they're double-deckers. Deuce rides will cost you $3.00 per ride, and there are stops in front of every

The Deuce bus works well for Strip travel and offers a great view from the upper deck. Charo Burke

Strip property. Buses run 24 hours a day, seven days a week, and the maximum wait time between buses is from 7 to 17 minutes, depending on the time of day and day of the week.

> INSIDER TIP: Get on the Deuce around sundown and take an upper-deck seat, the closer to the front the better. It's a great way to take in the Strip and catch the lights just as they go on.

By Monorail

The Las Vegas Monorail runs from the MGM Grand on the south end of the strip to the Sahara on the north, taking about 14 minutes to travel 3.9 miles. The Monorail is open from 7 AM until 2 AM daily, and a one-way pass is $5. Twenty-four-hour passes and three-day passes are available at $15 and $25 respectively and can be purchased in advance. Be forewarned that the Monorail does not load and unload on the strip; stations are generally on the east side of the hotels, so riders end up walking about a block west to the Strip.

GUIDED TOURS

With all there is to see and do in and around Las Vegas, guided tours are very popular ways to get out and experience the area while letting someone else do all the driving. There are many options and types of tours available; for example, you can have a real desert adventure in a four-wheel-drive vehicle or interact with an entirely different kind of wildlife on a "Vegas nightlife" tour. Whatever your speed, you can find a tour that suits your needs.

Desert Adventures (702-293-5026; www.kayaklasvegas.com) Perhaps you'd like to experience the beauty of Lake Mead, the grandeur of Hoover Dam, and the majesty of the mighty Colorado river, but flying over in a helicopter or driving by in a 4x4 is just a little too removed for you. Desert Adventures specializes in guided kayaking, hiking, ATV, mountain biking, and horseback riding trips, all of which take place in the Lake Mead National Recreation Area, the Hoover Dam area, Bootleg Canyon, Eldorado Canyon, and Valley of Fire State Park. And beginners, fear not. Many of Desert Adventures' clients start their trips as novices; basic paddling instruction is provided on each excursion, and their lightweight, ruddered kayaks are easy for even the newbies to handle. Desert Adventures also offers Adventure Fitness training and kayak and canoe instruction. Canoe, kayak, and bicycle rental is available for those preferring self-guided adventure trips. Meals are provided on trips, and hotel pickup and return is complimentary. Group trips are available. Prices range from $69 for the Moonlight Paddle on Lake Mead to $369 for the three-day Overnight Kayak paddle and camping trip in Black Canyon.

Gray Line Las Vegas Tours (800-634-6759; www.graylinelasvegas.com) Gray Line Tours offers tours by luxury motor coach and minibus of points of interest both in and out of Las Vegas proper. You can cruise in air-conditioned comfort to the Grand Canyon and Hoover Dam or float down the mighty Colorado on their Colorado River Raft tour. If you're keen to see the neon and sparkle of Las Vegas, try the Neon Lights tour. If you're looking to sample both Vegas glitz and desert beauty, maybe the Deluxe city and Red Rock canyon tour is for you. Meals are provided on most tours, and some tours can be upgraded to include helicopter rides. Not all tours are offered year-round; check the Gray Line Web site for tour details. Complimentary hotel pickup and return is also available. Gray Line also offers 24-hour airport shuttle service to and from all major Strip and downtown resorts. Reservations for tours and shuttle services are available online. Prices range from $55 per guest for the Neon Lights Tour to $190 per guest for the Grand Canyon West Rim with Skywalk Entrance Tour.

Pink Jeep Tours Las Vegas (800-900-4480; www.pinkjeep.com) For those looking to get out of the city and experience some of the fantastic natural wonders of the Mojave and beyond, Pink Jeep Tours provides a wide selection of off-road family friendly adventures in their air-conditioned 10-passenger Tour Trekkers or 6-passenger SUVs, driven by their knowledgeable Certified Interpretive Guides. Tours of Hoover Dam, Mount Charleston, Valley of Fire, Zion National Park in Utah, and the Eldorado Valley are available, as well as unique seasonal trips, such as the Flower Power Trekker Tour, which runs from around March 1 to around April 30 and takes visitors through Death Valley and its spectacular annual spring wildflower bloom. Lunch is provided on all Grand Canyon, Death Valley, and Zion tours, and a snack is provided on the Valley of Fire tour. Group tours are available and reservations can be made online. Hotel pickup is available at most properties; check with the clerk when you make your tour reservation. Prices range from $86 per guest for the Hoover Dam Classic tour to $317 per guest for the West Rim Drive, Fly, and Float tour.

Rebel Adventure Tours (800-817-6789; www.rebeladventuretours.com) Rebel Adventure Tours offers a variety of tours for the outdoor enthusiast, via a variety of modes of transport: you can travel by Hummer, ATV, river raft, Jet Ski, and even helicopter. Some of their tours give you the chance to travel by multiple methods within one trip: "The Big One" is an 8-hour tour in which you'll travel by Hummer to Lake Mead, then discover the beauty of the largest man-made lake in America on your own personal watercraft, and "The Great Escape" begins with a helicopter tour of the Grand Canyon, and culminates with a Hummer and Jet Ski trip on the Colorado. Prefer to drink in the desert's majesty the old-fashioned way? Their Horseback Adventure Tour is a two-hour ride through sage and yucca-studded wilderness, with breakfast, lunch, or dinner provided depending on the hour. Water is provided on all tours; meals are provided on most. Hotel pickup and return is available, and all over-the-road vehicles are air-conditioned. Some trips may not be available year-round—call for up-to-date tour information. Prices range from $149 to 159 per guest for the Horseback Adventure Tour to $499–559 per guest for the Great Escape Tour.

HeliUSA Airways (800-359-8727; www.heliusa.com) A unique way to view the Las Vegas Strip is from above, and that is only one of the helicopter tours offered by HeliUSA Airways. On their Apollo Night Flight Strip Tour, you'll first be treated to a champagne toast at the Hughes Executive Air Terminal, then you'll take flight and see all the lights and sights of Las Vegas from their A-Star Executive Jet Helicopter. They offer a helicopter wedding package and a range of Grand Canyon tours, some including overnight stays on the west rim and meals at the Grand Canyon West Ranch. Complimentary hotel pickup and return is included, and reservations can be booked online. Group rates and packages are available. Prices start at $99 per guest for the Apollo Las Vegas Night Flight and range to $429 + $50 fee per guest for the Pegasus Chariot of Fire by Helicopter and Grand Canyon Voyage tour.

EASY SIDE TRIPS

Grand Canyon West

Until recently, a visit to the Grand Canyon from Las Vegas was more than just a day trip. It involved an overnight stay and a long drive. But not any more. Thanks to the Hualapai tribe, you can take in spectacular close-up views of the Grand Canyon without having to change hotels.

To say that any view of the Grand Canyon is picturesque is redundant. However, these views are a bit different in that they are personal to the tribe. The Hualapai are the only area tribe that was allowed to stay on some of their original land right up to the canyon edge, one million acres total. All of the other tribes were pushed to more remote areas. Sadly, those tribes do not have the same tourism opportunities that the Hualapai do. This land and easy-to-reach views are why a Las Vegas businessman came to them with a proposal to build **Skywalk**. Skywalk is a glass bridge that was designed to make you feel as though you are walking on air 70 feet above of the rim of the canyon. It is an engineering marvel. It's so good that your eyes play tricks, making you think that the Colorado River doesn't look like much from here. Then a helicopter tour takes off near the water's edge and the truth materializes. These same tricks have made the owner of Skywalk and the Hualapai tribe set some strict ground rules. There are no cameras, backpacks, purses, or any other carried items allowed on the bridge. There are stories about folks dropping them into the canyon and onto the glass bridge itself. Although it's several inches thick, it can still be scratched. Personal lockers are provided free of charge. No cameras means no pictures, right? Oh, you can get a picture of yourself on the bridge, but for a price. And there's the $30 ticket to walk onto the bridge as well. But no matter, the majestic beauty can be appreciated without buying up the place.

The west rim of the Grand Canyon is closest to Las Vegas. Crystal Wood

This isn't to say that there aren't activities worth spending money on. The helicopter ride is well worth the $149. You're taken to the bottom of the canyon for a boat ride on the famous river and then flown back up. These are views that can't be described, but must be witnessed firsthand. If the prospect of dizzying heights is frightening, the horses for rent at the Hualapai Ranch are calm and know the trail along the canyon like the back of their hoof. They even have a celebrity living there. In the film City Slickers, Billy Crystal has to carry a baby bull named Norman through the water. The young guy has grown up and now resides at the ranch.

Next to Skywalk is **Eagle Point**. This is not one of those spots where you wonder why they named it after an eagle. It really jumps out at the viewer. No squinting or tilting of the head to see why. The tribe tells the story of a young boy who could see marauders of another tribe coming his way. Rather than be taken by them, he jumped into the canyon and was turned into the eagle in the rocks.

After Skywalk is **Guano Point**. Named after the guano mines directly across the canyon, this spot has some absolutely remarkable views. A small but moderately steep hike gives you a view that Omnimax movie directors would envy. Bat guano was used in the manufacture of makeup, fertilizer, and explosives due to its high nitrate content. Guano mining happened at a faster pace than the bats could replenish the reserves, so the operation was shut down in the 1960s. Standing at the equipment left behind, look carefully across and find the cave. Now imagine riding a pull-car system across the canyon.

The reservation opened to tourists in 1988. So unlike the immensely popular South and North rims, facilities and services are still being developed. The food choices aren't too many. The barbecue at **Hualapai Ranch** is rustic but definitely edible. At Guano Point, the food—basic and with few choices—is similar to that at other stops on the reservation. The difference here is the view. The most important information about visiting Grand Canyon West is to seriously consider taking a tour that leaves from Las Vegas and does the driving for you. Fourteen of the last 21 miles of road to the west rim are unpaved and very bumpy. Almost any car and many trucks are going to suffer damage taking this trip. The recommendation here is to take a Hummer tour like the ones offered by **Big Horn Wild West Tours** (702-385-4676; www.bighornhummertours.com). There are many tour companies available such as bus, plane, and helicopter to Grand Canyon West from Las Vegas, but Big Horn's Hummer tour gives anyone new to the desert an individual tour. Your personal tour guide knows the history and quirks of the areas you'll pass on the way there. They are also well versed in spotting local fauna and wildlife. All that information is perfect for their "special" road. The road they take to the rim is not the one all the tour buses take. It's a privately held road used for ranching. Taking it really gets you into the heart of the desert's uniqueness, as opposed to speeding past it on a highway. It may technically be a shortcut, but due to the terrain and the opportunities for pulling over to have a picture taken with an ancient Joshua tree, travel time is about the same. Don't let the $239 price tag of the Big Horn Grand Canyon West tour deter you. Add up what you would pay to rent a car, park, have lunch, and fill the tank. Then figure in the guide's knowledge, driving skills, and opportunities to experience what other tours don't.

If you are driving yourself, be aware that lodging on the area is short on supply. There are plans for more but for now there are a few newly constructed, sparsely decorated cabins at the Hualapai ranch. What they lack in amenities they make up in proximity to the rim, and no large crowds in the evening and early morning.

Please keep in mind that visitors to Grand Canyon West are on sovereign land belonging to the Hualapai nation. These aren't just rules like at an amusement park. They are laws that are to be respected. The Hualapai people depend on tourism to ensure their tribe's present and future survival. They have opened up their lands and are willing to share their most precious commodity. This endeavor provides them with jobs that help to keep them near home and with funds that help build needed infrastructure. Millions visit the other rims each year, while only a few hundred thousand make it to Grand Canyon West.

INSIDER TIP: Read your car rental contract carefully before driving to Grand Canyon West. Many have added stipulations regarding cars damaged on unpaved roads, like that leading to the west rim.

The best "dining with a view." Crystal Wood

MESQUITE, NEVADA, TO ST. GEORGE AND CEDAR CITY, UTAH

MESQUITE

On a northbound journey on Interstate 15 toward Salt Lake City, visitors will encounter Mesquite, Nevada. Poised approximately 80 miles north of Las Vegas and located on the Nevada/Arizona border, Mesquite is the final stop for gamblers traveling toward Utah looking to win their fortunes.

Mesquite, however, is far more than a mere stop along a longer journey—it's a place where many of the locals go when they need to get away for the weekend. About an hour's drive out of Las Vegas, Mesquite is home to seven golf courses, four casinos, a handful of spas, horseback riding, a motocross park, and a shooting range—a large offering for a town that is home to fewer than 20,000 people. As a result, the top-notch golf courses often have cheaper fees and readily available tee times. Similarly, the spas are often cheaper and appointments are easier to obtain.

MESQUITE CASINOS

CasaBlanca Resort, Casino, Golf & Spa (702-346-4041; www.casablancaresort.com; 950 West Mesquite Boulevard, Mesquite, NV 89027) The Casablanca Resort boasts 500 freshly remodeled hotel rooms, table games, slot machines, a sports book, an 18-hole golf course, full-service spa and salon, and live entertainment.

Eureka Casino and Hotel (800-346-4611; www.eurekamesquite.com; 275 Mesa Boulevard, Mesquite, NV 89027) Known as a locals' casino and hotel, the Eureka has table games, slot machines, Let it Ride, bingo, and more. Gregory's Steaks and Spirits, its fine dining room, has luxurious entrées such as hearty all-American prime cut steak, Australian lobster tail, and osso buco.

MORE IN MESQUITE:
Mesquite Motocross Park (928-347-4176; www.mesquitemx.com; Peppermill Palms Boulevard, past Palms Golf Course;) Rider: $30 per session, 9 AM–4 PM Spectators: $5.00, 5 and under are free. Thursday Practice, $20 per rider, Noon–4. Gates open one hour before practice.

Falcon Ridge Golf Club (702-346-6363; www.golffalcon.com; 345 Calais Dr, Mesquite, NV. 89027) This course has a 6,550-yard, par-71 rating.

The Palms Golf Club (711 Palms Boulevard, Mesquite, NV 89027) This course has a 7,008-yard, par-72 rating. The front nine has extended fairways, while the back nine is marked by mountainous terrain.

Wolf Creek Golf Club (866-252-4653; www.golfwolfcreek.com; 403 Paradise Parkway, Mesquite, NV 89027) The course has a par-72 rating and has a 7,018-yard layout.

> INSIDER TIP: The CasaBlanca Resort, Casino, Golf & Spa offers packages where visitors can save money on a night's stay and golf/spa treatments. Make sure to ask about them.

ST. GEORGE, UTAH
St. George, a major gateway to nearby Zion National Park, as well as many other natural beauties, is about 40 miles north of Mesquite, Nevada, and about 120 miles north of Las Vegas. The city's winters are mild, and it is an ideal destination for golfers who can revel in any of their 10 golf courses. The city is also home to a notable Mormon temple, an arts amphitheater, and dinosaur tracks.

Tuacahn Amphitheatre and Center for the Arts (800-746-9882; www.tuacahn.org; 1100 Tuacahn Drive, Ivins, UT 84738) The Tuacahn stages outdoor theatrical musicals, big-name concerts, and other performances nestled in a dramatic. red rock amphitheater on the edge of scenic Snow Canyon. Performances are scheduled throughout the year, but the summer season has the most offerings. The performances are family friendly and tickets range from $12.50 to $59.50, depending on the show.

Dinosaur Discovery Site (435-574-3466; www.sgcity.org/dinotrax; 2180 East Riverside Drive, St. George, UT 84790) The St. George Dinosaur Discovery Site at Johnson Farm was deemed to be the most significant dinosaur track site discovered within the western United States. The some 2,000 individual tracks, found in 2000 and believed to be between 195 and 198 million years old, display impressively clear details such as skin impressions. The tracks stem from animals believed to be Dilophosaurus-like creatures, which are three-toed and between 13 and 18 inches long, and also have accompanying impressions made by tail drags and swimming movements. The Johnson Farm also boasts a 15,000-square-foot museum that contains hundreds of dinosaur remains, fossil fish, plants, and invertebrates. Mon.–Sat. 10 AM to 6 PM. Adults 12 and older $6. Children (ages 4 through 11) $3. Children under 4 are free.

St. George Temple for The Church of Jesus Christ of Latter-day Saints (435-673-3533 250 East 400 South; St. George, UT 84770) The Mormon temple is the oldest operating temple in the Church of Jesus Christ of Latter-day Saints. Construction began in 1871, soon after the Mormons arrived in southern Utah. This was the only temple that was fully constructed during the 30-year tenure of Brigham Young, a prominent historical and religious leader of the Mormon faith. This inspiring 110,000-square-foot structure sits on six acres and is not open to visitors, but a free tour is available at the visitors' center next door.

INSIDER TIP: Utah is one hour ahead of Nevada. If you buy tickets to a show or set up a tee time, make sure you adjust your watches and travel schedule.

CEDAR CITY, UTAH

Cedar City, Utah is a small town 295 miles north of Las Vegas on Interstate 15 and about 175 miles north of St. George, Utah. At 5,840 feet, it has a significantly higher elevation than Las Vegas, Mesquite, and St. George, and it is an exciting cultural retreat from the severe heat in Las Vegas during the summer months. Cedar City is home to the Utah Shakespearean Festival and is a centralized location to many of the outdoor parks and recreation areas in the area such as Zion National Park, Bryce Canyon, and Brian Head, Utah.

Utah Shakespearean Festival (435-586-7878; www.bard.org; 351 West Center Street, Cedar City, UT 84720) Making the trek to the Utah Shakespearean Festival in southern Utah is an annual Las Vegas resident tradition. Each year since 1962, Las Vegans have driven to Cedar City, Utah, to see and be a part of one of the largest Shakespearean festivals in the country. The Festival is located on and around the Southern Utah University campus and is spread over three separate theaters—the Adams Shakespearean Theatre, the Randall L. Jones Theatre, and the Auditorium Theatre—and features three Shakespearean and several modern plays each year. Featured is the Adams Shakespearean Theatre, an authentic replication of Shakespeare's original Globe Theatre in London, and it takes place from June through August for the Summer Festival and September through October for the Fall Festival.

The festival comes in two parts—a summer and a fall segment. The Summer Festival offers free nightly Greenshows as an appetizer to the evening performances; the Greenshows feature singing, storytelling, and audience participation. The Fall Festival has free literary seminars, actors' seminars, and costume seminars.

INSIDER TIP: Take the backstage tour. It's only $8 and you get to talk to wig makers, costume designers, lighting and design technicians, and the people who work hard to put the show together. It is amazing. Know that you must take stairs to see everything.

BRIAN HEAD, UTAH

Brian Head, Utah, is a great place for travelers who love the outdoors. Close enough to Cedar City to be counted as a part of the community, its high elevation makes for a perfect locale for skiing in the winter and mountain biking in the summer. And if you don't like participating in sports, it's still a wonderful place to get away from the sounds of the city and stargaze.

Brian Head Resort (435-677-2035; www.brianhead.com; 329 South Highway 143, Brian Head, UT 84719) Brian Head Resort gets more than 400 inches of powdery snowfall annually and has 500 skiable acres, 53 runs, and a 1,707-foot vertical drop. The resort has runs suitable for all ability levels and is open usually from late November until mid-April, weather permitting. Brian Head Resort has more than winter skiing—it has snowmobiling, tubing, snowshoeing, sleigh rides, snowboarding, and a cozy lounge area for sipping coffee, cocoa, or something with a little more kick. It also has a camp for children ages 3 through 12 and a day-care facility for children aged 6 and up. Rental equipment is available at $27 for skis and $32 for snowboards. A full day's lift ticket costs $45, a relatively inexpensive day on the slopes. Starting in late June or July and lasting through October, Brian Head's mountain biking season offers fun trails through mountain forests.

INSIDER TIP: When driving between St. George and Cedar City, make sure to detour through Hurricane (pronounced Hur-uh-kin by the locals) and have lunch at the Main Street Café (435-635-9080; closed Sundays) downtown. It offers a full coffee bar, sandwiches, breakfasts, homemade breads, and vegetarian meals. Ponder the art on the wall or listen to one of the local bands, but definitely dine in the tree-lined garden area with the hummingbirds.

When choosing your hotel, it's all about location. Crystal Wood

3

Hotels and Resorts

Something for Everyone

There are close to 150,000 hotel/motel rooms in Las Vegas. Between the four hotels at the corner of Tropicana and Las Vegas Boulevard—MGM, New York, New York, Excalibur, and Tropicana—there are more than 12,000 rooms. The good news? There's so much to choose from. The bad news is there's so much to choose from. So where does one begin?

While the different resorts and rooms have some variations like themes, materials, and colors, they really are very much alike. Each property has good views and bad. More than likely there's construction nearby, since something new is always being built here. And almost all resorts have a steakhouse. The mega-resorts have such lengthy distances between parking, front desk, elevator, and guest rooms, you'll feel like you're on an Australian walkabout. They also have the most fun contained in their walls, making it easy to stay in one place for excitement. Activities at mega-resorts are tailored to the tastes of their dominant clientele—you'll want to acquaint yourself with the different offerings before making your choice.

The best way to choose where to stay is to whittle away those off the list that don't appeal to what you're looking to do. For instance, avid shoppers will be happiest staying near a mall. Of the Strip's malls, Miracle Mile has more stores closer to a "normal" price range. If this is the mall of choice, then Planet Hollywood works best. Looking at the locations for hottest shopping spots can help you with where not to stay, such as The Palms, Excalibur, or The Hard Rock. These hotels have limited shopping on-site and are a distance from the aforementioned malls.

Lately, many of the hotels in Las Vegas have started charging a "resort fee" or "resort charge" similar to the charges airlines have been implementing. The fee can include the fitness center, daily newspaper, parking, shuttles, swimming pool, spa facilities, and any number of different amenities, whether used or not. When the bill for your stay is tallied, the total may be very different from the steal of a deal found on an Internet site. Make sure you are informed of these fees when you check in. That paper you're signing may be for more than phone calls and room service. Check it carefully or ask directly.

Many guests of Las Vegas hotels are flabbergasted that views often cost more, even for just a smidgeon of the Strip or fountains or pool. The fact that the rooms of most major Strip hotels lack coffeemakers is also a point of contention. Also, a short wait at the check-in desk would be a pleasant surprise. An important caveat: Las Vegas room rates can vary wildly depending on events and holidays. Pricing guidelines do not include room taxes and fees, and prices are based on standard rooms, double occupancy.

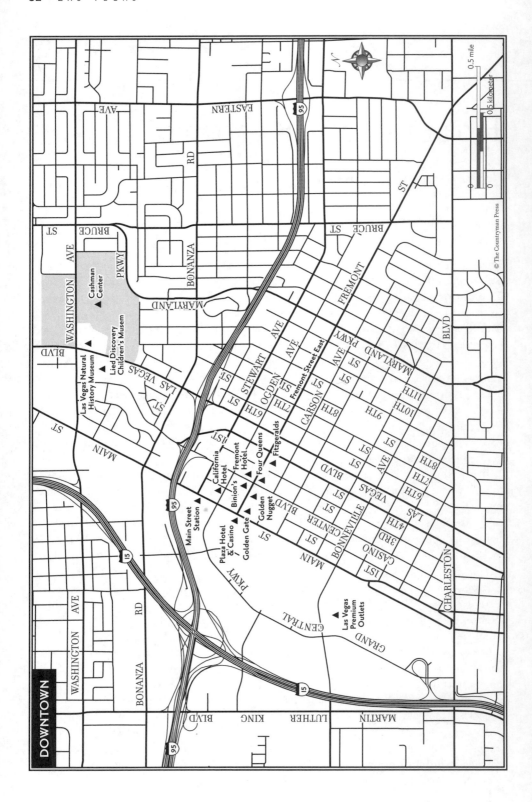

DOWNTOWN

© The Countryman Press

THE STRIP

Bally's Las Vegas

3645 Las Vegas Boulevard South, Las Vegas, NV 89109

877-603-4390 or 702-967-4567

www.ballyslasvegas.com

Price: Expensive.

An "old" resort by Las Vegas's newer-is-better standard, the recently remodeled Bally's Las Vegas remains a 30-year favorite along the Strip. Bally's is home to Donn Arden's Jubilee!, a traditional "showgirl" show at 7:30 and an acclaimed topless revue at 10:30. If partial nudity offends you, this is not the show for you. But, if you're into sparkly costumes and a little extra skin, then you'll have a good time. This show is definitely classic Vegas and spotlights singers, dancers, elaborate million-dollar sets, and dazzling costumes by famed designer Bob Mackie. Tickets range from $50 to $100 each. Bally's also features The Price is Right, a live-audience version of the popular TV game show where randomly selected members of the audience participate in winning cash and prizes. If you're at least 21 years old, you are eligible to challenge yourself in games such as Plinko, Hole in One, Race Game, and the showcase showdown for appliances, vacations, and even cars. Tickets are $49.50 each. Game times are 2:30 PM except on Fridays, when the game begins at 7:30 PM. Guests under 21 may buy tickets, but they can only watch. Bally's has more than shows and its standard fare of gaming; it also has a Las Vegas Harley-Davidson store that is sure to get any motorhead's heart pumping and wheels smoking. Don an array of Harley-Davidson apparel, leather, and sunglasses, pick out a few collectibles and home decorations to remember your stay, and then ask about Harley rentals for cruising around town during your visit. Bally's is a stop along the Las Vegas Monorail system.

INSIDER TIP: Located on the southeast corner of Las Vegas Boulevard and Flamingo Road, Bally's is on prime Strip real estate. It is not only across the street from the glamorous Bellagio but also next door to Paris Las Vegas and its Eiffel Tower, near the historic Flamingo hotel, and kitty-corner from Caesars Palace. It is also highly accessible, as it is located right next to one of only two pedestrian-friendly walkway areas in town (Las Vegas Boulevard and Tropicana Road is the other).

Bellagio Las Vegas

702-693-7111 or 888-987-6667

www.bellagio.com

3600 Las Vegas Boulevard South, Las Vegas, NV 89109

Price: Very Expensive.

Bellagio, a favorite of tourists and locals, alike, proudly hosts many fine shows, restaurants, shops, and things to see. Guests and gawkers can watch the Fountains at Bellagio at the front entry—a stunning choreography of water, music, light, and grandeur against the nighttime sky. Once inside, visitors can watch the show O, a Cirque du Soleil aquatic, European-styled production, featuring acrobats, synchronized swimmers, divers, contortionists, and trapeze acts in and out of the water. O is performed twice nightly at 7:30 PM and 10:30 PM, Weds. through Sun. Tickets are $150.00, $125.00, $99.00, and $93.50. While waiting for your show, make sure to step inside the Conservatory and Botanical Gardens. A visual and olfactory buffet, the conservatory is decorated to reflect the season with gorgeous plants, flowers, and trees in the height of their splendor surrounded by enchanting ponds, gazebos, bridges, and water features. Wonderful for a romantic moment or gorgeous backdrop for a photo, this floral oasis is a free and definite must-see inside the Bellagio. Also be certain to schedule a visit to the Bellagio Gallery of Fine Art, which

Caesars Palace has kept up well with the changing times. Leah Koepp

showcases magnificent works from widely renowned painters, sculptors, and more. Tickets are $15 and children under 12 are free. Be sure to gaze upward to the Dale Chihuly art installation in the lobby to see the sparkle of the 2,000 hand-blown glass flowers meant to welcome hotel guests. Need a little nighttime excitement? Stop at The Bank for a few drinks from this bottle-service nightclub with a high-energy atmosphere and glass dance floor, but bring a full wallet because bottle service is not cheap. If you're more of a daytime person, take a round of golf at Shadow Creek, the Las Vegas valley's most exclusive course, complete with limousine service and a personal caddie. Make sure to peruse Via Bellagio, a row of high-end shopping featuring Giorgio Armani, Chanel, Dior, Gucci, Hermès, Tiffany & Co., Yves Saint Laurent, Prada, Fendi, and more.

INSIDER TIP: If you plan on seeing any of the Cirque du Soleil shows at the Bellagio or any of its sister properties, make reservations as soon as you can. Tickets for these shows are far more expensive than any other on the Strip, but are usually well worth it. As such, they can sell out months in advance, though hotel guests can call their local ticket offices to see if any last-minute tickets have been released.

Caesars Palace Las Vegas

866-227-5938
www.caesarspalace.com
3570 Las Vegas Boulevard South, Las Vegas, NV 89109
Price: Very Expensive.

If you're a fan of top celebrity performers and the feel of classic Vegas, then Caesars Palace is the place for you. Known for its beauty and luxury since the day it opened in 1966, the hotel has 3,300 rooms, 26 restaurants, 240,000 square feet of convention space, a 4.5-acre Garden of the Gods pool and garden area, and 4,300-seat theater, all to ensure the proper relaxation and entertainment of its guests. The Colosseum, the primary performance hall at Caesars, has featured all of the big-name icons, including Liberace, George Burns. Dean Martin, Frank Sinatra, and Celine Dion, and now showcases performances from legendary performers Cher, Bette Midler, Elton John, and Jerry Seinfeld. Tickets range from $86 to $250 each, and advance purchases are recommended. Before going to the show, make sure to stop for a bite to eat at any one of the many fine restaurants there for the cuisine of your choice: Rao's (Italian), Restaurant Guy Savoy (French), Bradley Ogden (seasonal, farm-fresh American), Mesa Grill (Food Network's own Bobby Flay and his Southwest-inspired cooking), Payard Pâtisserie & Bistro (French bistro), Neros (dry-aged premium steaks), Bejing Noodle No. 9, and Hyakumi (Japanese), just to name a few. Make sure to eat well—you will need your energy, as there is plenty of shopping to be done. Caesars Palace is home to the Forum Shops, featuring 120 stores and upscale boutiques, comprising one of the largest shopping malls in the entire city. Or burn off those calories by dancing all night at PURE, a 40,000-square-foot nightclub with four venues in one—each with its own DJ and sound system, bringing you intense energy and a heart-pounding night out. Club wear is expected. Take a moment to rest your dancing feet and take the twisting staircase or ride the glass elevator to the Terrace, where you can catch your breath and, at the same time, breathe in the incredible panoramic views of the Strip. And if you time your visit right, you can catch a boxing match at the outdoor Roman Plaza or a one-of-a-kind event that makes Las Vegas so unique. Caesars has been home to some of the most widely publicized events in the city's history, including the failed motorcycle jump over the front water fountains by stunt daredevil Evel Knievel in 1967, later successfully attempted by his son Robbie Knievel in 1989 and Mike Metzger in 2006 at the resort's 40th-anniversary celebration. Caesars Palace is also a stop along the Las Vegas Monorail System.

Circus Circus

800-634-3450 or 702-691-5950
www.circuscircus.com
2880 Las Vegas Boulevard South, Las Vegas, NV 89109
Price: Inexpensive.

Be a kid again, or at least act like one with your own kids at Circus Circus Las Vegas. Built as one of the first family-oriented resorts on the Strip, Circus Circus is definitely an older property. It still has its share of gaming and fine restaurants that any adult can enjoy but also has many kid-friendly things to do, starting with the Midway. Step right up and play your favorite carnival game and win fun prizes. While playing, gaze up every so often and catch a glimpse of any one of the free trapeze and acrobatic acts that take place between 11 AM and midnight. After you collect your carnival prizes, visit the Adventuredome, an indoor theme park. The Adventuredome provides decent rides for adults and kids, alike, but does not have the hair-raising rides that true adrenaline junkies would adore. Ride the Canyon Blaster, a 55-mph, double-loop, and double-corkscrew roller-coaster ride, or the Rim Runner ride, but only if you don't mind getting wet. Thrill seekers can't resist rides like the Sling Shot, Inverter, and Chaos or heart-pounding activities like Lazer Blast. Rides are also available for junior adventurers as well. Rides range from $4 to $7 each, or a regular all-day pass is $24.95 and a junior pass is $14.95. If you prefer a different kind of game, visit the golf course at any of the Walters Golf club facilities—the Royal Links Golf Club, Desert Pines Golf Club and Bali Hai Golf Club. After you are done working up your appetite, stop by THE Steak House

for prime rib, lobster, crab, and lamb chops; the Garden Grill for traditional American fare; or Mexitalia, with a menu that offers a compromise to the picky eaters in your family—Italian and Mexican cuisines.

Excalibur Hotel Casino

702-597-7777
www.excalibur.com
3850 Las Vegas Boulevard South, Las Vegas, NV 89109-6778
Price: Inexpensive.

Excalibur arrived on the scene in 1990 as a family-friendly casino, a rarity among the multitude of gaming establishments meant for the 21-and-over crowd. The most popular attraction at the Excalibur is the twice-nightly Tournament of Kings, a dinner and jousting show, complete with brave knights, fair maidens, and gallant steeds at $61 per ticket. Then, tour the Fantasy Fair midway, where you can test your skill at carnival games and win prizes. If the kid stuff isn't for you, however, then there is still plenty to see and do. Catch a few laughs with Louie Anderson at the Thunder Showroom Lobby for only $54 or $79 per ticket. Let those belly laughs continue at Dick's Last Resort for traditional American fare and a rowdy, wisecracking staff serving up an extra order of sarcasm—not intended for the easily offended. If insults and witty banter aren't risqué enough, then gather your friends and go for a wild night with some of the most handsome, nearly naked Australians around at Thunder Down Under. Imagine a sexy Jack Sparrow, a Spartan, a fireman, a cowboy, or even a soldier in his finest uniform, and then imagine him out of it. Tickets are $39.95 or $49.95 and the show is always a treat, even on a repeat visit. If your sense of adventure is more on the mild side, then be sure to arrange a visit to the Royal Treatment Spa for some pampering, a fine cut of beef at The Steakhouse at Camelot, or 18 rounds at Bali Hai, Desert Pines, or Royal Links Golf Clubs to calm your mind and fill your spirit.

Flamingo Las Vegas

888-902-9929
www.flamingolasvegas.com
3555 Las Vegas Boulevard South, Las Vegas, NV 89109
Price: Moderate.

The Flamingo, as locals call it, is the casino that nefarious mobster Bugsy Siegel built, starting the resort-style boom in Las Vegas. True to its early days, the Flamingo still hosts many well-known performers such as Donny & Marie and even television psychic John Edwards. Tickets range from $90 to $225 each. If singing and spirits aren't for you, see comedian George Wallace for tickets at $40 to $75. Hungry? There a multitude of restaurants including Voga, an American bistro, and Jimmy Buffett's famed Margaritaville. If you're looking for something mellower, try Hamada of Japan, a longtime Las Vegas sushi favorite, or Steakhouse46, for a fine cut of beef. Bugsy Siegel opened the Flamingo in 1946; since then it's been through numerous reincarnations in order to keep current: the most recent innovation is Go Rooms. The updates included the technological with iPod compatible sound system, bathroom in-mirror flat-screen televisions, and electronic draperies. The décor is retro chic with a smattering of Austin Powers fun thrown in. The Go Rooms must be specifically requested as part of the reservation booked through the Flamingo and only represent 500 or so rooms of the more than 3,000 in the resort. Part of the attraction of the Flamingo is what lies not only within its walls but also outside them. Arrange a round of golf at nearby Cascata golf course, or stay on-site, as the Flamingo hosts a wildlife habitat on the premises and is home to a flock of pink Chilean flamingos, as well as swans, ducks, turtles, and koi living in lush landscapes and sparking waterfalls. And if you like wildlife of a different sort, visit the GO Pool, an "adult alternative" party pool, complete with cocktail service, DJ music, topless sunbathing, and large cabanas for rent with air conditioning, 52-inch plasma televisions, Xbox 360

The Flamingo has updated some rooms in a 60s spy-movie style. Courtesy Harrah's

gaming stations, and specialty menus. Leave the kiddies at home for this trip. The Flamingo is also a stop along the Las Vegas Monorail system.

Four Seasons Hotel Las Vegas

702-632-5000 or 800-819-5053
www.fourseasons.com/lasvegas
3960 Las Vegas Boulevard South, Las Vegas, NV 89119
Price: Very Expensive.

The luxury doesn't get any finer than the Four Seasons Hotel, but then the price tag certainly matches the quality. Physically attached to the Mandalay Bay, but run separately, the Four Seasons is one of the only major hotels on the Strip that does not have a casino floor. As a result, the Four Seasons is noticeably quiet and serene, and a welcome respite from the constant, intense energy found in many of the other resorts. The rooms are also highly refined, and there are plenty of specialty suites, such as the Presidential Suite, 180-Degree Strip-View Suite, and Executive Suite. Schedule an afternoon in the spa to get your fill of flower-stone massages and facials, collagen treatments, and mud wraps and ooze comfort and relaxation. Or get out your big hat and fancy pearls and have high tea in Verandah, the resort's informal dining room that overlooks the garden and pool, from 3:00 to 4:00 PM each afternoon. The full menu at the Verandah contains fresh juices, exotic fruits, a mix of contemporary American and Italian dishes, and favorites like spiced duck, Maine lobster ravioli, and lemon chicken pappardelle. Make sure to have the lobster bisque—it's incredibly creamy and delicious. If you like your cup to runneth over with more than hot tea, stop by the Verandah Bar and Lounge after playing a round of golf at either the Bali Hai or Royal Links golf courses. Work up that appetite for a visit at Charlie Palmer Steak, an American steakhouse, which prides itself on creative twists on traditional beef fare. Charlie Palmer's

kitchen prepares its ever-changing menu with fresh fish and seafood options, as well as artisan aged beef. There is no such thing as a bad meal at Charlie Palmer Steak.

Harrah's Las Vegas Casino & Resort

702-369-5000 or 1-800-427-7247
www.harrahslasvegas.com
3475 Las Vegas Boulevard South, Las Vegas, NV 89109
Price: Moderate.

Harrah's is known for its entertainment, and with a comedy lineup of Rita Rudner, Mac King, and a fresh new batch of faces at the Improv each week, the laughs keep rolling in.

Rita Rudner tickets are $54 each, Improv tickets are $29 and $45 each, and Mac King, comedian and magician, are $25 each. And if you'd rather see singing and dancing by your favorite celebrities, you can watch them in the longest-running celebrity tribute show in town, the 20-year-old classic, Legends in Concert. These live re-creations of the most amazing superstars of different decades can be seen on one stage, and features impersonators of a changing roster of talents such as Elvis Presley, Rod Stewart, Madonna, Jay Leno, Garth Brooks, Whitney Houston, Britney Spears, Justin Timberlake, Karen Carpenter, Ray Charles, George Strait, Barry White, Prince, ABBA, and Gwen Stefani. Have a cocktail served with style from some of the best flair bartenders around at the Carnival Court, or drop in at Toby Keith's I Love This Bar and Grill for great grub and live entertainment, all inside the restaurant and appropriately named after his famous song. Come for a fine meal at the Range Steakhouse, Ming's Table for Asian cuisine, Penazzi for Italian fare, or fresh steamers and calamari at the Oyster Bar and Penzzi and get in the spirit of fun at this Carnival-styled resort. Harrah's is also a stop on the Las Vegas Monorail system.

The windows in the Luxor pyramid rooms have an unusual slant. Courtesy MGM.

Luxor Las Vegas

702-262-4444
www.luxor.com
3900 Las Vegas Boulevard South, Las Vegas,
NV 89119
Price: Moderate.

The Luxor is among the most recognizable resorts on the Las Vegas Strip because of its design as the Great Pyramid of Giza. Encased in a 30-story pyramid of black glass with a fixed spotlight emanating from its apex, the hotel can be seen from anywhere in the Las Vegas Valley and is also reported as being seen as far as Los Angeles and Kingman, Arizona, on clear nights. The hotel's engineers also claim that the bright light can even be seen in space. Despite its lights and seemingly odd shape as a hotel, the Luxor's Egyptian-themed interior contains a surprising 405 guest rooms and 487 suites. After checking in, visit some of the restaurants for some great food: TENDER, a steak & seafood house; Backstage Deli, for sandwiches with meat stacked so high on marbled rye that any New Yorker would be proud; and Fusia Luxor, an Asian-inspired lounge offering an unusual twist on traditional Asian cuisine. Come to CatHouse—no, not that kind of cathouse—a new dining experience created by *Iron Chef* victor Kerry Simon. Dine, dance, and relax in an upscale restaurant/lounge with two separate DJs and dance floors, all highlighted by a beautiful staff dressed in racy lingerie. Or skip the food and go directly to the Los Angeles–inspired nightclub, LAX, complete with plenty of posh VIP tables. Fans of magic can check out Criss Angel Believe, a Cirque du Soleil show, as he explores magic and the surreal world of the human imagination in his nightly show, starting at $59 and up to $160 per ticket. Too intense for you? Go for a few laughs with Carrot Top, as he presents his witty observations through the use of crazy props and wacky inventions. Tickets are $50 each. Or visit FANTASY, a show of wild fantasies and seductions as an adult, topless revue, featuring singing, comedy, and choreography for men and women. Tickets are $45 to start.

Mandalay Bay Hotel & Casino

877-632-7800
www.mandalaybay.com
3950 Las Vegas Boulevard South, Las Vegas, NV 89119
Price: Very Expensive.

Mandalay Bay is one of the more luxurious resorts on the Strip and has plenty for visitors to see and do. Begin with its 12,000-seat Events Center for performances by entertainers such as Beyoncé and events like the Latin Grammys, world championship boxing, or Ultimate Fight Championships. Visit the House of Blues, a more intimate performance venue where local bands and international megastars can be seen. Or go to Disney's award-winning theatrical version of the *Lion King,* exclusively at Mandalay Bay. Walk through the Shark Reef tunnel aquarium and come eyeball-to-eyeball with some of the world's fiercest predators—sharks, piranha, moon jellies, and rare golden crocodiles. Tickets are $17 for adults and $11 for children. Mandalay Bay is also home to one of the better spa facilities on the Strip at both its Bathhouse and the Spa at Mandalay where the services are as grand as the facilities are elegant. Dine at several of the hotel's fine restaurants: Aureole, an award-winning steak and seafood eatery with its trademark four-story wine tower and wine angels to retrieve your vino selections; Red Square, a Russian-inspired world of intrigue, complete with caviar, exotic entrées like Strozapretti Stroganoff and Salmon Kulebyaka, a private vodka vault, and an icebar featuring more than 200 vodkas, martinis, and Russian-inspired cocktails; Wolfgang Puck's first foray into Italian dining, Trattoria del Lupo, featuring fresh pasta made daily and tastes from all over the country; Rick Moonen's RM Seafood, a great place for delicate seafood dining upstairs and a sushi bar downstairs; STRIPSTEAK, offering three kinds of beef—certified Angus, American Kobe, and "A5" Japanese Kobe—to cook on its two wood-burning grills and six slow-poaching chambers for the ultimate in flavor and tenderness; or dine in rumjungle, a restaurant and nightclub mix where guests pass through a wall of fire and a waterfall to eat the greatest in Brazilian, Caribbean, and Cuban entrées, followed by a drink from the world's largest rum bar.

MGM Grand Las Vegas

877-880-0880 or 702-891-7777
www.mgmgrand.com
3799 Las Vegas Boulevard South, Las Vegas, Nevada 89109
Price: Expensive.

The second-largest hotel in the world, the MGM Grand touts itself as The City of Entertainment, and quite frankly, it really could be a city unto itself. With 16 restaurants, 5 pools, 4,293 hotel rooms, 751 suites, 576 Signature suites, 51 lofts, 29 villas, a 17,000-seat event arena, over a dozen high-end boutique shops, a spa, a wedding chapel, a nightclub, a health club, a lion habitat, a performance theater, and 171,500 square feet of separate casino floor space, the only thing missing is a duly-elected mayor. KA, a Cirque du Soleil theatrical production, is a story of twins lost and journeying to return home to their families, encountering many dangers and predators throughout the Chinese lands. There is dramatic dancing and acrobatics, intense drumming, fiery scenes, chanting and singing, incredible costumes, and a moving stage that all lend themselves to the telling of this epic journey. Tickets are $78 to $160 each. Visit the MGM Garden Arena web site for a full list of concerts, sports, and special events that cannot be found anywhere else. Stop by the Las Vegas version of New York's Studio 54 nightclub, or see *Crazy Horse Paris,* an adult revue, as it "celebrates the artistry of the nude." MGM Grand management also shares a pro-restaurant philosophy, believing that a hotel's fine dining

The tanks behind the check-in desk at the Mirage help pass the time. Crystal Wood

experiences are what can truly shape the quality and character of a resort, and they have pulled out all the stops on its restaurant options: Craftsteak, a steakhouse with veal, salmon, lobster, and Kobe beef; Nobhill Tavern for modern American cuisine and elegant cocktails; SEABLUE, a Mediterranean seafood grill; Pearl, cuisine celebrating the Canton and Shanghai provinces; Wolfgang Puck Bar & Grill, a reinvention of American fare by its legendary namesake; FiamMA Tattoria and Bar, a modern Italian eatery with fresh, handmade pastas, award-winning wine list, and fireside lounge; Shibuya, a sake and sushi haven in an airy and ambient setting; Emeril's, serving his famous Creole and Cajun specialties; Diego, serving traditional recipes from the Mexican countryside; and two restaurants from Joel Robuchon, one a traditional French restaurant serving 16-course dining experiences and the other a cafe serving French tapas.

The Mirage Hotel and Casino

702-791-7111 or 800-374-9000
www.mirage.com
3400 Las Vegas Boulevard South, Las Vegas, NV 89109
Price: Expensive.

The Mirage, most famous for its iconic volcano that erupts every 15 minutes, has been seen on television shows around the world. Recently redesigned, the volcano has a new fire pattern and striking drumming music that accompanies its new intensity—a free show not to be missed. Once inside, check in at the hotel's front desk and view the 20,000-gallon saltwater aquarium, filled with angelfish, sharks, stingrays, eels, gobies, sea bass, puffer fish, tangs, and other exotic sea creatures including nearly one thousand specimens of coral reminiscent of Australia's Great Barrier Reef. Walk through the lobby and into the hotel's misty and aromatic atrium and step into a lush rainforest filled with palm trees, orchids, bird of paradise trees, and cascading waterfalls. Keep walking and stop at Siegfried & Roy's Secret Garden & Dolphin Habitat Experience, where you can see white lions, white tigers, panthers, leopards, Atlantic bottlenose dolphins, and the latest arrivals—at the time of writing, baby tiger cubs and a new baby dolphin. Continue onward to the customized theater that was built for LOVE, the Cirque du Soleil show with the powerful and passionate sounds of the legendary Beatles. Listen to the Beatles' timeless music, as interpreted by international dancers, aerial performers, and extreme sports athletes in an audio and visual sensation. Feel the dancing arise within yourself and explore JET, a multilevel nightlife experience with lights, lasers, and a cryogenic effects system intended to create an exotic party mood within its three distinct rooms. Full bars and European bottle service are also featured in each room. Need a little food to fill your body, not just your soul? Eat at any one of the several signature restaurants inside the Mirage: Japonais, for contemporary Japanese; Stack, an American Bistro; Fin, for contemporary Chinese cuisine; Kokomo's, for prime steaks, chops, fresh seafood, and giant lobster tails; Onda, for classic-rustic Italian cuisine; and Samba, a Brazilian-style barbecue offering endless portions of marinated meats, poultry, and seafood.

Monte Carlo Las Vegas Resort and Casino
888-529-4828 or 800-311-8999
www.montecarlo.com
3770 Las Vegas Boulevard South, Las Vegas, NV 89109
Price: Moderate.

The Monte Carlo is home of Master Magician Lance Burton, who uses both prop magic and sleight-of-hand tricks to mesmerize his audience. He starts with small tricks to lure in his audience at the beginning of his show, and once he has you caught up in the excitement, he builds up his act and graduates to larger and grander illusions, leaving people gasping for more. Unlike many magicians in town, Lance talks to his audience and is extremely charming and unassuming, which is part of his appeal. Tickets are $67 and $73 each. After the show, stop by the Monte Carlo Brew Pub for a draft beer. Once a fully operational brewpub, the room is now just a bar, but is still, nonetheless, a great place to throw a few back with some friends. Not a beer drinker? Stop by Diablo's Mexican Cantina for a full bar and specialty frozen drinks. It's great place to people-watch, especially on the patio, or a place to watch the next big game on any of their large plasma televisions. Nibble some Mexican food favorites with your margarita, or stop by any one of their signature restaurants, including BRAND steakhouse, a restaurant/lounge fused into one; Andre's Restaurant & Lounge, traditional French cuisine featuring Rack of Colorado Lamb, Filet of Beef au Poivre Vert, and Live Maine Lobster Thermidor; or Dragoon Noodle, an Asian and tea emporium, offering beef, chicken, seafood, and even sushi; or the Market City Caffe, an Italian eatery filled with the sweet aroma of simmering tomato sauces and brilliant spices. Afterward, connect with the hotel's own Golf Concierge, who is more than happy to arrange a round of golf at nearby courses such as the Bali Hai, Desert Pines Golf Club, and Royal Links Golf Club. Or visit The Spa at Monte Carlo to recharge your body and soul in an intimate spa with a fully attentive staff.

New York, New York Hotel Casino
800-689-1797 or 866-815-4365
www.nynyhotelcasino.com
3790 Las Vegas Boulevard South, Las Vegas, NV 89109
Price: Expensive.

Not surprisingly, New Yorkers think this hotel is just plain silly and far too clean to be the Big Apple. But for those not familiar with the real thing, the Disney-fied version may bring some joy. The Central Park theme on the gaming floor was recently trimmed back. Now there are far fewer fake trees, which is good. Now the casino looks revived as opposed to dusty with counterfeit foliage, and the location, with the MGM Grand and Excalibur across the street, is good. The property's footprint is unusual due to the facades of NYC's famous buildings on the outside. This relatively small hotel is laid out like a labyrinth, and if lounging by the pool for hours on end is important to you, stay elsewhere—the pool here feels like an afterthought. Cirque du Soleil's sexiest show, Zumanity, is found here. The Coney Island Arcade and roller coaster are fun for families. The restaurants are mostly affordable and casual, Gallagher's steakhouse being the exception. For partying through the night, there's Coyote Ugly, Rok Vegas, and Nine Fine Irishmen.

Rooms can be found in petite replicas of New York City's famous skyscrapers. Courtesy MGM

The Palazzo Las Vegas Resort-Hotel Casino

877-883-6423
www.palazzolasvegas.com
3325 Las Vegas Boulevard South, Las Vegas, NV 89109
Price: Very Expensive.

The Palazzo is the sophisticated sister property to the Venetian and is located next door. If you desire to, you can get from one to the other without ever walking outside. This property is all about living it up in style. From the largest Canyon Ranch Spa Club in the Americas to the multiple celebrity-chef-owned restaurants, you can spend all your time and money here. There are more than 3,000 suites, most of which are more than 700 square feet. The rooms are twice as large as the standard hotel room. If given the opportunity to upgrade your stay to the Concierge level, ask to see the facilities and the total price for your stay before deciding. It's a very nice option for business and convention travelers, but may be unnecessary for vacationers. There are a dozen different restaurants helmed by chefs of notoriety. They may not be at this particular location very often, but you can say you ate there. The pool area is a delight and with seven to choose from, the view can be ever-changing. They offer a very nice shuttle ride from the airport for $6, per guest of the hotel (cash only). The shuttle arrives at the airport at the top of the hour, just outside door number eight. The big show here is *Jersey Boys*, the story of Frankie Valli and the Four Seasons. Next door at the Venetian, it's *Phantom—The Las Vegas Spectacular*, Blue Man Group, and Wayne Brady.

Paris Las Vegas

877-603-4386
www.parislasvegas.com
3655 Las Vegas Boulevard South, Las Vegas, NV 89109
Price: Moderate.

Paris Las Vegas is a very popular hotel and it's a mystery as to why. The suites are

Standard rooms at Planet Hollywood include genuine movie memorabilia. Courtesy Planet Hollywood

extravagantly decorated in what can only be described as French gaudy, but with no whimsy or realism. The basic rooms are fine but may not be worth the extra effort and price. The location (across from Bellagio) can be a draw, and certain rooms have a view of the famous dancing fountains; however, these rooms are likely to cost extra. The issue with the location is the traffic. The traffic lights at the street entrance and those at the next corner are timed too close together. Add gawking at the Bellagio fountains and it is mayhem. If you're not driving, this isn't a concern. The only eating establishment worth recommending is La Creperie, even if it is a bit inconsistent. The freshly made crepes served with an assortment of fillings, ranging from the traditional to the experimental, make a pleasant and inexpensive breakfast or lunch.

Planet Hollywood Resort & Casino

702-785-5555
www.planethollywoodresort.com
3667 Las Vegas Boulevard South, Las Vegas, NV 89109
Price: Expensive.

Planet Hollywood Resort somehow gets it right. They're able to make their resort fresh, young, and hip, and yet anyone could enjoy staying here. Whatever it is you want to do while staying on the Strip, Planet Hollywood has it. Dining choices include the Las Vegas outlets of the legendary Pink's Hot Dogs and the renowned Strip House. Other restaurants include Koi, Yolos Mexican Grill, and Earl of Sandwich. Headlining concert entertainment is found in the 7,000-seat theater. Peepshow is a burlesque style show with rotating headliners who have included Holly Madison, Kelly Monaco, and Mel B. The nightlife options are plenty here. Privé is the main dance club, while the Living Room and Heart Bar are more about relating to one another. There are more than 2,500 rooms here. The standard Hollywood Hip Room has genuine movie memorabilia as part of the décor. The room also includes a 42-inch flat-screen television and CAT high-speed data-port. The bathroom is larger than one would expect and has a soaking tub. However, the armoire is small and, as there is no closet, this can be a hindrance. For more space, there are the Deluxe, Resort, and Vista rooms. There's loads of shopping, dining choices from fine to casual, and multiple bars to hop at the attached Miracle Mile mall. Planet Hollywood is a member of Starwood Hotels.

Sahara Hotel & Casino

702-737-2111 or 888-696-2121
www.saharavegas.com
2535 Las Vegas Boulevard South, Las Vegas,
NV 89109
Price: Inexpensive.

In Las Vegas time, the Sahara Hotel and
Casino has been around a very long time—
since 1952, to be exact. It's one of the last Rat
Pack–era casinos left. For those looking for
genuine vintage Las Vegas, not modern glitz
and glam, this may be the hotel for you as
long you're willing to tolerate a few older
quirks. An advantage to staying in an older
hotel is what you hear once you get up to your
room: Not a thing. There are no nightclubs at
the Sahara and the entertainers are skewed
toward a more mature audience. Unless the
Coasters are having some kind of revival
with the in-crowd, the odds of the whipper-
snappers whooping it up as they pass your
room are unlikely. The rooms are definitely
dated but are also large and tidy. Because
there is a NASCAR Café and simulation ride
here, it's best to keep your distance when the
big races are in town, unless that's your
thing. For dining, the House of Lords
Steakhouse is perfect for those not looking
for celebrity chefs and high modern décor.
The portions are large and the servers are
experienced professionals. The Sahara's
location at the north end of the Strip may be
difficult for some, but with a monorail stop
here, getting to the action is just a ride away.

Stratosphere

702-380-7777 or 800-998-6937
www.stratospherehotel.com
2000 Las Vegas Boulevard South, Las Vegas,
NV 89104
Price: Moderate.

Different casino resorts cater to different
crowds. Some aim for the glamorous, others shoot for the business class. Some
attract those who want to spend a lot of
money, even if in everyday life they don't

live like this. Some visitors enjoy coming
to Las Vegas looking to spend as little as
they can. The Stratosphere was opened
during the "family destination" phase of
Las Vegas marketing. And while other
hotels just replaced their family fun with
more alluring attractions, the
Stratosphere planted its feet firmly and
tried to weather the storm. The result is a
property that is not only less expensive
than others but also caters to folks who
choose not to see the artsy Cirque shows
or dine at restaurants featured on cable
channels. The location at the far north end
of the Strip can be inconvenient, but
there's a monorail stop a few blocks away
in the Sahara. Not surprisingly, the rooms
are not updated and the bathrooms are
unexpectedly small, even for a hotel.
When traveling with others or with children, this can be an issue. Due to a lack of
workspace, these rooms are not recommended for business travelers. Guests of
the hotel have free access to the observation deck atop the tower each afternoon.
The Top of the World restaurant obviously
offers a wonderful view, but, for the price,
a better meal can be found elsewhere. If
the view is a necessity, have drinks at the
restaurant's bar.

Treasure Island Hotel and Casino

800-288-7206 or 702-894-7111
www.treasureisland.com
3300 Las Vegas Boulevard South, Las Vegas
NV 89109
Price: Expensive.

Treasure Island, or "TI" as it asks to be
called, has worked very hard at morphing
from a families-welcome resort to a hot
spot for the fashionable and young. And it
worked. The prime location is perfect for
those looking to take in all that the Strip can
offer. For shopping fanatics, the Fashion
Show Mall, Palazzo Shoppes, and Grand
Canal Shoppes are across the street.

17 Miles Across the Desert: Lake Las Vegas

In Las Vegas, there's only one thing more powerful than money. It's not looks and it's not youth. It's water. Wherever this liquid gold is controlled, money and prestige are sure to follow. Just seventeen miles east of the Strip at Lake Las Vegas, the water (3 million gallons of Henderson, Nevada's, Lake Mead allotment) made the lake, which made a golf course, palatial celebrity homes, shopping, and two of the classiest hotels in all of the Las Vegas valley. For other activities, there's the small **Casino MonteLago (702-564-4766),** gondola rides, and dinner cruises.

The luxurious but not stuffy Loews Lake Las Vegas Resort doesn't have a casino.   Courtesy Loews Lake Las Vegas

Loews Lake Las Vegas
877-285-6397 or 702-567-6000
www.loewshotels.com
101 Montelago Boulevard, Henderson, NV 89011
Price: Very Expensive.

There are just 18 Loews properties around the country and once you've stayed at this one, you'll want to visit the other 17. There are few refined hotels where feeling comfortable and welcomed are the status quo, but Loews pulls it off. From the greeting at valet parking straight through the entire stay, you are treated to what true customer service should be. The décor in the public areas and rooms is Turkish Kasbah but not to the point of looking like a fashion-conscious teenage girl's bedroom. It's sedately

Nightclubs located in the property include Christian Audigier The Nightclub and Social House. The latter also makes it to the list of eateries, which includes Kahunaville, Canter's Deli, and the only Vietnamese Pho menu on the Strip. The original Las Vegas Cirque du Soleil show, *Mystère,* is here and the Beatles version, *LOVE,* is at the Mirage next door. If inclement weather keeps the outdoor show *Sirens of TI* from going on, scope out the casino for cast members available for memorable pictures. Sadly, the pool area is small when compared to those at other resort hotels. The rooms are conscientiously clean, though the bathroom lighting is not the most flattering. The petite suite with king bed has two separate bathrooms and is excellent for two friends looking to share a Strip room.

done with gentle hues and textiles. Of the rooms with a lake view, it's best to request a garden level for the patio. However, if the hotel is busy or if there's a wedding or other private function, the noise level can increase. The higher floors have Rapunzel balconies, which provide no place to sit or stand. And for those infuriated by the lack of coffeemakers in most Las Vegas hotels, Loews is one of the few exceptions. Two restaurants, **Rick's Café** and **Marssa**, offer unusual choices along with regular fare. Marssa is blessed with a highly awarded executive sushi chef whose creations deserve every accolade received. The quiet desert nights can be thoroughly enjoyed at the public fire pit overlooking the lake. If the winds are kicking up there are comfortable chairs, couches, and credenzas just inside but with the same view. The walk-up bar makes cocktails with fresh juices and offers some quenching specialties of the house. As high-end as Loews is, families are not only welcome but also encouraged to stay here. The amenities focusing on families include the pool with waterslide and basketball court and cooking and sushi classes. Fly-fishing lessons, bike rentals, kayaking, and lake cruises are available nearby, too.

Ritz-Carlton, Lake Las Vegas

702-567-4700
www.ritzcarlton.com
1610 Lake Las Vegas Parkway, Henderson, NV 89011
Price: Very Expensive.

It is almost redundant reviewing a Ritz-Carlton hotel. How are the rooms? Sublimely gorgeous yet exceedingly comfortable. And the amenities? Most of the ones you are charged for at the Strip resorts are included here. And the service? Come on, it's a Ritz-Carlton. This is a hotel company known the world over for their attention to a customer's needs, sometimes before the customer even knows they need something. If it's so fantastic, then why write about it? Because most visitors don't even know it's here and that is why it is worth writing about. It's here, it's wonderful, and, best of all, it's serene. The weekend brunch buffet is streamlined when compared to the Strip's behemoths, but the quality far surpasses those others. The spa draws you in with promises of feeling like a renewed individual and then delivers with extravagance. The spa's Lunar Rhythm Massage ($350 per person) is available according to the lunar calendar and is said to enhance the intensity, calmness, or energy of the massage, depending upon the phase of the moon. This Ritz-Carlton is so tranquil it would make the perfect ending to a two-leg Las Vegas stay. First, a few days on the Strip, living it up where it's vibrant and happening. Then, a few days at the Ritz-Carlton, Lake Las Vegas, winding down and recharging before returning home. The best of both vacation worlds.

The Venetian Resort Hotel Casino

877-883-6423
www.venetian.com
3355 Las Vegas Boulevard South, Las Vegas, NV 89109
Price: Very Expensive.

The Venetian is as showy as it gets in Las Vegas. From the architecture—outside and in—to the attractions, every single aspect is over the top. And since Las Vegas is known for this, the Venetian fits in very well. This is the one hotel you could stay in, never leave the resort, and hit most every must-try item on your vacation list. Most of the stores in Grand Canal Shoppes are ritzy, to say the least. From classic art to Zippo lighters, it can be found here. If that doesn't satiate the spending bug, the Palazzo Shoppes are just steps away. There are so many restaurants in the Venetian, leaving for a meal is by choice, not necessity. Within the 11 fine-dining restaurants, there are three serving Italian cuisine, two serving seafood, and one serving Italian seafood. And no stay in Las Vegas would be complete without seeing a big production show. *Phantom—A Las Vegas Spectacular* pleases those wanting to see a musical. Wayne Brady's *Making ^&*# Up* tickles all the funny bones with a different show every night. And if both comedy and music are desired, there's the Blue Man Group. What about a ride or attraction? Try a gondola ride in the Grand Canal Shoppes. It's no roller coaster, but whiplash isn't to everyone's vacation liking. There is one reason not to stay each and every minute here and it's the pumped-in fragrance. The baby-powder floral scent can be debilitating. Once you are in your room, show, or restaurant, it dissipates, but as you are walking from one to the other (and it's a long walk) it overwhelms. The rooms are a matter of personal taste. To some the opulent stylings are comforting, while to others the room may have the appearance of a home belonging to someone trying too hard to appear continental.

OFF THE STRIP BUT OH, SO CLOSE
Gold Coast Las Vegas
702-367-7111 or 800-331-5334
www.goldcoastcasino.com
4000 West Flamingo, Las Vegas, NV 89103
Price: Inexpensive.

The Gold Coast has been a locals hangout since its grand opening in 1986 and boasts a variety of local and tourist-oriented attractions that almost everyone can enjoy. First is the Cortez Room, the property's high-end restaurant that serves steak and fresh seafood, all at a reasonable price in a casual atmosphere. The prime rib is surprisingly delightful, given its low price, and is highly recommended. Or visit Ping Pang Pong, the hotel's Asian restaurant, which serves up authentic dishes stemming from the various provinces around China. Save

room for dessert and stop by Kate's Korner, an old-fashioned ice cream parlor, serving up traditional and inventive flavors in a multitude of delicious ice cream creations. Work off that dinner by ballroom dancing in the Gold Coast Showroom or listening to the various live music acts that perform there weekly. If you'd rather exchange your dancing shoes for bowling shoes, the Gold Coast has you covered. Gather your friends for a night of bowling at the Gold Coast's 70-lane Bowling Center and knock down some pins. When you're done there, catch the shuttle to the Orleans, the Gold Coast's sister property.

From the front doors to the submerged speakers in the pool, The Hard Rock Hotel is about rock and roll.
Charo Burke

Hard Rock Hotel & Casino Las Vegas
702-693-5000 or 800-HRD-ROCK
www.hardrockhotel.com
4455 Paradise Road, Las Vegas, NV 89169
Price: Expensive.

If you don't like to party, the Hard Rock Hotel is not for you. This hardcore casino is home to some of the most amazing live performances by current bands, megastars, and rising talents. The lineup of performers changes each night, but superstars such as Paul McCartney, Aerosmith, Kenny Chesney, Bon Jovi, Mötley Crüe, and The Killers are just some of the performers showcasing their music there. The primary concert venue, The Joint, is an intimate locale for an up-close feel for every fan. If you want to dance, visit Body English, a nightclub filled with waitresses barely clad in their best lingerie offering bottle service in a backdrop of lavish leather and dark woods and a posh 41-booth VIP area open from 10 PM to 4 AM. If loud, booming music and the line at the velvet ropes are not for you, come to Wasted Space, a unique rock club with a backstage feel. Perfect for the person who adores a sophisticated lounge setting where you can get the chance to get close and personal with some of the featured rock legends or the up-and-coming bands before they hit it big. After a night of partying, visit Rehab, the poolside party place in the sun, to recharge your energy and to be where the beautiful people hang out. Cure that hangover with a margarita on the patio deck of Pink Taco, a Mexican cantina, or cruise inside in the main dining area to continue the party in a bedazzled setting with folk art, low-rider motorcycles, and heart-pumping tunes. Visit Nobu for sushi in a sleek, urban setting, or stop at AGO for Tuscan-style Italian food, opened by renowned restaurateur Agostino Sciandri and his partner and Hollywood icon Robert DeNiro. The restaurant attracts an A-list clientele and is known for its prime meats, organic salmon, customized cocktails, and even an underground wine cave dining area.

Las Vegas Hilton

888-732-7117 or 702-732-5111
www.lvhilton.com
3000 Paradise Road, Las Vegas, NV 89109
Price: Expensive.

The Las Vegas Hilton is a great resort for the conventioneer. Located next to the Las Vegas Convention Center, the Las Vegas Hilton, though not directly on the Strip, is convenient and even accessible to and from other hotels, as it is a stop on the Las Vegas Monorail system. The Las Vegas Hilton has also had a long-standing tradition of big-name entertainment since its grand opening in 1969, starting with its debut act of Barbara Streisand and Peggy Lee. Not long afterward, Elvis Presley performed there, breaking all attendance records, followed up by showman extraordinaire Liberace. Not to disappoint in its entertainment tradition is icon Barry Manilow, performing nightly, with tickets ranging from $95 to $225 each. Feel inspired by his music and get to Tempo, the Las Vegas Hilton's high-energy lounge. Belting out music of the '70s, '80s, and '90s and contemporary hits, Tempo offers a fun night out with its sexy bevertainers and perfect cocktails. Or have a fine dinner at TJ's Steakhouse; Casa Nicola, an Italian and Mediterranean eatery; as well as 888 Noodle Bar, Garden of the Dragon, and Teru Sushi, three restaurants celebrating a variety of Asian cuisines.

Palms Casino Resort

866-942-7777 or 702-942-7777
www.palms.com
4321 West Flamingo Road, Las Vegas, NV 89103
Price: Very Expensive.

The Palms is designed for those who revel in the club scene. Everything from the rooms to the restaurants is about being cutting-edge cool and young, oh so young. The rooms are appointed with the assumed modern décor, but what guests are really paying for is to say they stayed here. The sportsbook catches a bettor's eye due to odds available on sporting events that stray from the norm. This may be due to the Palms being owned by sports team owners, the Maloof brothers. As much as the Palms caters to folks under 30, there's very little shopping compared to other youthfully minded casinos. The fantasy-inspiring Playboy Club with high-stakes gaming is here. There's a cover charge, which is odd for gambling, and serious blackjack players may not appreciate such an inexperienced, though beautiful, dealer. Also in the Palms are nightclubs The Pearl and Ghostbar and restaurants N9ne, Little Buddha, and Garduno's.

Rio All Suite Hotel and Casino Las Vegas
866-746-7671
www.riolasvegas.com
3700 West Flamingo Road, Las Vegas, NV 89103
Price: Moderate.

As the first all-suite hotel in Las Vegas, the Rio model has been copied since then. Now the Rio could stand to do some mimicking of other all-suite properties. The suites originally used quality materials and design, now the rooms look worn and could benefit from updating. Time and many guests have taken their toll. The property is laid out well—it's easy to get around. One of the smartest shows in town, Penn and Teller, has their regular home here. The Rio is not one of the more family-friendly resorts. There's a lot of adult-themed fun here, with the Voodoo Lounge providing one of the best views in town. Lucky Strike Lanes uses a vintage look and feel for big kids only and the grown-ups-only Sapphire Pool was created by a local gentlemen's club. The Wine Cellar is a hidden oasis of wine served in a quiet, relaxing, and classic atmosphere that is absolutely worth the time off the casino floor.

South Point Hotel, Casino, and Spa
702-796-7111 or 1-866-791-7626
www.southpointcasino.com
9777 Las Vegas Boulevard South, Las Vegas, NV 89183
Price: Moderate.

Though the address for South Point is Las Vegas Boulevard, most would not consider this the Strip. A newer property, the location makes it a great spot for locals, as well as visitors. The distance from the Strip can be driven in five minutes. The lack of sidewalks makes the possibility of a walk a bad idea, but a cab or bus is a viable option. The rooms are subtly and tastefully decorated and include 42-inch flat-screen televisions. There's no themed décor, just good solid amenities and some nice views. If you're too tired to make the trip to the Strip, there's a 32-lane bowling center, a 16-screen movie theater, and a sand volleyball court. There are plenty of restaurant options to choose from, including Michael's, which the owner moved from a previously owned property. This beloved restaurant has only two seatings each night, for up to 50 people. This is one for gourmands who like dining the way it used to be. South Point does have one amenity to offer that no other property can, an equine event center with stables. It is the only one in the country connected to a hotel. When the National Finals Rodeo is in town each December, the horse events here draw a large crowd.

Trump International Hotel and Tower Las Vegas
866-646-8164 or 866-939-8786
www.trumplasvegashotel.com
2000 Fashion Show Drive, Las Vegas, NV 89109
Price: Very Expensive.

Having no casino has its perks—the biggest is that there are no smoke-filled gaming areas to walk through. Another advantage to no casino is a nicely navigable hotel, since there is no maze of slot machines and craps tables to meander through. The hotel opened in March of 2008 and is still looking pretty spiffy. The rooms are sleekly decorated and surprisingly in good taste considering the hotel's glass is wrapped in 24-karat gold. The oversized windows offer nice views of the Strip. The kitchenettes, even found in the studio suites, are the most appreciated amenity and one rarely seen in Las Vegas. The same for the wireless Internet. The marble bathroom is stocked with upscale furnishings including separate shower and jet stream tub. The Guestroom has a double vanity. The location is touted as a "mere stroll" from the Strip. In the daytime, this is fine but at night the hotel's next-door neighbor, the Fashion Show Mall, closes, making for a lonely and poorly lit walk. The cab ride from most any Strip resort wouldn't take too long or be too expensive as there is a back way to the hotel on Industrial Road.

Westin Casuarina Las Vegas Hotel, Casino & Spa

www.starwoodhotels.com
702-836-5900
160 East Flamingo Road, Las Vegas, NV 89109
Price: Very Expensive.

Running around Las Vegas can result in an impression of overkill. From the sights and sounds, to the dining out every meal, to the walking up and down the Strip, it can be too much after a bit. Getting back to your room for a rest is yet another journey. You'd like to just lie by the pool, but there's a DJ spinning and folks partying it up in their expensive cabanas. At the Casuarina, none of this is an issue. The placidly decorated rooms are small and basic, as are the bathrooms, but since the hotel is a Westin, the beds are comfortable and the showers have dual heads. Poolside cabanas are available here, and they're far less expensive than those at other hotel pools, but there aren't any food

choices other than room service. This is the only hotel in Las Vegas that doesn't allow smoking in any of the rooms or public areas, except the small casino. The hotel is a four-block walk from the Strip and Caesars Palace, Bally's, and Bellagio. For a shortcut to Paris and beyond, enter Bally's through the rear entrance (directly across from Casuarina) and head toward the Paris/Bally's connecting walkway.

DOWNTOWN

Four Queens Hotel & Casino

800-634-6045 or 702-385-4011
www.fourqueens.com
202 Fremont Street, Las Vegas, NV 89101
Price: Moderate.

The Four Queens, which opened in 1966, is one of the oldest and most notable downtown properties. The casino, named after the original owner's four daughters—Faith, Hope, Benita, and Michele—is known as the jackpot capital of the world and features a Nickel Palace, where the 5-cent slots are a highlight. It is known to have cheap accommodations, but the quality of the rooms is hit-and-miss and guests either love it or hate it there. Nonetheless, the Four Queens is a perfect place to stay if you plan on being so busy that it is merely a place to store your stuff where you can catch a simple snooze and shower before going back out. It is also connected to the Fremont Street Experience, a large light and visual downtown show; some rooms face the excitement, some don't. When booking a room, be certain to clarify which type of room you would like, especially since the property is

Convenient for Racing Fans and the Utah Bound

As you head north out of Las Vegas, hotel resorts dwindle to nonexistent. Until now, this has been a hassle for racing fans heading to the Las Vegas Motor Speedway and those going to or coming back from Utah's majestic beauty and ideal skiing. Though the rest of the city is still catching up the Aliante Station Casino and Hotel, the place gets hopping for NASCAR in the early spring.

The Golden Nugget is the nicest property downtown. Courtesy Golden Nugget

so large at 40,000 square feet that it takes up the entire block bordered by Fremont Street, Casino Center, Third Street, and Carson Avenue. Whether you stay at the hotel or not, Hugo's Cellar, the shining star of the Four Queens, is widely known by locals as a premier gourmet room. Beef Wellington, Chateaubriand, escargot, prawns, scallops, lobster bisque, duckling anise flambé, and rack of lamb are just a few of the exquisite selections on the menu. If you're not feeling so upscale, visit the Chicago Brewing Company with their handcrafted microbrews, entrées, pizzas, sliders, and even cigars on the menu. Sip a cool Ultimate Weiss Hefeweizen (highly recommended), Red Rocker amber ale, Old Town Brown ale, All Nighter light ale, or Pale Rider pale ale, for a delicious way to cool down on hot summer days.

Golden Nugget Hotel
702-385-7111 or 800-634-3454
www.goldennugget.com
129 East Fremont Street, Las Vegas, NV 89101
Price: Moderate.

The Golden Nugget hotel, built in 1946, is one of the city's oldest resorts. Despite its age, the property is considered the swankiest of the downtown hotels. Once owned by casino mogul Steve Wynn, the property has a reputation for elegance and was rated as being a four-star resort. The Golden Nugget has since changed hands, but the hotel's reputation for high quality remains. It is considered to be a boutique hotel, and it is maintained very well, down to the original marble flooring. This dedication to upholding its reputation for refinement can be seen in Vic & Anthony's, a Houston-based steakhouse company. The restaurant features succulent beef and lobster entrées and a delightful wine list. Grotto, an Italian restaurant; Lillie's Noodle House, a traditional Cantonese, Szechwan, and pan-Asian eatery; and Red Sushi, a Japanese specialty and sake room and sushi and sashimi house all provide guests with dining options that will be sure to please even the pickiest of eaters. But the Golden Nugget has more to offer than a good meal; it has plenty of entertainment, too. Gordie Brown, an impressionist, comedian, singer, and entertainer, is featured at the property as a permanent performer on its docket. Tickets are $44 and up. Looking to create your own action? Stop by the Gold Diggers nightclub and have a few cocktails while checking out the go-go dancers and overlooking the balcony views of the Fremont Street Experience. For a thrill, visit the Tank, a swimming-pool complex with a shark tank and a secure water slide that allows you to get close, but not too close, to some of the ocean's deadliest creatures. And of course, you can't stay at a resort named the Golden Nugget and not actually see one. Visit the Hand of Faith, the world's largest gold nugget in existence at a whopping 61 pounds, inside the hotel lobby. Who knows? Maybe it will bring you a little extra luck. Shuttle service is provided to and from the Las Vegas Premium Outlets.

Aliante Station Casino & Hotel

702-692-7777 or 1-877-477-7627
www.aliantecasinohotel.com
7300 Aliante Parkway, North Las Vegas, NV 89084
Price: Moderate.

Aliante Station Casino is a sleek and chic resort in the far desert north region (I-15 and 215) of Las Vegas. This ultramodern casino is set in a dramatic backdrop of desert mountains that caters to both tourists and locals and is just minutes away from the Las Vegas Motor Speedway, Aliante Golf Club, and Silverstone Golf Club. Stay in one of the suites and drift off into dreamland with your own 42-inch plasma TV lulling you to sleep. But before you do, dine at MRKT, Aliante's signature steak and seafood restaurant, offering indoor and outdoor patio dining, porterhouse steaks, prime rib, lobster tail, shrimp scampi, Alaskan king crab, lamb chops, and veal, as well as a wine list with over 5,000 bottles, 300 labels, and 20 wines by the glass. Not feeling like a carnivore? Pips Cucina & Wine provides an authentic Italian dining experience, complete with an eclectic and affordable wine selection that matches anything on the menu. And if that doesn't suit you, try Camacho's Cantina. It has many of the traditional Mexican favorites, but whatever you do, make sure to order the fresh guacamole prepared tableside and order a drink made with any of the 100 premium tequilas. After a drink, visit the Access Showroom, an intimate venue that hosts many big-name entertainers, seats up to 650 guests, and boasts a full-service bar, or catch a movie at any one of Regal Cinemas's 16 screens.

THROUGHOUT LAS VEGAS

Boulder Station Hotel Casino

702-432-7777 or 800-683-7777
www.boulderstation.com
4111 Boulder Highway, Las Vegas, NV 89121
Price: Inexpensive.

Boulder Station is located on what locals call "The Boulder Strip" in east Las Vegas. Popular with the residents, it is minutes away from Nellis Air Force Base and the cities of Henderson and Boulder City. Visit the Broiler, a locally acclaimed steakhouse that touts its carefully selected beef, aged for tenderness and grilled over mesquite charcoal, creating a savory steak experience. While there, peruse the menu and select from any one of its fresh seafood dishes flown in daily, including Australian lobster and Alaskan king crab. It really is possible to get fresh seafood in the middle of the desert. Or cha-cha a few steps down for a little south-of-the-border fare at Guadalajara Bar & Grille for cheap margaritas and well-priced Mexican cuisine. If you're feeling like garlic and not chili pepper, then enjoy fresh pasta entrées, antipasto, and pizzas from the Pasta Palace, also a reasonably priced restaurant. Afterward, drop the kids off at Kids Quest, a fully supervised child-care facility, so you can hit the casino floor, as it is definitely not the place for the kids to linger. Kids Quest cares for little ones from 6 weeks to 12 years old, and they can enjoy an indoor playground, nonviolent video games, arts and crafts, karaoke, or even quiet play zones and a Tiny Tot Room. While they're in there, make sure to catch a movie at Regal Cinemas or live music at the Railhead, a mini-showroom known for bringing in the hottest names of blues, jazz, country, and rock.

Fiesta Rancho Casino-Hotel
702-631-7000 or 888-899-7770
www.fiestarancholasvegas.com
2400 North Rancho Road, North Las Vegas, NV 89130
Price: Inexpensive.

Located in the northwest area of the Las Vegas Valley, miles away from the Strip, the Fiesta Rancho definitely caters to the locals. It offers reasonable room rates and local entertainment and is a lot less tourist-oriented than most others. In fact, the Fiesta Rancho appeals so much to the locals that many of its events are weekly football betting and ice rink activities such as lessons for little ones and hockey leagues for the adults, all meant for regularly visiting guests. Yes, we did say there was an ice rink in the middle of the desert! There are also times open for public skating or even the hosting of events, so if you don't belong to a league, don't worry about it—you're still welcome. Of course, there is still plenty for out-of-towners to see and do there, particularly if being cold isn't your thing, like having an authentic Mexican dinner at Garduno's. Visit the fresh salsa bar or have fresh, tableside guacamole as an appetizer—the guacamole is out of this world. Pick from any of their 200-plus tequilas to have a drink with your meal. But whatever your entrée pick, whether it is their fajitas, burritos, or tacos, make sure to save room for the sopapillas—they are served warm, soft, and heavenly. At the Blue Agave Steakhouse, where fine steaks and live Maine lobster are served, diners can enjoy a show by an acrobatic girl on a red velvet swing performing stunning maneuvers over the bar. When your belly is full, visit Club Tequila, a dance club and stage, to work off those calories and watch featured local performers in reggae, Latin, and R&B. The Fiesta Rancho also offers a Kids Quest child care facility.

Fiesta Henderson Casino Hotel
702-558-7000 or 888-899-7770
www.fiestahendersonlasvegas.com
777 West Lake Mead Parkway, Henderson, NV 89015
Price: Inexpensive.

Like its counterpart in the northwest part of the city on Rancho, the Fiesta Henderson also caters to locals but in the nearby town of Henderson in the eastern part of the Las Vegas Valley. It, too, has inexpensive (translated as "average") rooms and all of the amenities locals enjoy, like a 12-screen Regal movie theater and a food court featuring favorites like Subway, Starbucks, Villa Pizza, and Fat Burger. In its casino, it also has several smoke-free poker tables and a new 137-seat race and sports book that is touted by the locals as being a "good one" to go to. But just because it has an affinity for the locals doesn't mean it that lacks good restaurants. Fuego Steakhouse, which boasts a cozy environment complete with a fireplace for cool nights, offers upscale entrées in a casual environment. Try the Steak Diane, the 20 oz. porterhouse steak, or even the Chateaubriand at reasonable prices. It also offers a Kids Quest, a child-care station, inside the casino.

Green Valley Ranch Resort Spa Casino
702-617-7777 or 866-782-9487
www.greenvalleyranchresort.com
2300 Paseo Verde Parkway, Henderson, NV 89052
Price: Expensive.

A very chic place to be, the Green Valley Ranch Resort in the nearby city of Henderson has it all. Where else can you land your private helicopter, book a room, and have a fine meal, all at the same place? It is utterly impossible to go hungry at the Green Valley. Eight restaurants celebrate cuisines from around the world and can please any appetite: Hank's Fine Steaks and Martinis, complete with live piano-bar entertainment; Terra Verde for wood-fired pizzas and homemade pastas with a 1,500-bottle wine list; Sushi + Sake, a contemporary sushi and Japanese specialty house featuring infused sakes; Tides Oyster Bar, capturing the spirit of New Orleans with gumbos, po'boys, and a raw oyster bar; and more. Have a pint at Quinn's Irish Pub and dance a jig to the music sounds of Darby O'Gill and the Little People, a band with a mix of traditional Irish music and modern rock. Drop in at the Drop Bar for cool

drinks, a funky atmosphere, and eclectic tunes to get your evening rocking. Or have a relaxing day at the spa after a full day of shopping at The District. a shopping villa that has more than 70 shops, boutiques, and restaurants including Aveda, Brighton, Coach, Coldwater Creek, Pottery Barn, Williams-Sonoma, Talbots, and Ann Taylor Loft. Visit the Grand Events Center to catch a glimpse of your favorite band and definitely visit the pool area at Green Valley Ranch. Dip into the sand-bottom pool for relaxed swim and calm atmosphere, or sunbathe in privacy at the European-style, secluded beach The Pond, where sun worshippers can cool off underneath the waterfall or enjoy bottle service—not the place for little children, gawkers, or the stiff-upper-lip types.

JW Marriott Las Vegas Resort & Spa
702-869-7777 or 877-869-8777
www.marriott.com/hotels/travel/lasjw-jw
-marriott-las-vegas-resort-and-spa/
221 North Rampart Boulevard, Las Vegas, NV 89145
Price: Very Expensive.

Located in Summerlin, a master-planned community in the western portion of the Las Vegas Valley, JW Marriott is only 15 minutes from the Las Vegas Strip and is close to many of the city's off-the-Strip attractions often overlooked by tourists. Nearby is Red Rock Canyon, which provides hiking, climbing, and biking in a beautiful desert mountain range and dramatic scenery. Or stay on the property and indulge yourself with a visit at the Aquae Sulis Spa and Salon with all of the amenities a tired body and mind could possibly need to recharge the spirit. When you're done, continue the relaxation with a pint or a shot of whiskey with your shepherd's pie at the authentic Irish pub, J.C. Woologhan's. Live Celtic music is featured, and it is a great place to have a few drinks and swap tall tales with your mates.

The Red Rock Resort is best for those interested in golf, cycling, and desert beauty. Crystal Wood

Gustav Mauler's Gourmet Tobaccos & Lounge, another great hangout, offers premium spirits, vintage ports, hand-rolled cigars, and a private humidor club. There is a dress code for guests, as this is a place for true sophisticates wanting to unwind from their day. Gustauv Mauler, renowned master chef and restaurateur, makes a second appearance at the JW Marriott in his Spiedini Ristorante with his classic Milanese menu and wine list. Visit Shizen, a Japanese steakhouse and sushi bar with teppanyaki-style dining, or enjoy a soothing night out at Round BarAway, for a quiet cocktail and music at an intimate piano bar.

Orleans Las Vegas

702-365-7111 or 800-675-3267
www.orleanscasino.com
4500 West Tropicana, Las Vegas, NV 89103
Price: Moderate.

When it comes to Las Vegas sometimes less known is better simply because the business has to try harder. The Orleans is another "locals" casino and, though it is located a few minutes off the Strip, it's a straight shot if you're driving. The property also offers a complimentary shuttle. The traditionally decorated accommodations are spacious. Request a room on the east side of the hotel for a nice view of the Strip. The fitness facility is clean and included with your reservation. Though the pool doesn't turn into a swanky nightclub or offer nude sunbathing, it's a swell spot. Though there is no widely popular show, there are headliner entertainers scheduled a few times a month with very reasonable ticket prices. There's more to do, with an 18-theater movie house and 70-lane bowling center that's been voted the best in town. For families, Kid's Tyme is a way for you to see a show while the kids have supervised fun. The Orleans is a good Las Vegas bargain and perfect for those who like to get to the Strip, but don't need to stay on it.

Red Rock Casino Resort Spa

866-767-7773
www.redrocklasvegas.com
11011 West Charleston Boulevard, Las Vegas, NV 89135
Price: Expensive.

Here's a place off the Strip and with just enough Vegas in it to remind you you're here. Sitting in the casino, you may notice that the air just seems nicer. As a newer property, the air filtration system is top notch. The whole property is smaller than the mega-resorts of the Strip but it has most things they do and some they don't. For instance the rooms aren't garish but subdued, in chocolates and grays. And if you request it, you may get one with a view of the beloved Red Rock Canyon. Don't worry, you can also get one with a view of the Strip. One is prettier during the day and the other at night. The spa and pool are sublime in the ability to cater to their clients, but the Red Rock Casino Resort Spa is still a comfortable place to be. This property is recommended to those who live a more active lifestyle and don't plan on spending every moment here inside. Besides being close to the canyon and Mt. Charleston, the **Adventure Spa** (702-797-7877) will assist guests in taking rock-climbing and kayaking adventures. The Spa at Red Rock can be rejuvenating or tran-

quil, depending on your needs. A view of Red Rock Canyon and a massage were meant to go together. There's also the poshest bowling lanes in town, a movie theater with 16 screens, and a pool to make you feel like a celebrity.

Suncoast Hotel and Casino

702-636-7111 or 877-677-7111
www.suncoastcasino.com
9090 Alta Drive, Las Vegas, NV 89145
Price: Moderate.

Suncoast is a great hotel and casino for those not looking to be seen but rather to see. It is on the far west side of Las Vegas, and the mountains, desert, and Red Rock Canyon are very near. The surrounding neighborhoods (Summerlin) are some of the best in town. While not walkable from the hotel, the high-end shopping and dining are only a quick drive away. Six of the area's best golf courses are on this side of town, too, including the Tournament Players Club Canyons. The hotel also has a movie theater and bowling center. A courtesy shuttle to the Strip and back (about 10 miles each way) runs every 2 hours and with 48 hours' notice can transport guests to and from McCarran International Airport. Considered quaint by Las Vegas standards, the Suncoast has fewer than 400 rooms and suites, making this an easy property to navigate. The rooms and bathrooms are nicely sized, but the bland décor is nothing to write home about. The rooms are well maintained and many have nice views of the mountains and golf courses.

Try Staying off the Radar

The giant casino resorts of Las Vegas aren't for everyone. For some, it's the mile-long hike through the casino and then again from the elevator to your room. For others it's never really getting rest, as there's always a reason to get out of bed or avoid going to bed completely. Rooms on the Strip are not thought of as a place to while away the hours but as a spot to store your things. For those looking for somewhere a bit more quaint, consider one of these options. Each has rooms (or trailer) meant to be languished in by those in need of true rest and relaxation.

Stay somewhere really different with KOA's fully stocked Airstream trailers. Charo Burke

KOA Campground

800-562-7270 or 702-733-9707
www.koa.com
500 Circus Circus Drive, Las Vegas, NV 89109

At the KOA Campground near Circus Circus, you're not expected to bring the trailer. A stationary Airstream trailer is already set up with linens, kitchen items and utensils, outdoor fire pit, and propane grill. There are so many benefits to this method of hospitality. For one, you aren't sharing walls with the boisterous room on either side. As you walk to your "room," there's no smoke nor do you have to walk the North Forty to get to and from the elevator. It's best to request one farthest from the front entrance in hopes of less noise. Some Airstreams have a tiny patch of grass in front and all have chairs and table outside. The drawback? No room service and a cleaning deposit is required. Circus Circus and Riviera hotels are nearest, so it's not the most glamorous location.

Bed & Office

702-290-2546

www.bedandoffice.com

2176 Pueblo Circle, Las Vegas, NV 89169

Bed & Office is another spot where you can enjoy Las Vegas and a little bit of quiet time as well. There are two sites, each converted into Las Vegas's version of a bed-and-breakfast. The location is an older residential postmodern neighborhood that is very convenient to the convention center and less than 10 minutes away from the Strip, unless there's convention traffic. Included is use of a fully equipped kitchen, queen-size bed, complimentary wi-fi, and continental breakfast. The personal service is one thing that no Strip resort is going to able to match. The owners reside in Las Vegas and are happy to share their knowledge of the city's eccentricities and attractions and make suggestions.

Milos Inn at Boulder

702-294-4244

www.milosinnatboulder.com

534 Nevada Way, Boulder City, NV 89005

This demure and romantic spot, one of the area's few bed-and-breakfasts, has just four rooms, which are decorated in the spirit of and named after the wines of Tuscany. The rooms surround a patio with pond and waterfall and each has a fireplace, private bathroom, and whirlpool tub. A fresh cooked and hearty breakfast is included. The 30-minute drive to the Strip can be a bit long but for those looking to visit Hoover Dam, the location is convenient. A masseuse licensed in Reiki, Swedish, and aromatherapy is available for appointments. For further relaxation, a wine bar is attached to the inn.

Natural light and charming decorations make the Conservatory at Bellagio a pleasant diversion and lovely photo spot. Crystal Wood

4

On the Strip

Keeping Busy on the Boulevard of Lights

While you can't really get a feel for Las Vegas by staying strictly on the Strip, you can stay busy for an entire trip without any lags in fun things to do. Most important, bring comfortable shoes. Although the Strip is one street and on a map it may look easily walked, it's not just the boulevard that must be taken into consideration. Seventeen of the largest hotels in the United States are in Las Vegas and just getting from the arcade on one end to the shopping on the other is a healthy jaunt. There's no making a beeline either when there is gaming, other visitors, and more to look at between each stop. Each resort is its own labyrinth and it will behoove your tootsies for you to pay attention to the posted signage, so as to keep from unnecessary backtracking.

There's plenty to see by just keeping to the outside of the resorts as well. Visible for 250 miles, the Luxor's Sky Beam is the strongest beam of light in the world. Not to be outdone by the Great Wall of China, this light can be seen from space as well. On warm summer nights, it becomes every bat's bug buffet fantasy. There's more world-famous free entertainment on the boulevard, like *Sirens of TI* at Treasure Island, the Fountains of Bellagio, and the spectacularly over-the-top architecture of almost every casino and hotel on the Strip. If you plan on seeing everything from the sidewalk, don't forget to bring a bottle of water during the warmer months. You'll be hard pressed to find a drinking fountain anywhere on the entire Strip.

For the purpose of this book, the Las Vegas Strip runs from the south end with Mandalay Bay and continues on to the Stratosphere on the north end. All of the resorts on the Strip have a Las Vegas Boulevard South address, though. If you intend to see as much of the Strip as possible during your visit, check out the Las Vegas Monorail running from the MGM Grand to the Sahara, with stops in between. More information on the monorail can be found in the Transportation chapter of this book.

Adventuredome Theme Park

(702-794-3939; www.adventuredome.com; Circus Circus) The coolest family attraction in Vegas is literally cool—The Adventuredome theme park is 5 acres of thrill rides and carnival games, all under a giant pink climate-controlled dome at Circus Circus Hotel and Casino. You'll be amazed at the number of rides and attractions under the dome, and there's something here to delight kids of all ages, from the Circus Carousel, a traditional merry-go-round, to the Disko, which rotates at a hectic speed while also swinging to and

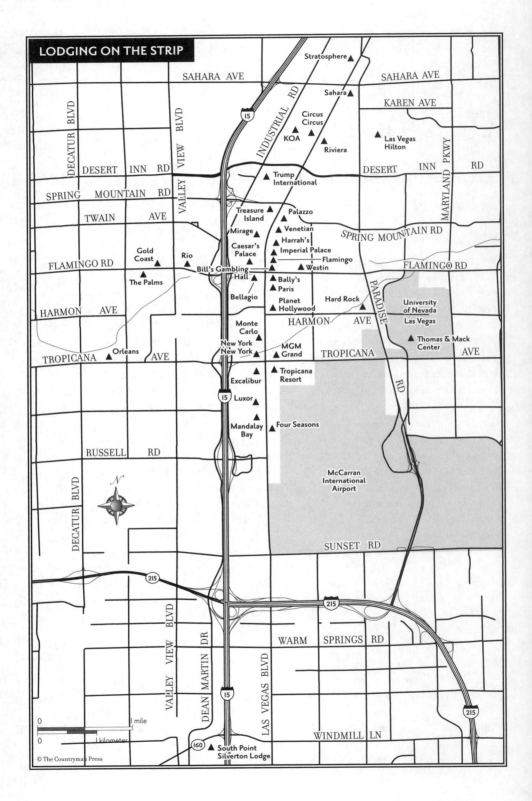

LODGING ON THE STRIP

SAHARA AVE
SAHARA AVE
KAREN AVE
DECATUR BLVD
VALLEY VIEW BLVD
INDUSTRIAL RD
DESERT INN RD
MARYLAND PKWY
DESERT INN RD
SPRING MOUNTAIN RD
TWAIN AVE
SPRING MOUNTAIN RD
FLAMINGO RD
FLAMINGO RD
HARMON AVE
HARMON AVE
PARADISE RD
TROPICANA AVE
TROPICANA AVE
RUSSELL RD
DECATUR BLVD
SUNSET RD
VALLEY VIEW BLVD
DEAN MARTIN DR
LAS VEGAS BLVD
WARM SPRINGS RD
WINDMILL LN

Stratosphere
Sahara
Circus Circus
KOA
Las Vegas Hilton
Riviera
Trump International
Treasure Island
Palazzo
Mirage
Venetian
Caesar's Palace
Harrah's
Imperial Palace
Gold Coast
Rio
Bill's Gambling Hall
Flamingo
Westin
The Palms
Bally's
Bellagio
Paris
Planet Hollywood
Hard Rock
University of Nevada Las Vegas
Monte Carlo
Thomas & Mack Center
New York New York
MGM Grand
Orleans
Excalibur
Tropicana Resort
Luxor
Four Seasons
Mandalay Bay
McCarran International Airport
South Point
Silverton Lodge

0 — 1 mile
0 — 1 kilometer

N

© The Countryman Press

fro on huge rails. Don't miss the Sling Shot, which propels riders rapidly skyward while leaving their stomachs on the ground. Roller-coaster enthusiasts will love the Canyon Blaster, which takes you up to the highest point in the dome before zooming you down through its two loops and two corkscrews. This is the only double-coaster, double-loop indoor roller coaster in the world. Altogether there are 26 rides under that pink glass dome. Featured attractions include Pikes Pass miniature golf, Midway Games, and the Xtreme Zone, where you can climb a rock wall or bungee yourself silly on a trampoline, and free clown shows are scheduled throughout each day. Regarding admission: The All-Day Ride Pass wristband is your best bet. It is possible to pay for rides "à la carte," but going this route you will quickly spend more than the cost of the All-Day Pass. Please note, the featured attractions are not included in the price of the All-Day Pass, but all the rides are, including Lazer Blast laser tag. Group rates are also available, as are party facilities. Mon.–Thurs. 11 AM–6 PM; Fri.–Sat. 10 AM–midnight; Sun. 10 AM–9 PM. Hours may vary for events and holidays. Call for updated times. $4–7 per ride. Day passes are $24.95 for adults and $14.95 for children 33–47 inches tall (free for toddlers under 33 inches with a paying adult).

Animatronic Fountain Shows
(The Forum Shops, Caesars Palace) Inside the Forum Shops are two sets of statues that come to life and tell their tale to shoppers passing by. Festival Fountain is the older of the two and located nearest the strip entrance. Here Bacchus, Apollo, Venus, and Pluto have a light conversation, which—due to mall noise—is not always easy to understand. There's a laser show with this one, too. It's all a bit dated but in a wholesome, fun way. At the opposite end of the mall is the *Fall of Atlantis* show with King Atlas pushing his kids toward an ill-fated sibling

rivalry for the control over Atlantis. There's more bells and whistles on this one, with a fire battle and Atlantis sinking. And as loud as it is—and it is very loud—it can still be difficult to understand the dialogue. Then again, it's not like they're reading Chekhov. You should have no trouble getting the gist of the stories. On the backside of this statue's base is a 50,000-gallon saltwater fish tank with more than 100 species. Feeding times at 1 and 5 PM are fun to watch. The statue shows are every hour on the hour during mall hours.

The Auto Collections
(702-794-3174; www.autocollections.com; Imperial Palace) Car enthusiasts will be amazed at the automobile collection on display in this funky casino. There are more than 250 cars, worth over $100 million, covering 125,000 square feet. Where can they fit so many cars in an older casino? Why, the sealed-off fifth floor of the parking garage. While their collection of antique cars is famous, there is also an impressive collection of not-often-seen cars such as the Alpha Romeo BATS. There are also modern cars such as a 2002 Collector's Edition Trans Am that was the first to roll off the assembly line. It's difficult to pin down exactly what cars can be seen because most of them are available for purchase. Those not for sale include Johnny Carson's 1939 Chrysler Royal Sedan, one of only two Cadillac Ghia Coupes, and Al Jolson's 1928 Mercedes-Benz S Tourer. Check the Web site for coupons on admission. Daily 10 AM–6 PM, Adult $8.95, kids 12 and under $5, 3 years and under are free.

Conservatory and Botanical Gardens
(www.bellagio.com; Bellagio) Each well-known holiday and season, 140 expert horticulturists decorate the atrium, located just past the check-in desk and Chihuly blown-glass sculpture. The atrium is stories high with something rarely seen in a Las Vegas

casino—windows. The room is filled with plants, water features, and whimsical garden art all dedicated to the same theme. For Chinese New Year, there are topiaries shaped like pandas, huge red lanterns hanging from the glass ceiling, and footbridges. The fall season brings jewel tones from nature, a mill with turning waterwheel, and a tunnel made of fall foliage to walk through. This can be a wonderful spot for a superbly colorful vacation photo.

Bellagio Gallery of Fine Art
(702-693-7871; www.bellagio.com; Bellagio) For some, art is better in small doses. It can be difficult to observe, take in, appreciate, and remember all the art one sees in a mega-museum. The Bellagio Gallery of Fine Art is just right for such occasions. Not to worry—this gallery doesn't feature LeRoy Neiman sports figures, Thomas Kinkade's twinkling fairy sceneries, or Wyland whales. This is honest-to-goodness art. From Cézanne to Monet to O'Keeffe, the touring collections scheduled here are not huge, but they are impressive nonetheless. The prerecorded guided tours are worth trying. Some are better than others in information and if it's crowded, getting close enough to read the typed description isn't necessary. But often the recording doesn't give any more information about the painting or artists. Like every museum, it has a gift shop featuring books, posters, and cards pertaining to the art you've seen and other exhibitions that have visited in the past. Sun.–Thurs. 10 AM–6 PM; Fri.–Sat. 10 AM–9 PM. The last admission is 30 minutes before closing. General admission $15, children under 12 free.

The Birdman of Las Vegas
(Hawaiian Market Place; 3743 Las Vegas Boulevard) Though this shopping center claims to be modeled after the International Marketplace in Hawaii, that couldn't be farther from the truth.

However, it has one redeeming quality and that's the Birdman of Las Vegas, Joel Krathwol, and his assortment of performing birds including parrots, cockatoos, eagles, cranes, owls, and rare Andean condors. Rest assured that these and all his feathered friends are well taken care of, as he is also the director of the World Center for Exotic Birds, a rescue and breeding sanctuary. It's amazing how much you can learn from a free bird show. Fri.–Sun. 1:30 and 3:30 PM. Free.

Circus Acts
(Circus Circus; www.circuscircus.com) There are aspects of old Las Vegas that will always be missed and then there are those that are inexplicably still around. With a couple exceptions, Circus Circus belongs to the latter. One of those exceptions is the free circus acts. There is a rotating group of acts including trapeze artists, acrobats, jugglers, and contortionists. If you're at Circus Circus in the evening, get some classic Las Vegas kitsch at the rotating Horse-a-Round bar as seen in the film *Fear and Loathing in Las Vegas*. Daily, about every 30 minutes, 11 AM–midnight. Free.

Crazy Girls Statue
(Riviera; www.rivierahotel.com) There is a claim that the bronze statue of the Crazy Girls' posteriors is the most photographed statue in Las Vegas. And it's true that a lot of people have had their picture taken with it, but there are a lot of statues in Las Vegas. Many years ago, the same view of the show's dancers' backsides (and in G-strings) was a Crazy Girls ad. The first billboard caused a bit of a huff in Las Vegas. Residents fully accept where they live, but until then, it rarely crept off the Strip and downtown. So, to "remedy" the situation, very short and ruffled skirts were attached to the billboard. Of course they fluttered up in the wind, making the whole thing silly and futile. Now the ad appears dated and the

Riviera has seen better days, but the statue gets rubbed for luck and photographed 24 hours a day. Free.

Eiffel Tower Experience

(www.parislasvegas.com; Paris) Riding a mini–Eiffel Tower may not appeal to everyone. This half-scale exact replica has a glass elevator trip that tops out at 460 feet in the air. For sure, the best time to ride is at night but it is a couple dollars more and crowded. The observation deck is a prime vantage point to watch the Bellagio Fountains. Because this is so popular, it's best to position yourself as the last show ends and wait for the next one. The view from above adds a whole new dimension to the watery choreography below. Daily 9:30

AM–12:30 AM, weather permitting. $10 for adults; $7 for seniors 65 and older and children 6–12; free for children 5 and under. Family packages are available for $30 from 9:30 AM–7:30 PM (two adults and two children). From 7:30 PM–12:30 AM, admission is $12 for adults and $10 for seniors and children.

> INSIDER TIP: Check out those coupon books inside cabs and found around the Strip. There can be two-for-one offers good for attractions or free Las Vegas merchandise with purchase. The savings can really add up.

Fiori Di Como

(www.bellagio.com; Bellagio) There are a lot of things Las Vegas can say about Steve Wynn, not all of them kind. But one thing to thank him for is his commissioning of master glass artist Dale Chihuly to create this spectacular hanging glass bouquet. In total there are more than 2,000 hand-blown glass elements in the 70-by-30-foot ceiling box. It weighs more than 40,000 pounds and was fully constructed in Chihuly's Seattle studio before being dismantled and hung in its new home. It's well worth sitting down in the lobby seating, across from check-in, and taking in this marvel for as long as you wish. Free.

Fountains of Bellagio

(www.bellagio.com; Bellagio) When one does any research on what to do in Las Vegas, a picture of the Fountains of Bellagio comes up. They've become one of those Las Vegas emblems and well deserve the notoriety. They don't just move with the music. The choreography and technology are so good the water sprays appear to be dancing to the music. The Bellagio was originally a Steve Wynn property, and he's never been known for skimping on what people like. He personally chose each piece of the music, ranging from opera to show tunes. Traffic on the Strip almost stops when they

Dale Chihuly's floral glass sculpture at Bellagio's lobby is mesmerizing. Crystal Wood

The Fountains of Bellagio are worth watching multiple times during the day and especially at night.
Courtesy MGM

perform and the crowds can really build up on the sidewalk in front. If the crowd beat you to the good vantage points, just wait for the next show. Or, consider watching from the pedestrian bridge connecting the Bellagio corner to the Bally's. If you're shopping inside, there's a small balcony near the top of the escalators that looks out over the water. Lights are this town's trademark, so the fountain's 4,000 lights look better at night—but seeing them during the day is better than not at all. If there are high winds, the show can be canceled. After all, they wouldn't want to waste water in a desert. The show is every 30 minutes during the day and every 15 minutes from 8 PM to midnight. Free.

INSIDER TIP: The free shows in front of casinos and in shopping malls attract professional pickpockets, too. It's a smart idea to close purses and shopping bags. Guys, consider putting your wallet in your front pocket. Enjoy the show!

Gameworks

(702-432-4263; www.gameworks.com; 3785 Las Vegas Boulevard) While the original concept of Gameworks had Steven Spielberg involved, gaming giant SEGA purchased the chain in 2005. With so many good arcades in Las Vegas, it's perplexing why this one doesn't keep up. Location maybe? It's next to MGM Grand and M&M World, across from New York–New York, and catty-corner from Excalibur. If it isn't SEGA, including the classics, you most likely won't find it here. Well, except for pool tables and air hockey. While they like to talk about no cover charge, games can only be played with a debit card purchased there. This card has an automatic fee. Isn't that a cover charge? Sun.–Thurs. 10 AM–midnight; Fri.–Sat. 10–1 AM.

Jubilee! Backstage Walking Tour

(702-946-4567; www.ballyslasvegas.com; Bally's) There are fewer and fewer showgirls on the Strip—not models dressed in feathered headdresses and sequins used for publicity photos but honest-to-goodness showgirls. For decades they were Las Vegas's crowning jewel. Their class, dancing abilities, and strict career regulations were the reasons residents defended them to the outside world, which tended to misunderstand them. For instance, a pretty face and skyscraper-length legs aren't

enough. *Jubilee!* showgirls must audition every six months. Your tour hostess is a veteran *Jubilee!* showgirl who knows all the ins and outs of the stage, dances, costumes, costume changes, and all the nuances of her world. You'll get to see how the stage's elevators are tricky to walk on, let alone twirl on in 3-inch heels. Be forewarned that this tour takes roughly an hour and is made up of a lot of walking and standing. You will have to walk upstairs; there are no ramps. The tour is available by reservation only on Mon., Wed., and Sat. at 11 AM. *Jubilee!* ticket holders' cost is $10; without a show ticket, the tour is $15.

Houdini Museum

(702-798-4789; www.houdini.com; The Forum Shops) Maybe museum isn't the most accurate term—it's more of a collection—but there are some interesting artifacts of Harry Houdini to be seen here. Head straight to the back of this magic shop to where the items are showcased, including props this country's first great magician used in his famous escapes and illusions. There's also a full-size hologram of Houdini performing simple tricks. If you're planning on a special trip to the mall just for this display, be sure to call ahead first. The owner of the items intends to take them back to Wisconsin, if he can fund a museum there.

Las Vegas Cyber Speedway

(702-737-2111; saharavegas.com/NASCAR/cyber-speedway; Sahara, NASCAR Café) Oh, if only you could drive like a NASCAR driver. At Las Vegas Cyber Speedway you can get pretty close. This is a simulator drive that takes place in a 7/8-size stock car—16 to choose from—that's been mounted on a hydraulic motion base. Enthusiasts can adjust the tire pressure, angles of the wings on the back, suspension, and brakes, and choose between automatic and stick shift. A 20-foot screen

The serenely entertaining Living Garden at the Shoppes at the Palazzo—arrive early for a good seat.
Crystal Wood

surrounds the drivers, as does a 16-channel, 15-speaker sound system. Ask about the "Race through Las Vegas" simulation. Driving through the Forum Shops and tearing down Fremont Street is somehow empowering. For a better bargain, consider purchasing the all-day package, which can include "Speed—The Ride." If you're finished with the NASCAR simulators but still looking to quell the video game longing, the Pit Pass arcade is located on the first floor of the NASCAR Entertainment Center. This arcade is open 24 hours a day and has 120 player stations and standard video games. Use the Dance Dance Revolution Super Nova to get ready for your big night out. The Pit Pass was named the Best Arcade of 2008 by the *Las Vegas Review-Journal* staff. For more racing fun, Carzilla starts the engines

and honks the horn every hour in the NASCAR Café. Sun.–Thurs. 10 AM–midnight; Fri.–Sat. 10 AM–1 AM. One race, $10.

Living Garden
(www.theshoppesatthepalazzo.com; Shoppes at Palazzo) Most of the free shows on the Strip are fun but raucous, which is appropriate amid the neon. However, if it's time to take it easy on the senses for a few minutes, the Living Garden is the only one that's both entertaining and calming. There is a little bit of seating, but it can be taken up quickly, so get there early. Between the escalators is a waterfall with a meditative pool across from it; this is the best place to sit. The performers come from the floor above, so keep an eye on the down escalator. Three woman dressed in gray tunics

and face paint are the garden's statues. Once they descend, they stand in the waterfall and become choreographed water art. Their mystical appearance, the music, and the sheer charm of the idea evoke stories and fables from childhood. Once the performers are done, get your camera ready. You are permitted to take photos while posing with them. Keep your eye out for some terrifically high topiary vines that come to life, too. Free.

Lion Habitat

(www.mgmgrand.com; MGM Grand Hotel and Casino) The original MGM Grand Hotel and Casino has a special place in the hearts of many longtime Las Vegas residents. One memory is Leo, the MGM Grand lion. While he is long gone, the MGM lion tradition continues but in a more insightful and caring manner. The lion habitat in MGM Grand is surrounded by clear 1 1/2-inch

Most likely the lions will be sleeping, but the clear tunnels make it possible to see the lions at many angles. Courtesy MGM

glass and has a walk-through tunnel as well. This is good because these big cats are good sleepers, making them difficult to see in action. The lions do not live on premises but on an 8-acre ranch outside of town with their trainer and owner, Keith Evans. He has a total of 26 lions that are rotated through the exhibit. Daily 11 AM–10 PM, except 3:30 PM to 4:30 PM. Free.

Madame Tussaud's Wax Museum

(702-862-7800; www.madametussauds .com; The Venetian) Wax figures can be eerie. It doesn't matter if they're celebrity look-alikes or not. And there is a reasonable argument that the price is too high. But with coupons available in different spots around town, added to the fact that you are allowed to photograph the figures as well as get up close and personal, it's not so bad. Many attractions in Las Vegas offer to take your picture in the hope that you will purchase the prints after the show, ride, or other event. At Madame Tussaud's, you can justify the high cost of admission by considering it an up-front charge for as many poses as you want. The entrance to Madame Tussaud's Wax Museum is outside, in front of the casino, near The Palazzo.

Roller Coaster at New York–New York

(www.newyorknewyorkcasino.com; New York–New York) Roller coasters are an attraction left over from the "Las Vegas as a family destination" days. They appeal to the crowd seeking fun and exhilaration and are not dependent upon children, and because of their construction price tag, the roller coasters and thrill rides stayed while the costumed characters left. New York–New York's roller coaster was designed by a well-respected Japanese firm known throughout the world for their work and for the safety records of their rides. But what's really important to riders are the numbers. First you're lifted 203 feet, then dropped to

Outside and inside New York–New Yorks's casino, the roller coaster gives ample opportunity to experience g-force excitement. Courtesy MGM

144 feet at a speed of 67 mph. This is followed by a 180-degree barrel roll and a hang that's 86 feet up. This is followed by the well-loved "heartline" twist and dive. The entire coaster is 4,777 feet in length and takes 2 minutes and 45 seconds to complete. The ride starts inside the casino (upstairs, near arcade) heads outside and then returns briefly through the casino. This last leg can be viewed by bystanders at the Greenwich Village eateries at the casino's north entry. If you rode this when it was named the Manhattan Express, the only thing that's changed is the name.
Sun.–Thurs. 11 AM–11 PM; Fri.–Sat. 10:30 AM–midnight. $14 per person, $7 for a second ride. Must be 54 inches tall to ride.

Secret Garden and Dolphin Habitat

(www.mirage.com; Mirage) Both the Secret Garden and Dolphin Habitat were started by the hugely influential Siegfried Fischbacher and Roy Horn (Siegfried & Roy) as an alluring way to educate the public about the beauty and plight of wild animals. There are six dolphins in the 2.5-million-gallon tank surrounded by lush flora and fauna. If enjoying the dolphins playing and interacting isn't enough to satisfy the yearning to be near them, you can be a **Trainer for a Day** (702-792-7889). Guided by a trainer, you'll get to feed and play with dolphins from the morning through the afternoon. Photos will be taken of you and Sgt. Pepper, Duchess, Lightning, Huff 'n Puff, Maverick, or Bella throughout your "working" day. The photos will be presented to you on CD. The $550 price tag includes the photos and is limited to only four people per day. From the ocean to the jungle, the Secret Garden has six showcases featuring lions, tigers, panthers, and leopards. Of course, the biggest stars of the Strip, the white tigers (striped and pure), are here as well.
Mon.–Fri. 11 AM–5:30 PM; Sat.–Sun. (including major holidays), 10 AM–5:30

PM. Admission includes both attractions, $15 for adults, $10 for children 4–12, and free for children under 3. Last admissions are sold 30 minutes prior to closing.

Shark Reef Aquarium

(702-632-4555; www.mandalaybay.com; Mandalay Bay) The Shark Reef Aquarium never ceases to inspire amazement and awe. It's well executed with something for everyone. The displays are well thought out and provide opportunities to see the beautiful and the creepy creatures within. This is North America's only predator-based aquarium and only place in the United States to see tiger sharks up close. Just as thrilling is having two inches of glass between you and a Komodo dragon or a school of piranha or a golden crocodile. If the Shark Reef is your only plan for Mandalay Bay that day, park in the lot at the far south end (convention center parking). The entrance here is much closer to the aquarium than the parking garage.

Cool and humid, the Shark Reef Aquarium at Mandalay Bay is educational and comfortable.
Courtesy MGM

However, if it's summer, this is uncovered parking, and your car will becoming scorching hot. Certified divers can experience the sharks close up with Dive with Sharks. Only two people may participate in the once daily dive for $650 per person. Sun.–Thurs. 10 AM–8 PM (last admission at 7 PM); Fri.–Sat. 10 AM–10 PM (last admission at 9 PM). Adults $16.95, children 12 years old and younger $10.95, children 4 and younger admitted free.

Sirens of TI

(www.treasureisland.com; TI, Treasure Island) Ah, the lure of scantily clad women, pirates, and a free show with pyrotechnics. The original pirate show, which ran for 10 years, could have used some updating but had been just fine. Instead the show was totally revamped to match the young affluent crowd that the newly renamed TI is going for. The 18-minute show was created by Kenny Ortega—the man behind the obscenely popular *High School Musical*—and pits the guys' ship (The Bull) against the gals' ship (The Song). There's fire, explosions, dancing, lingerie, stunts, and high dives. Daily at 7, 8:30, 10, and 11:30 PM. Any show can be canceled due to inclement weather or high winds. Free.

Speed—The Ride

(www.saharavegas.com; Sahara) This roller coaster uses an electromagnetic force to slingshot the coaster over the first set of rising tracks at a spectacular speed of 0 to 70 mph in four seconds. This is followed by a steep 25-foot drop that plummets riders below the surface into an underground tunnel before catapulting back above the ground and through a breathtaking loop. Accelerating from 35 to 70 mph in just two seconds, the coaster then whisks through the Sahara's 192-foot-tall marquee before stopping 224 feet above the ground. And like any good roller coaster, it goes backward through the same path. This is one ride for which being there before the crowd may not help cut down your wait time. The ride requires a certain amount of riders in order to go. Also, Speed—The Ride is exhilarating but only 45 seconds long. If you've got the stomach for it, you can get two free rides on the coaster by finishing the Bomb, a 6-pound, 2-foot-long burrito at the NASCAR Café next door. They're kind enough to throw in a T-shirt and place your photo on the Winner Wall, too. The minimum height is 54 inches. One ride $10. Speed—The Ride runs daily noon–10 PM.

Titanic

(702-492-3960; www.luxor.com; Luxor) What was it like on the Titanic before and during its fateful sinking? This was the largest moving object of its time and it was not only filled with individuals but also their personal items and stories. This exhibit used to be across the street at the Tropicana. In the new location, the exhibit has added 20 or so never-before-seen items, including pieces of a grand staircase, gaming chips, passenger papers, and personal pieces. Most impressive is the largest Titanic artifact ever recovered. Called the Big Piece, it is more than 25 feet long and weighs more than 15 tons. It took 48 hours just to get it inside the Luxor. Some might think this too depressing to do on a Las Vegas vacation, but most leave feeling a connection with an important event of the past. Tickets are $27 and are good for seven days from date of purchase. Daily 10 AM–10 PM with the last admission being sold at 9 PM.

Venetian Gondola Rides

(702-414-4908; www.thegrandcanal shops.com; Grand Canal Shoppes, The Venetian) Take a ride on a genuine Italian gondola down the quarter-mile canal that winds its way through the Grand Canal Shoppes or out to the lagoon in front of The Venetian. Because being the lone gondola wouldn't be quite realistic, there are more

Make your reservation for a gondola ride at the Venetian. Courtesy The Venetian

than one at a time in the canal or in the lagoon. They were after all Venice's main mode of transportation. The gondola is steered by a singing gondolier. There is a lot of talent in Las Vegas, so they can really sing, rather than faking it. So popular is this ride that the Venetian immediately had to hire more gondoliers after opening. Each gondola fits up to four passengers, so there is a possibility of sharing the ride if yours is a smaller party. A higher price can ensure a private, more romantic, ride, although the busier the mall, the louder the crowds. Same-day reservations are taken in person at the Emporio D'Gondola on a first-come, first-served basis starting at 9 AM each day. Reservations cannot be taken over the phone. Outdoor rides are available as weather permits. The full trip takes about 15 minutes for the indoor ride and a few minutes shorter for the outside version. Sun.–Thurs. 10 AM to 11 PM; Fri.–Sat. 10 AM to midnight.

The Volcano

(www.mirage.com; Mirage) The volcano in front of the Mirage is iconic. In 1989, it was the first "live" free show in front of any resort in Las Vegas and it influenced all that came after. As the free entertainment offerings of the Strip's other casinos blossomed, the volcano started to feel a bit dated. The other offerings were longer and with more showstopping effects. What's an ol' fake volcano to do? Well, it could be imploded, like everything else in Las Vegas that's starting to look past its prime. After 20 years, the Mirage made the right decision: keep the historic emblem and gussy it up. First, it was given its own musical score created by Grateful Dead drummer Mickey Hart and Indian tabla legend Zakir Hussain. Next, the flames were replaced with more than 100 Fireshooters developed specifically for this project. These shoot flames 12 to 15 feet in the air. The Fireshooter used as the finale can shoot up to 60 feet. While these are fun to watch, consider the outside temperature during your viewing. The heat from the flames can be felt and make the

Fans of India's tabla and the Grateful Dead will enjoy the new music heard at The Mirage's updated volcano show. Courtesy MGM

A new parking lot makes visiting the recognizable sign safer, but lines can form for photos. Crystal Wood

scorching evening seem more so for a few minutes. Depending on the season, the volcano goes off each evening about once an hour with the performance lasting 4½ minutes. Free.

Welcome to Las Vegas Sign

(Las Vegas Boulevard, south of Mandalay Bay) Worshipped and adored, the Welcome to Las Vegas sign has been the best spot for a vacation photo since 1959 and was only just nominated for placement on the Register of Historic Places. But only recently was a small parking lot constructed nearby, giving folks a less dangerous route to the iconic sign. This isn't an enormous lot, just big enough for 12 cars (including two handicapped spaces) and two buses. The lot can only be entered from the north (with Mandalay Bay behind you) and exiting you can only head south. This is so much better than taking your life into your hands by crossing one of the most dangerous streets for pedestrians in the nation. The sign was designed by Betty Willis, whose father was Clark County's first tax assessor. Since the sign is part of the public domain, it can be perpetually copied, which explains why it's in every souvenir shop. For a one-of-a-kind souvenir (aside from your photo), check out **www.officiallasvegaslight.com**. As the sign's lightbulbs burn out, they can be specially boxed and sent to you.

Wildlife Habitat

(www.flamingolasvegas.com; Flamingo Hilton) In a surprisingly beautiful garden full of imported tropical foliage, a lagoon, waterfalls, and footbridges, there is a large collection of Chilean flamingos, ibis, colorful parrots, cranes, and nearly 300 other birds. Benches here and there provide a place to relax and enjoy some tranquility on an otherwise chaotic boulevard. If you're looking for the penguins, they've gone to a Dallas zoo. While at the wildlife habitat, look for the memorial for Bugsy Siegel, the original owner of the Flamingo who was gunned down in front of his girlfriend's home six months after the casino opened. It can be found near the wedding chapel near the pool. The wildlife habitat is open 24 hours (though obviously animals do sleep) and free.

Nightlife

Nightlife in Las Vegas may seem a bit redundant. Isn't everything in Las Vegas part of the nightlife? Well, yes, that is a good point. However, not everyone wants the same thing from their nightlife fun.

The Bank

(702-693-8300; www.bellagio.com; Bellagio) If you've come to Las Vegas to be seen or to hang with the other beautiful people and you're awash with confidence, The Bank is the place for you. It goes without saying that the hottest club wear is necessary. And although a no-jeans dress code was mentioned, plenty of pricey dungarees may be seen. There are tables available, but as well as being costly and cash only, they're difficult to get. Don't blame the gentlemen manning the door. They're pulled in every way and pounced on each time they turn around, but they were always courteous and professional during our visit. Try your concierge or casino host and be ready to tip for this. A table is not necessary to enjoy The Bank. The dance floor is crowded and hopping, and there are plenty of walkways and nooks and crannies. Periodically throughout the night, cage go-go dancers join in. The DJ was fantastic at mixing the best of ol' school with the new. As you walk past the private tables, keep your eyes peeled for a celeb or two. But don't blow your cover as one of the beautiful people by trying to get their attention.

Christian Audigier the Nightclub

(702-894-7580; www.audigierlv.com; Treasure Island, TI) With everything in Las Vegas huge and overwhelming, it's nice when a nightclub is designed to be more intimate than all the others. Ask the jelly-fish in the two tanks along the back wall—they'll agree. Cozy is a rare find on the Strip. This isn't to say that this isn't one swank hot spot. It is after all the project of Christian Audieger, designer of the ultrafamous Ed Hardy fashion line, as well as Crystal Rock and Smet. It isn't just about liquor and thumping music here—the look is all Audigier. His tattoo-inspired designs can be seen throughout the club including the wall art and staff uniforms. A second bar on the patio gives a great view of the Strip and of the Sirens show in front of Treasure Island.

Cleopatra's Barge

(www.caesarspalace.com; Caesars Palace) Ah, sweet memories of old Vegas and Rome. With all the new clubs on the strip, it's nice to know that this one is still around. Shaped like the name states, the dance floor is contained on the bow and rocks up and down. It's difficult to pin down a schedule, but there will either be a DJ spinning music from the '80s and '90s or a live band covering songs from the same era. This was the first themed nightclub in America. There is no cover charge, but there is a two-drink minimum on Friday and Saturday.

Forty Deuce

(702-632-9442; www.fortydeuce.com; Mandalay Bay) This is a finicky club that relies heavily on the reputation of the original Los Angeles location. If you visit during one of the town's slower weeks, you could get a great show by the dancers and the top-notch live band accompanying them. If you visit on a busy night and pay the $20 cover charge, then disappointment is a possibility. If you desire a place to sit during the show, then bottle service is necessary at a very hefty price tag. If dancing between shows is more your style, the minuscule dance floor will definitely not suffice. The dancers are wonderful striptease entertainers and stunning to look at. If you want to return home and say you visited that cool club seen on *Jimmy Kimmel Live!* and *Entertainment Tonight,* then be aware that the first show isn't until midnight or so but arriving early will help ensure a better spot to stand for close to two hours. The Thursday show, Royal Jelly, is more rock and roll than the classic burlesque found here on weekends. Thurs.–Sun. 10 PM.

Nightclubs in Las Vegas can be very pricey and cash gets more notice. Courtesy PURE Management

LAX

(702-262-4529; www.laxthenightclub.com; Luxor) Yes, LAX is hip. And yes, just like the Los Angeles original, LAX is where celebrities can be found. But everyone is there looking for the hip spot where the stars are. So the place is very, very crowded. All that time in line, a paid cover charge, and for what? Standing around packed together like cattle in an abattoir but with a DJ spinning mad beats. If where you went is more important than if you really had a good time, this is the spot for you.

Minus 5 Ice Lounge

(702-632-7714; www.minus5experience .com; Mandalay Bay) What comes immediately to mind when you think of Las Vegas? Heat. Sidewalks hot enough to fry eggs, and sunshine so bright you need welder's goggles to cut the glare. But not everything here is hot. Imagine a place that's below freezing at all times, even in the desert. Starting at $30 per person (price of admission gets you 30 minutes in the ice lounge and one very cold drink), you can chill out in the coolest lounge in town. Not dressed for the cold? No problem. The nice folks at Minus 5 fit you out in parkas, mittens, and mukluks and usher you first into a cool room, to help you acclimate to the lower temperature, then into the lounge itself, where the temperature is kept at a constant 27 degrees Fahrenheit, or (you guessed it) minus 5 degrees Celsius, and everything, from the furniture to the sculptures, is made of ice. Belly up to the ice bar and order one of Minus 5's signature vodka cocktails (nonalcoholic drinks are available as well) served in a glass made entirely of ice, but don't worry about your lips sticking to the glass—unique technology is used to remove all humidity from the air and without moisture, your lips don't stick. The lack of humidity is also what gives the ice sculptures and furniture their amazing clarity. There's an ice couch for lounging, and next to it a whimsical ice lamp. For prospective brides and grooms looking for an unusual place to tie the knot, the rear of the lounge is an ice wedding chapel that can accommodate up to 50 people. Thirty minutes is the comfort limit at these temperatures, and once your time is up (you're given a badge that lights up to let you know when it's time to leave), you can continue the party in the Minus 5 Lodge, a rustic ski lodge that was still under construction at the time of our visit. This is a great way to kick off a night of revelry, because the one drink included in the admission will feel like two when you return to the warmer temperature of the casino. This is not, however, a place to spend the evening. Besides the time limit, the ice bar/lounge is diminutive. Larger packages are available and include the price of a unique souvenir— a cool logo'd hat with earflaps.

Noir Bar

(702-262-5257; www.luxor.com; Luxor) Did you skimp on dessert at dinner tonight because you were overstuffed and now as the night is progressing, a little something sweet would go nicely right now? Then, with any luck, you made reservations here because the Noir Bar has a carrot cake martini that's shockingly good. The reservations are worth it. The entrance is a snaking long corridor emptying into a bar with more lit candles than the *Phantom of the Opera* stage show. It's a "secret" entry, making the bar reminiscent of a speakeasy. Don't bother asking for a menu, just let the mixologist know your pleasure and some time later, it's in front of you. Though it will be a very pricey drink, this for them is a gourmet art. No photos allowed.

The Piano Bar

(702-369-5000; harrahslasvegas.com; Harrah's) While Las Vegas has been crazy for dueling pianos for a while now, this one starts the night with karaoke and then transitions to the twin ivory ticklers. Yep, these musicians are female and identical twins to boot. The karaoke starts at 6 PM and goes to 9 PM. That's when the piano players take 10 paces, turn, and start dueling. Remember, tips ensure that your song request is taken seriously.

Red Square

(702-632-7407; www.mandalaybay.com; Mandalay Bay) The Red Square serves vodka for sipping and enjoying, not for throwing back shots and yelling in a simian fashion. There are 150 types of vodka to choose from and a mini Siberia of ice running down the center of the bar to keep your choice nice and frosty cold. The martinis are considered some of the most sublimely ideal on the Strip. To truly complete your *From Russia with Love* moment, order some caviar. The menu offers choices for most every tax bracket. Groups might want to check about buying a bottle and enjoying it in the freezer with provided fur coats, hats, and gloves. While this isn't a place designed to get wild and crazy, it can get loud on busy nights due to its smaller size.

Seahorse Lounge

(www.caesarspalace.com; Caesars Palace) This is an over-the-top but poshly decorated lounge that is all Las Vegas, from the well-endowed mermaid statues to the 1,700-gallon cylindrical aquarium that sits in the middle of the room and is filled with Australian Potbellied seahorses. There is abundant comfy seating, with chairs, couches, and low tables throughout. If you're nearby during the day, the lounge is a coffee bar. Video poker can be found on the bar top.

Stoney's Rockin' Country

(702-435-2855; www.stoneysrockin country.com; 9151 Las Vegas Boulevard) This is the place to go if you need room to get your groove on and if blue jeans is your "out of town" ensemble. The dance floor is immense, and if you're intimidated by country line dancing, there are free lessons on Thursday and Friday nights. The lessons are for pairs dancing as well. The music from either a live band or DJ is a lot of country and a little bit of rock and roll but all danceable. It just wouldn't be a country bar without a mechanical bull, and Stoney's has one. While there's no charge to ride it, a tip for the operator might increase the length of your ride. There are also four lanes of machine bowling and electronic darts for those not bitten by the dancing bug. Free shuttle service offered on available dates with reservation.

At Noir Bar, the cocktails are high-end, there's ample seating, and reservations are highly recommended.
Courtesy Kirvin Doak Communications

XS

(702-770-0097; www.xslasvegas.com; Encore) Looking like the set of a Roger Moore—era James Bond film with gold-foil nudes decorating the walls, XS is poising itself to be THE club on the Strip and is said to be the most expensive one ever built. The dance floor is really small, giving up most of the space to table service. For extra space and some fresh air, the club opens up onto the pool area. Even with reservations, guests of the hotel can wait up to an hour in line. If you are successful and get into XS, there's a special cocktail called the Ono, made with Dom Pérignon Enotheque and Louis XIII Rémy Martin Black Pearl cognac. The front door staff is very stringent with the dress code, so look the part.

Yard House

(702-734-9273; www.yardhouse.com; 6593 Las Vegas Boulevard South) It's about the beer here—with 160 beers on tap it should be about nothing else here. Admittedly, Yard House is a chain, but that doesn't stop them from having the most remarkable selection of brews in Las Vegas. If genuine beer is still new to you, just let the staff know what you like to drink and let them take care of the rest. They're all trained to assist in pairing what you like now with what you will like before you leave. Fans of the traditional Black & Tan will be happy with the Yard House's own eight blends for a little variety. There's no dance floor, but there is classic rock a-plenty.

Fremont East has taken shape as the local's hippest hangout area. Charo Burke

5

A World off the Strip

Going Past the Glitz

Questions like "Do people really live there?" and "Is your mom a showgirl?" or "Do you live in a hotel room?" rarely get asked of Las Vegas residents these days, but there was a time when they often were, and with a serious face.

Getting off the Strip is a sure way to see the rest of the city, from downtown to Boulder City to the mountains in the west. Las Vegas has many of the same attractions other cities of comparable size have—museums, institutions of higher learning, natural wonders, and so on. There are also things that are only found in Las Vegas, especially with the renovated downtown area.

Catch a bus, a cab, or a shuttle, or take the car, but be sure to check out at least a few things off the world-famous Strip.

Antique Collection at Main Street Station Casino

(702-387-1896; www.mainstreetcasino.com; 200 North Main Street) "Antique collection" might be a strong term for this free self-guided tour of some odd, although historical, collectibles at Main Street Station Casino. To make sure you don't miss any, stop by the front desk for a map. The bell desk has them, too. What type of antiques do you find in a Las Vegas casino? The eclectic list includes a fireplace from Prestwick Castle of Scotland, eighteenth-century lamps from Brussels, a piece of the Berlin Wall located in the men's room (this one may be difficult for women to get to), antique rail cars, Parisian opera-house chandeliers, and more. The casino's décor has a "Victorian train station in the ol' West" theme, so the peculiar mix of antiques works as part of its charm.

Atomic Testing Museum

(702-794-5161; www.atomictestingmuseum.org; 755 East Flamingo Road) The Nevada Test Site is the single most influential piece of Las Vegas history. From 1951 to 1992, below- and aboveground tests numbered close to 1,000, all just 65 miles from Las Vegas. Las Vegas rarely had earthquakes, but sometimes the classroom windows shook a bit. The Nevada Test Site Historical Foundation has been chosen as one of the first museums to take part in the Smithsonian Institution's affiliates program. While there is a slight sense of humor here, with admission staff wearing test site smocks, the museum is respectful of the importance of this part of American history without showing ideological preferences. The interactive exhibits, videos, and photographs are easy to follow thanks to a time-line illustrating events going on in the world concurrently. Listing when the Lego was invented also helps to make it more tangible and interesting for younger visitors. The Ground Zero Theater, designed to resemble an aboveground testing zone, is not to be missed. Be sure not to sneak in after it has started. It's worth the wait to experience it from the countdown straight through to the end. The exhibits continue, including modern inventions that had their origins at the test site, as well as what is being done there now. Revolving exhibits and lectures make regular stops at the museum. The kitschy back-in-time fun does return at the gift shop. From T-shirts to Area 51 salt-and-pepper shakers to Albert Einstein action figures, this is a great spot to pick up a souvenir. Mon.–Sat. 9 AM–5 PM, Sun. 1–5 PM Adults $12, seniors, military, youth $9.

Aquarium at Silverton Lodge

(www.silvertoncasino.com; Silverton Lodge, 3333 Blue Diamond Road) Saltwater fish aficionados will really enjoy this tank. While it may not be on the Strip, it's the best-executed tank for watching and learning about its aquatic residents. The 117,000-gallon octagonal tank is home to 4,000 tropical fish, three stingrays, and three species of shark; it can be viewed from all sides. The Silverton Lodge has been gracious enough to place some comfortable chairs facing the aquarium. If it's not too busy, it's relaxing and tranquil, even for a casino entrance. The aquarium is right next to the Bass Pro Shop entrance, so the seats are welcomed by those who like to watch fish, and catch them. Three times a day, marine biologists wearing microphones feed the fish and answer questions. In the Mermaid Lounge, located next to the aquarium, are two jelly-fish tanks. Feeding times at the aquarium are 1:30, 4:30, and 7:30 PM.

Clark County Heritage Museum

(702-455-7955; www.accessclark county.com; 1830 South Boulder Highway, Henderson)

The Clark County Heritage Museum is a sweet spot to learn about the inhabitants of Southern Nevada, from the Anasazi tribes to the enormous surge of population growth there today. If you're a history buff interested in the old West, then this is a recommended destination. If you're not, this may feel like you're on a middle-school field trip. There's a history-of-gaming exhibit (with a 1918 wooden slot machine) and a gallery featuring rotating Nevada-themed historical collections. The highlight of the museum is Heritage Street: historic houses, businesses, a Paiute village, and mining equipment from the region have been brought here and refurbished. The 1930s train depot, complete with 1918 Union Pacific steam engine and caboose, draw many a train devotee. Daily 9 AM–4:30 PM. Adults $1.50, seniors and children $1.

Desperado

(702-679-7433; www.primmvalleyresorts.com; Buffalo Bill's) Desperado, the roller coaster at Buffalo Bill's, is 40 miles west of Las Vegas in Primm, Nevada. To some that may seem like an awful long way to go for a thrill ride. Keep in mind this is one of the fastest (up to 80 mph), highest (225 feet with a 55-degree descent) and most loved rides in the country. Nowhere else in town can you experience weightlessness nine times in a single ride. The ride is even longer than the others in Las Vegas at 2 minutes and 43 seconds. The experience starts before you've bought tickets as the roller coaster zips through the covered valet area at full speed. Be sure to secure your belongings. Many a pair of sunglasses, purse, or cell phone has paid the price for this much fun. Other attractions available for separate admission are the Turbo Drop, Adventure Canyon Log Flume, The Vault 3D Simulator, and Attraction Zone Arcade. Must be 48 inches to ride. One ride is $8.

Erotic Heritage Museum

(702-369-6442; www.eroticheritage museum.com; 3275 Industrial Road) While it's true that many jokes and innuendos could easily be made regarding this collection of erotic art and materials, it's all taken quite seriously at the Erotic Heritage Museum. After all, as long as there has been art, artists have painted, sculpted, and drawn the naked human figure. This is a museum, not a peep show, although it is located on the same road as many of Las Vegas's strip joints and even shares a parking lot with one. The 24,000 square feet are filled with everything from silent-era pornography to an ancient carriage used as a mobile striptease show. And while there are many historically significant items and excellent examples of fine erotic art here, there are also displays of fetishes and life-size replicas and castings of adult movie stars that may make some squirm. Mon. 10 AM–3 PM; Wed.–Thurs. 5 PM–11 PM; Fri.–Sun. 12 PM–midnight. Adult: $20.00; Senior: $15.00; Student (18 and older): $15.00.

Ethel M Chocolate Factory & Botanical Cactus Garden

(888-627-0990; www.ethelschocolate.com; 2 Cactus Garden, Henderson) The beauty of cacti and other aridity-loving plants is often sadly underappreciated. About 10 miles from the Strip, this 2.5 acres chockful of more than 300 varieties of cactus, succulents, and other desert vegetation could change opinions. A stroll through one of the world's largest gardens of this type provides ample opportunity to learn from informational signs and plaques throughout the garden. If you are visiting during the Christmas and New Year's season, the display of lights is phenomenal and worth braving the desert's winter wind. Since M&Ms took over the company in 2005, you'll have to pass through a store dedicated to that candy. The new bosses got rid of the Living Machine, which was used to clean reclaim water from the factory and use it in other areas like washing the delivery trucks. It is to be hoped that they'll leave the rest of the garden alone. The self-guided factory tour includes a free piece of Ethel M Chocolate at the end. Workers on the candy assembly line are not there on weekends or after 3 PM on weekday afternoons. Other issues like maintenance can affect viewing of the candy production, so call ahead if this aspect is important to your visit. It's hard to say what you'll see as you peer through the windows at the assembly kitchen. Ethel M produces 50 kinds of chocolates and all the fillings are made here. If you aren't familiar with these chocolates, Forrest Mars (yes, of that candy bar company) had passions for gardening and chocolates. His dream was to produce a high-end chocolate similar to his mother's creations during his childhood—that's why her name, not his, is on the boxes. Daily 8:30 AM–6 PM. Free.

First Friday/Art Galleries

(www.firstfriday-lasvegas.org) First it started with artists and galleries reclaiming the older section of downtown businesses and homes. They had an uphill battle ahead of them but persevered until they achieved success. As the Art District started to grow and be taken seriously, Las Vegas followed in the footsteps of other cities and developed its own First Friday. What started as an event that drew a few hundred people each month now attracts crowds of thousands. Celebrated as a gathering of artists, performers, and the folks who love and support them, First Friday is 20 city blocks of 80 galleries, street artists, live music, fire breathers, ice sculptors, fortune tellers, and plenty of colored chalk with which to create a masterpiece of your own. The food available ranges from the expected kettle corn and funnel cakes to the surprisingly tasty and inexpensive H & H Hawaiian barbecue stand. First Friday of each month, 6–10 PM $2 entrance fee. Complimentary shuttles from the Clark County Government Center (Grand Central Parkway), El Cortez Hotel (600 Fremont Street), and Holsum Design Center (241 West Charleston Boulevard) run about every 15–20 minutes.

Tiki carving is just one of the many art forms found at First Friday. Charo Burke

Fremont Street Experience

(www.vegasexperience.com) Before the Fremont Street Experience, downtown Las Vegas was not the most relaxing place in Las Vegas. It provided some unusual people-watching, but that and penny video poker were the extent of its fun. There were a lot of justified concerns about the methods and philosophy employed to clear out the more unattractive inhabitants of the area. But, all in all, the Fremont Street Experience did what it set out to do—revive Las Vegas's downtown. The area keeps getting better but still has a lot of "character." Fremont Street was the beginning of the city—not just the gambling, but the beginning of the town itself. It was the city's first paved road, site of its first traffic light, and the spot where the self-proclaimed Mr. Las Vegas, Wayne Newton, launched a career at the Fremont Hotel. Now it's a blocks-long canopy covered in 12 million lights and there's almost always free entertainment going on. How can there be such a large outdoor pedestrian-friendly light show right in the heart of downtown Las Vegas? In 1994, the area was permanently closed to car traffic. To see what the area looked like in the day, check out 1971's James Bond film *Diamonds are Forever.*

Gondola Adventures

(877-4466-3652; www.gondola.com; Lake Las Vegas Resort, Henderson) You took the casino shopping-mall gondola ride; now take one on the country's largest man-made lake surrounded by high-class hotels and ritzy, expensive homes. This is much more romantic than the Strip casino version. These gondoliers sing or play a musical instrument, and champagne, appetizers, and meals can be had. Meals are served just after you board. Once they are laid out by the local catering company, you can dine when you like. There is a lovely bridge to kiss under and seal your love for eternity. For large groups, flotillas can cruise together. Prices range from $135 for the Classic Cruise (1-hour cruise includes champagne and chocolates) to $395 for the Exquisite Dinner Cruise (2-hour cruise with three-course meal). Prices do not include gratuity.

Hand of Faith Golden Nugget

(www.goldennugget.com; Golden Nugget)

Along with the scheduled free light show, live music, car shows and sidewalk entertainers can sometimes be found at the Fremont Street Experience. Las Vegas News Bureau

Las Vegas has many of the world's biggest hotels, so the biggest nugget of gold (on display) in the world shouldn't come as a surprise. Discovered in Australia in 1980, the nugget weighs in at 61 pounds, 11 ounces. The nugget display can be found in the lobby of the north tower and presents a fun Vegas-y photo opportunity. Free.

Hoover Dam

(702-494-2517; www.usbr.gov/lc/hoover dam; 30 miles southeast of Las Vegas at the Nevada-Arizona border) The Hoover Dam is truly one of the wonders of the modern world. It took five years to build and cost 49 million dollars (676 million in today's dollars) and it is one of the grandest sights

there is to see. Originally called the Boulder Canyon Project, it was later officially renamed Hoover Dam in honor of President Herbert Hoover, who championed the project as a way to apportion the waters of the Colorado River among the western states through which it runs. There are many ways to see this monument to engineering and the American spirit: by car or bus, on foot, by air, and on the water. The most intimate way to experience Hoover Dam is on the Discovery tour, which takes you down inside the dam itself and outside onto observation decks that offer views that dazzle and amaze. You'll pass through the Hoover Dam Visitor Center, a three-story stone-and-glass

Hoover Dam attracts more than 1 million visitors each year. Las Vegas News Bureau

structure that houses exhibits, galleries, and a theater where you'll view a 12-minute video presentation at the tour's outset. From there, guides give talks at each of five stops, even taking you by elevator down to an area overlooking the dam's massive turbine room. The tour culminates with a visit to the visitor center's rooftop overlook, which affords incredible views of the dam and Black Canyon. The beauty of the canyon—blue desert sky above, the Colorado sparkling below, the impossible brilliance of the dam itself—combines to create a tableau that captures the imagination. During daylight hours, foot traffic is permitted on the dam. There is a gift shop, a snack bar, and an exhibit center where, as part of the Discovery tour, you'll watch a neat and informative 20-minute presentation about the Colorado River system and all the states and communities it serves. It's undeniably old school, but as at many stops on this tour you'll marvel at American ingenuity and the people that envisioned the system of dams that tamed the wild Colorado, paving the way for the expansion of the West. Daily 9 AM–6 PM, except Thanksgiving and Christmas. Tickets sold until 5:15 PM. The parking garage is open 8 AM–6 PM daily. Adults (ages 17–61) $11, seniors (62 and up) $9, juniors (ages 7–16) $6, children (ages 0–6) free. There is a special rate for military and adult dependents, which is $9.00, and a cash-only parking fee of $7.00 per vehicle.

Las Vegas Motor Speedway

(800-644-4444; www.lvms.com; 7000 Las Vegas Boulevard North) Just 12 miles north of downtown Las Vegas is a NASCAR and auto-racing pilgrimage destination. Whatever is going on at LasVegas Motor Speedway—and there is almost always something going on—they know what car race fans want and like. Of course, there's NASCAR, but on 1,600 acres of one of the world's most complete racing complexes there's also state-of-the-art dragster racing, Richard Petty Driving Experience, the Mario Andretti Racing School, huge souvenir shop, and a tour. The beloved darling here is the 1.5-mile D-shaped track, home of a 400-mile race on the NASCAR Nextel Cup Series, as well as Busch and Truck Series events. Drive and ride-along programs offered by the Richard Petty Driving Experience (www.1800bepetty .com) range from $160 to $2,600.

Mario Andretti Racing School

(www.877racelap.com) This school offers course drives in a BMW and Formula 2000 car from $129 to $3,000. If you're in Las Vegas just after the big March race week, check their Web sites for promotional offers. The drag strip or "The Strip" has racing every other Friday night called Midnight Mayhem. This is designed to help curb illegal street racing. The tour of LVMS is a good place to get your bearings on all that's here. The tour includes nine tracks at Las Vegas Motor Speedway, a visit to a luxury suite, and access to the infield of the superspeedway. Laps around the track are subject to track availability. Speedway tours leave at the top of each hour from the gift shop each Mon.–Sat. from 9 AM–4 PM and Sun. from 11 AM–4 PM. Tour prices are $8 per person. Children under 12, seniors over 55, military personnel, and Nevada residents are $6

From NASCAR to drag racing to private lessons, Las Vegas Motor Speedway has something for all racing fans. Crystal Wood

Le Cordon Bleu Cooking Classes

(888-551-8222; www.vegasculinary.com; 1451 Center Crossing Road) Taking a cooking class from a culinary professional and professor in a state-of-the-art working and teaching kitchen is the only way to cook. It's informative, classy, fun, and not a run-of-the-mill Las Vegas tourist attraction. The classes at Cordon Bleu College of Culinary Arts Las Vegas are offered twice a month, are limited in size, and fill up quickly. It's a good idea to sign up a soon as you can. The costs of the classes vary but tend to be about $150, which includes a continental breakfast and lunch. Class subjects have included: soul food, Latin cooking, cupcakes and candy, wine country cooking, party foods, and island holiday.

Liberace Museum

(702-798-5595; www.liberace.org; 1775 East Tropicana Avenue) There are those who snicker at the mere mention of Liberace, but he was an entertaining classical piano player and showman, and a friend to students of music from all economic backgrounds. He loved Las Vegas as much as it loved him. For 30 years the museum has showcased all that Liberace was known for, both his playing style (he referred to it as "classical music with all the boring parts left out") and his flashy flair for dressing. Liberace came from humble beginnings and knew how difficult it was to foster a musical talent without money. To date the Liberace Foundation for the Performing and Creative Arts has given well over 5 million dollars to 2,500 students at more than

Get to know Latin and Japanese cuisine, vegetarian dishes, cheeses, and more at the Le Cordon Bleu Culinary School classes for the public. Courtesy Le Cordon Bleu College of Culinary Arts—Las Vegas

Wine Country South

Many unlikely things are found in Southern Nevada—the Eiffel Tower, an active volcano, the Sphinx. It's a land of improbabilities, for sure. But would you think that you could happen across a winery in Southern Nevada? You absolutely can. About an hour's drive northwest of Vegas, in the small town of Pahrump, is the Pahrump Valley Winery (800-368-9463; www.pahrumpwinery.com; 3810 Winery Road, Pahrump), a charming privately owned winery and gourmet restaurant. Gretchen and Bill Loken bought the winery in 2005 and since then have made many much-needed improvements, including new winemaking equipment and a totally remodeled and updated tasting room and gift shop. The winery is their pride and joy, and they oversee its day-to-day operation and work right alongside the staff. It's a great place to spend an afternoon, strolling the grounds or picnicking under the lilacs and plum trees (especially nice in the spring and fall when the temperatures are in the 70s and 80s), or tasting their wonderful wines in the comfort of the lounge, with its dramatic fireplace and cozy leather sofas. While in the lounge, check out the display featuring the more than 90 medals won by Pahrump Valley Wines and the wines that earned them. Winery tours are available daily at 11:30 am, 1:30 pm, and 3:30 pm, and if you're there on bottling days, you can watch

The tasting room displays the winery's awards.
Crystal Wood

the magic happen. As beautiful as the winery is, the true stars are the wines themselves. If you like your wines white and light, try their rich Chardonnay, the crisp fruity Symphony, or their Desert Blush table wine, a semisweet blush that pairs easily with food. Red wine fans will enjoy themselves as well—the Pahrump Valley Winery features a unique American Burgundy, light-bodied and just slightly sweet; a rich, bold, Cabernet Sauvignon; and their Merlot, soft and fruit-forward, with cherries on the finish. Also not to be missed is their Syrah, their Pinot Noir, and the history-making Nevada Ridge Zinfandel, the first commercial red wine ever to be grown, produced, and bottled in Nevada.

Once you've tasted the wines, pair them with a lovely meal at **Symphony's Restaurant,** either out on their spacious deck or in the comfortable and elegant dining room. Start things off with their creamy lobster bisque, then move on to their grilled flatiron steak dressed with a burgundy wine sauce and bleu cheese crumbles, or the Winery Scampi, shrimp sautéed in their own Symphony wine, lemon juice, and garlic, and served with diced tomato and scallions over fettuccine. Their lunch menu features a host of sandwiches, such as the Turkey Reuben Panini, the Winemaker's Club, and the grilled

The Pahrump Valley Winery is one of the desert's many pleasant surprises. Crystal Wood

Kobe beef burger. They also offer lunch portions of a few of their dinner menu items, and their friendly servers can help recommend wine pairings for each of their menu offerings. (From Las Vegas, take Highway 160 [Blue Diamond Road] west into Pahrump. Turn right onto Winery Road, and continue on about one half mile; the winery is on your left.)

120 universities and colleges. The Liberace Museum is divided into two areas. The first building (closer to East Tropicana) houses the Historical Timeline with photos, his piano collection, and stage automobiles. Building Two showcases the glittering costumes, jewelry, and a re-creation of his outlandishly ornate Palm Springs bedroom. It's amazing that someone actually rested and slept in this décor. Also in this building is his rare Moser crystal collection, which features 14 glasses for a setting of twelve. The only other set like this is owned by Queen Elizabeth. In person, his elaborate pianos are mind blowing. Along with the well-known mirrored and rhinestone encrusted lovelies, there's also a sedately lovely grand piano once owned by George Gershwin. The jewelry is enough to make your jaw drop with platinum piano and candelabra rings. Rap stars have nothing on this bling. Swarovski collectors will ogle one of the world's largest, weighing in at 50 pounds. There is a complimentary shuttle from Riviera, Treasure Island, Mirage, Flamingo, Paris, and Tropicana. Call or check the Web site for pickup times. Tues.–Sat. 10 AM–5 PM; Sun. noon–4 PM Admission $15, free for children 10 and under. If you arrive by bus or cab, you can receive $2 off your admission, but not in conjunction with other coupon offers.

Lied Discovery Children's Museum

(www.ldcm.org; 833 Las Vegas Boulevard North) Like all good children's museums, there are many hands-on exhibits—more than 100 in the arts, sciences and humanities—at the Lied Discovery Children's Museum. The Everyday Learning Pavilion encourages kids to mimic everyday life by getting a job, receiving a paycheck, and budgeting money. There are car repairs and a grocery store to help parents explain why mom won't buy a new scooter "just because." Recently, the exhibit was made "green" by showing kids how recycling and solar and wind energy are important to everyday life. The plumbing exhibit demonstrates how to save water. It's Your Choice is about choosing food for a healthy life, and the Let's Make A Meal Deal is a definite highlight. These are important and lifelong lessons for any kid, resident or visitor. But it's all not about life's drudgery here: there are bubbles to blow, costumes to try on, and computer art to create. Tues.–Fri. 9 AM–4 PM; Sat. 10 AM–5 PM; Sun. Noon–5 PM. Adults $8, Children (ages 1–17) $7.

Natural History Museum

(www.lvnhm.org; 900 Las Vegas Boulevard North) For some, a natural history museum is a quiet adjournment from the busy, loud day-to-day life. Some even find them romantic in a quaint way. The reason to visit the Natural History Museum while traveling is learn about the area you're visiting, right? The E. L. Wiegand Wild Nevada Gallery focuses on the critters and plant life of the Mojave Desert. Unless you arrive at the same time as several school groups, this museum is akin to a hyperbaric chamber compared to the raucous atmosphere of the Strip. If you see a group of schoolchildren, though, stay away from the animatronic dinosaurs. Daily 9 AM–4 PM. Adults $8, Children (ages 3–11) $4.

Liberace was never known for being subtle in his wardrobe choices; at the Liberace Museum, his Pink Turkey ensemble gets notice. Courtesy Liberace Museum

The Neon Museum offers a close-up look at classic Las Vegas signage. Courtesy Neon Museum

Neon Museum

(702-387-6366; www.neonmuseum.org) Someday this museum is going to get so much notice, it will be difficult to get into. So before the entire world discovers and falls in love with it, schedule a tour. Call the museum in advance, as same-day appointments are rarely available and only a certain amount of reservations are taken each day. The Neon Museum is the proud recipient of vintage neon signs—1940s and after, either donated or loaned, for care, repairs, and archiving. These giant signs, with their faded lettering and coloring, resemble an end-of-the-world science fiction scenario. Walking among them with a eye-to-eye view really shows what works of art they were. While currently the museum is primarily the boneyard, construction is in swing on some great additions including a welcoming area set in the old La Concha Hotel lobby. This 1950s strikingly modern Googie-style building, designed by well-known architect Paul Revere Williams, was moved in its entirety to the museum and will one day hold exhibits and information. Williams was the first African American member of the American Institute of Architects. Due to the broken glass and rusty metal throughout the boneyard, closed-toe shoes are needed. This is also why this tour is not appropriate for young children. These will be your coolest vacation photos, but tripods are not allowed. Tour times vary according to the weather. During the warmest months (June–mid-September) they are at 10 AM. Throughout May, the tours are at noon. During the rest of the months, they're at noon and 2 PM. Minimum donation, $15.

Neon Walking Tour

(Fremont Street Experience) If you can't make it to the Neon Museum, then this walking tour will have to hold you over until you return to Las Vegas. The ten signs along Fremont Street Experience have all been restored and date from 1940 to the mid 1960s. They range from the recognizable Hacienda Horse and Rider to the virtually unknown dairy mascot, Andy Anderson. Since these are working signs, they are designed to be seen at night.

One Million Dollars

(800-937-6537; www.binions.com; Binion's Gambling Hall, 128 East Fremont Street) While the odds of you leaving Las Vegas a millionaire are slim to none, you can go home with a picture of yourself with million dollars. Think of what you'll save at tax time. At nearly 60 years old, Binion's is historically a landmark in Las Vegas terms and the "have your picture with a million dollars" has been their attraction on and off for many years. While now it's made up of a lot of small-denomination bills encased in pyramidal Lucite, at one time it was a frame containing 10,000 dollar bills in a horseshoe shape. It turns out that the bills were more valuable as separate collectibles. As has been pointed out throughout this book, things have changed in Las Vegas. In the past, to have your picture taken with the money was complimentary. At the writing of this book, it costs $20 and comes with $25 in slot play at Binion's.

Pinball Hall of Fame

(www.pinballmuseum.org; 3330 East Tropicana) Remember the pinball game you played on your first date? Or at the minimart by your grandma's house? At the Pinball Hall of Fame, there are roughly 200 different pinball games. Most are in working order, although at any time there are bound to be a few out of order. This place is a labor of love for owner Tim Arnold and

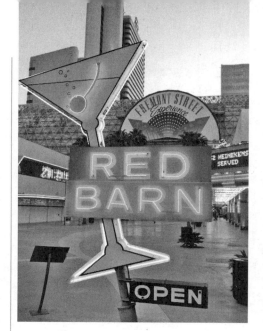

Always open, the Neon Walking Tour offers 10 fully restored signs. Las Vegas News Bureau

this includes the tinkering needed to keep the balls in play. Though nothing like the giant arcades found in casinos, this museum offers a trip down memory lane and a great place to show "antiques" to the gaming console generations. Most of the machines still only cost a quarter, so it's bargain entertainment as well. Each month, any profit made is donated to the local Salvation Army. For those looking for a particular game, check out the Web site, where a list of all the machines can be found. One that aficionados find interesting is Pinball Circus. Far from the oldest machine, it is one of only two of its kind that were ever made. Designed as a shot in the arm for the pinball industry, the upright machine was too cost prohibitive. The only two in existence were made for testing purposes. Don't bother looking for a big flashy sign for the Pinball Hall of Fame; there isn't one. Look for the cheap-seats movie theater next door instead. There's also no listed phone number. Sun.–Thurs. 11 AM to 11 PM, Fri. and Sat. 11 AM–midnight.

At the Pinball Hall of Fame, hundreds of games are still playable at their original prices.   Crystal Wood

Masquerade Show in the Sky

(866-746-7671; www.riolasvegas.com; Rio, 3700 West Flamingo Road) While officially the Rio Hotel and Casino is off the Strip, it's not far as the crow flies. However, walking on a very busy street and pedestrian bridge over a freeway may not be a relaxing stroll. There is a complimentary shuttle from Harrah's Casino on the Strip to the Rio about every 30 minutes. No ticket is needed for this show. Just find a spot to stand in Rio's Masquerade Village and look up. Anyone under 21 must stand on the second level, but others may sit at a slot machine on the ground level. Both levels have good views. Through the night, three different themed productions can be seen including Latin, naughty, and Hollywood burlesque. The show used to be centered on a Mardi Gras theme, but, though beads are still tossed into the audience, everything else has changed. The music is more modern with pop and hip-hop. The dancers are more scantily clad in corsets and lingerie. Except for the floats being attached to the ceiling and the customary throwing of beads in the finale, the entire show is different from the original. For $12.95, tickets can be purchased to ride in one of the parade floats and be part of a Las Vegas show. All minors under 16 must be accompanied by an adult. Shows are every hour, 7 PM–midnight. Free.

Marjorie Barrick Museum/Xeric Garden

(702-895-3381; hrc.nevada.edu/museum; University of Nevada, Las Vegas, 4505 Maryland Parkway) Quietly tucked away on the UNLV campus is a natural history museum and garden. The permanent collection focuses mostly on the craftwork of regional Native American tribes and Las Vegas area history. Temporary exhibits are found in the first section of the 2,500-square-foot hall and most often have something to do with the region. Past exhibits have included subjects like medicinal plants, artist-decorated hotel rooms, and Mexican dance masks and retablos. A particular highlight is the Xeric Garden at the museum's entrance. Designed to show how beautiful drought-tolerant plants and a water-conscientious irrigation plan can be, this 1½ acres has plenty of paved pathways and benches. Plant species include those from North America, South America, Australia, Mexico, and the Mediterranean. The bird-viewing ramada is especially relaxing, even for non aviary enthusiasts. Mon.–Fri. 8 AM–5 PM; Sat. 10 AM–2 PM Suggested donation, $5.

Old Las Vegas Mormon Fort State Historic Park

(702-486-3511; www.parks.nv.gov; 500 E. Washington Avenue) The Mormon Fort, built in June of 1855, was the first permanent structure in Las Vegas. Why this spot? A spring-fed creek and grassland attracted the Paiute, Spaniards, and anyone passing through on their way to California. The Mormons who built and settled this fort only remained for two years. After that it was bought and sold a few times before ending up in the hands of the San Pedro, Los Angeles & Salt Lake Railroad. This is a self-guided tour and whether or not the employee is able to answer specific questions depends upon luck of the draw. There are some interesting artifacts and photos, as well as an exhibition depicting the conditions for the Army soldiers staying here from 1867 to 1869. Because of its small size, the fort is best visited if you are visiting the nearby Neon Museum or Lied Children's Discovery Museum or taking in a Las Vegas 51s game at Cashman Field. Daily 8:30 AM–4:30 PM. Adults $3, children $2.

Nevada State Railway Museum

(702-486-5933; www.nevadasouthern.com; 600 Yucca Street, Boulder City) At about 45 minutes, it's a quick 3-mile train ride, and with air-conditioned and heated cars a pleasant one, too. The track was developed by Union Pacific Railroad in 1931 for materials and supplies needed to build Hoover Dam. The train consists of two refurbished Pullman cars, a 1963 Union Pacific locomotive, and an open-air car. The cars date back as far as 1911 and match very well with the vintage uniformed crew who provide an interesting narrative on the ride. There are also other locomotives and a railway post office on display. Plan on arriving at least 15 minutes before departure. Train rides, Sat.–Sun. 10 AM, 11:30 AM, 1 PM, 2:30 PM. Adult $8, Child $4.

Red Rock Canyon

(www.redrockcanyonlv.org; directions below) If you have time for only one off-the-Strip attraction, make it Red Rock Canyon. The park is the pride and joy of Las Vegas with its stunning colors, astounding views, easily navigable scenic drive (called "the loop"), and proximity to the city. It's a barometer of how much of the Las Vegas valley you experienced. If you traveled to all points in all other directions but not the 15 simple miles from downtown to Red Rock Canyon, then you might as well book a trip back so you can finish your vacation. Residents just call it Red Rock. The sandstone cliffs are brilliant southwestern shades of reds and oranges. Peaks here reach 8,000 feet high. The canyon can be enjoyed by car, bike, or on foot and features hiking trails, picnic spots, and rock climbing. It is Nevada's first National Conservation Area and has a very nice Visitor Center to let you know what you're looking at and what to look for. Restrooms can be found here and at a satellite building at the bottom parking lot. The 13-mile scenic loop drive is the most popular way to

The stunning Red Rock Canyon is too close to town to be missed. Crystal Wood

enjoy the canyon with easy parking at selected picturesque overlooks and vistas. All are easy to find and park in. Picnicking spots can be found at Willow Spring and Red Spring. Since the canyon is just five miles from the edge of the city, there will be plenty of places to stop for provisions. Ask at the visitor center if there have been a fair amount of recent rains. If so, the 0.3 mile hike to Lost Creek leads to a small but charming waterfall. More information on hiking, biking, and rock climbing in Red Rock Canyon can be found in the Recreation chapter of this book. If you are a photo buff, the best light at Red Rock is in the early morning with the sun behind you in the east. As there can be a stopped car or bicyclist around the bend, please adhere to the posted speed limits. There are two ways to get here from the Strip or Downtown. Which works best depends on your plans. If getting there rapidly is important, take I 15 north to US 95 west; exit Summerlin Parkway west to Rampart Boulevard and turn left (south); turn right on West Charleston and continue to park entrance. If you would like to see a bit of the city and stop for a bite or shopping, head west on West Charleston, which intersects with the Strip a few blocks north of the Stratosphere. Once on West Charleston, it's a straight shot all the way to the park entrance on your right. November–February, 6 AM to 5 PM; March, 7 AM–7 PM, April–September, 6 AM–8 PM; October, 6 AM–7 PM. Fee, $5 per vehicle.

INSIDER TIP: Driving through the desert, you may happen upon wild burros by the side of the road. As cute and tame as they appear, they have been known to bite and kick those who only mean to give them food or stand close for a picture. Enjoy them by photographing them from safe distance. Even if you don't have food to offer, they may think you do.

Shark Tank

(www.goldennugget.com; Golden Nugget) Yet another humongous tank (200,000 gallons) built in the middle of the desert, but, like the name says, this one has five species of sharks—sandtiger, brown, Pacific blacktip, nurse, and zebra. You may have heard about the waterslide that takes you through the shark tank. It is true—you can watch the sharks at the card tables or careen past them on an enclosed water slide. Guests of the hotel are welcome in the pool and tank area as an amenity of their hotel stay. Non guests will be charged a $12 fee. Daily 10 AM—6 PM.

Spring Mountain Ranch

(www.parks.nv.gov; 702-875-4141) Just up the road from the Red Rock Canyon exit is Spring Mountain Ranch Park, a lush, charming, and tranquil 520-acre state park that was once a star-owned home and working ranch. The grounds are very well maintained and have ample areas for picnics, walking, and relaxing. The amount of grass and trees (some 400 years old) may come as a surprise. They're especially picturesque with the glorious red sandstone backdrop. At 3,800 feet, the park can be 10—15 degrees cooler than the valley floor. Summer evenings are not only lovely but also can get very busy with theater program and cultural events. Each spring and fall, the living history programs include reenactments and demonstrations. The main ranch house has a self-guided tour and there are docents available to answer questions. There also a variety of guided tours. The main ranch house is open daily from 10 AM—4 PM. Guided tours are weekdays at

Take a water slide ride through sharks at the Golden Nugget's Shark Tank. Charo Burke

Once a celebrity home, Spring Mountain Ranch offers a respite from the hustle and bustle of town.
Las Vegas News Bureau

noon, 1 PM and 2 PM and weekends at noon, 1 PM, 2 PM, and 3 PM. Dogs on leash (no more than 6 feet in length) are allowed but not in buildings. Directions to Spring Mountain Ranch are the same as those to Red Rock Canyon. Just stay on West Charleston, pass Bonnie Springs, and the entrance will be on your right. $6 per vehicle, cash only.

Springs Preserve

(702-822-7700; www.springspreserve.org; 333 South Valley View Boulevard) Springs Preserve, built on the site of the desert oasis that refreshed the earliest explorers and denizens of the Las Vegas Valley, is a cultural center that celebrates the origins and history of Las Vegas and its environs. Built at a cost of $250,000,000 and opened in 2007 to great local fanfare, the Springs Preserve boasts several major attractions, including the ORIGEN Experience, the Desert Living Center, a nearly two-mile-long system of

trails, and an eight-acre botanical garden. In addition, within the Preserve lies the Cienaga, a wetland that is home to many species of native birds, plants, and animals; the original spring has been recreated here, in its original location. In the ORIGEN Experience, locals and tourists can enjoy

The Springs Preserve offers natural history, desert gardening tips, walking trails and organic pizza.
Leah Koepp

Mountain Flora—Ponderosa and Bristlecone Pines

Two important tree species found in the Spring Mountains are the ponderosa and the bristlecone pine; the ponderosa pine is very common, while the bristlecone pine is very unique. Found in areas totaling about 35 percent of the total acreage of the United States, the ponderosa pine (also called the western yellow pine or the bull pine) is the most abundant tree species in the Spring Mountains, as well as in the entire Western United States. Mature ponderosa pines grow to be quite tall, averaging 100–160 feet in height, with some trees topping out at over 180 feet. The bark of the ponderosa pine is unique in that it is orange in color, with black areas in between the bark's "plates," and its structure is such that the limbs that bear needles, cones, and seeds grow very high up on the trunk, leaving a lot of clear area between the lower tree limbs and the ground. The ponderosa pine is a majestic tree and a mainstay of every mountain landscape in Nevada. The bristlecone pine is much lower in physical profile than the ponderosa, but majestic in its own right—bristlecone pines can live to be thousands of years old, and are thought to be among the oldest living species on Earth. These dwarfed trees, their gnarled trunks and branches sandblasted by centuries of dry mountain winds, survive at very high elevations and on practically nothing—they are usually found in rocky areas near mountaintops with very little topsoil and almost no annual rainfall. In fact, scientists have found that the oldest bristlecone pines (found in the White Mountains of California) flourish in the harshest conditions, at the highest elevations. The oldest known bristlecone pine and indeed the second oldest known living tree on Earth, fittingly named "Methuselah," is found in California's Inyo National Forest, its exact location unmarked to protect it from vandalism. The bristlecone pines found in the Spring Mountains outside Las Vegas, while not the most ancient, are still quite spectacular and interesting; check them out if you find yourself hiking around in the higher elevations near Mt. Charleston.

interactive exhibits and recreations that depict how the Las Vegas Valley was discovered and settled, and the lives of the peoples that have populated this area, as well as learn about the geologic forces that created the Mojave Desert. Don't miss the "Flash Flood" exhibit, which puts you in the midst of a raging torrent (while keeping you safe and dry) and demonstrates the power of a flash flood. Outside the ORIGEN Experience is the Desert Wildlife exhibit, featuring many species of animals and insects that make the desert their home. The Desert Living Center houses two separate galleries: In the Sustainability Gallery, interactive exhibits educate visitors about recycling, composting, alternative energy and fuel sources, and conservation of natural resources; the Sustainable Home invites visitors to walk through examples of "green" living spaces (stop by the Design Lab and Training Center for assistance in planning your own "green" home). The "Inside Out" Gallery shows how sustainable building methods were used in building the Desert Living Center. Springs Preserve also has a gift shop and restaurant, the Springs Café by Wolfgang Puck, where you can dine while taking in a great view of the Las Vegas Strip and valley, perhaps after seeing a concert at the outdoor amphitheater, or a film in the Big Springs Theater (check their Web site for performance dates and times). A variety of guided walking tours is available; again, check their Web site for times. Lockers and strollers are available for rent, and standard wheelchairs are provided at no cost. Adult admission $18.95, children $10.95, kids 5 and under free. Daily 10 AM–6 PM.

Valley of Fire

(www.parks.nv.gov; 702-397-2088) The southwestern desert is like nowhere else in the world. Those familiar with it see it in the background of film or television and recognize it immediately. It's not recognized as just "the desert" but as Painted, Mojave, Monument Valley, Joshua Tree, or White Sands. Valley of Fire is that kind of unmistakably recognizable desert. Because it took a cauldron of situations like weather, water, earthquakes, and divine timing to create it, there is no other spot that can impersonate it. The colorful formations and sandstone combine with 3,000-year-old petroglyphs and petrified wood. Located 55 miles northeast of Las Vegas, this is Nevada's oldest (1935) and largest (36,000 acres) state park. Along with sites from the Basket Maker People and visual evidence of the Anasazi, the park has an excellent visitors' center. Stop here before venturing into the park. The park is much more than just another pretty face when you are equipped with

There's no shortage of beauty at Valley of Fire Las Vegas News Bureau

knowledge of its historical and ecological background. The center has good information on hiking trails as well. Those interested in rappelling need to stop here and notify the ranger. The sport is only permitted at Lone Rock and with natural tie-offs only. Unlike heading into the desert to the west of Las Vegas, this park is not located at a higher elevation and therefore offers no relief from the summer heat. Spring and fall are the best times to visit. For some relief, shaded areas with restrooms are located at Atlatl Rock, Seven Sisters, the Cabins, near Mouse's Tank, and White Domes. Even if you don't intend to picnic, be sure to pack food and water. There is no food or water sold in the park and the nearest town, Overton, is 15 miles northeast. There are water spigots for drinking, though. While driving the park's 20 miles of roadways, you may spot man-made stacks of rocks called "Hoodoos," a tradition meant to bring luck on the journey. The desert moves at a much slower pace than some environments, mostly due to lack of water. Moving the rocks to a formation unnatural to Valley of Fire is unappreciated by all those working to take care of it. The same goes for those thinking of taking a rock as a special souvenir. Take I-15 north to Exit 75, right to head east. The park is 18 miles from the interstate. Fee $6 per vehicle.

Nightlife

The bar scene in Las Vegas is varied enough that there is something for everyone. And as this is Las Vegas, there doesn't have to be a last call. There are many bars and clubs that have an opening and closing hour, just as there are plenty that don't. Another anomaly of the Las Vegas bar scene is that Friday and Saturday aren't necessarily the busiest nights. The accepted figure is that half of the town's employees work in the hospitality industry. Their industry doesn't operate on the nine-to-five, Monday through Friday workweek, so their fun doesn't, either. Many clubs and bars have industry nights where the cover charge, drink specials, music, and club vibe cater to the locals. A Tuesday can be as busy as a Friday in Las Vegas, on or off the Strip.

Another difference (unless you're from Reno, Lake Tahoe, or elsewhere in Nevada) is that local bars and clubs are known to have video poker, many with a progressive jackpot. Some bars ask that patrons not gaming try to not sit where there is a game when there are other open seats. Since there's gambling, are there free drinks? While all places have their own house rules, most will provide a drink if you sit and play awhile. The bartender can see from your machine's credits and of course, politeness and tipping can go far.

Gaming licenses can be difficult and expensive to obtain, which may explain the locally owned bar chains. Groups of local bars can be under one business group just like a chain of sandwich shops. Some of the chains can get quite extensive. **PT's Pub** (www.goldentavern group.com) has 35 locations throughout the Las Vegas metro area, including the posh **Sierra Gold Tavern** (6515 South Jones Road; 702-221-4120). And though the **Roadrunner Saloons** (www.roadrunnerlasvegas.com) total only four, all are open, bright, and lively bars with full restaurants.

If you happen to be in this town when your hometown team is playing, a little research could turn up a bar dedicated to cheering on your particular team. The transplants in Las Vegas are from everywhere and they all need a place to reminisce about the home they left. For instance, one Road Runner Saloon location (921 North Buffalo; 702-242-2822) is a well-known Denver fan hangout. And Buffalo fans can hightail it over to **Johnny Mac's** (842 South Boulder Highway, Henderson; 702-564-2121) for wings, beef on weck, and Canadian beers with other Buffalonians. You may not be home for the game, but you'll be close.

Many of the area's talented musicians enjoy dropping in to jam at the Bootlegger. Crystal Wood

Bootlegger

(702-736-4939; www.bootleggerlasvegas
.com; 7700 Las Vegas Boulevard South #1)
There are a lot of clubs on and off the Strip.
The Bootlegger might suit you just fine if
you don't want to wait in line for an hour
(or more) to pay a large cover charge so you
can buy overpriced drinks. Here, you can
listen to talented local musicians in a nice
atmosphere that doesn't have attitude or
cage dancers, and "table service" means if a
table is open it's yours. Though no longer in
its original location, the Bootlegger has
been a Las Vegas staple for decades and
celebrities have been spotted there for
most of those—not the here-today-gone-
tomorrow stars but legends. There's live
entertainment every night of the week,
including a far-above-average karaoke
night. Once again, there are a lot of talented
people living here. Along with the scheduled band, there's usually an open mic for
anyone who may drop by to sing or play.
Most often it's Las Vegas entertainers getting away from their "day job" by doing
their own thing: jazz, blues, ballads, whatever. If you're hungry, the restaurant serves
a full menu 24 hours a day. The Italian food
here is done in the southern style and
exemplifies the term "comfort food."

Crown & Anchor British Pub

(702-739-8676; www.crownandanchorlv
.com; 1350 East Tropicana Avenue) A pub
(even one in Las Vegas) should be warm,
comfortable, and well stocked with requisite beers. It should offer fun and cama-
raderie, as well as quintessential foods
from the Isles. All of this can be found
here, along with multiple televisions with
the football/soccer game almost always on.
The menu is replete with traditional fish
and chips, bangers and mash, kidney pie,
and real trifle. It's been said that visitors
from across the pond approve of the food.
The Crown & Anchor is right around the
corner from UNLV and a very quick
straight shot down E. Tropicana from the
Strip. The location is also very easy from
the airport, making it a great spot before
or after the flight. Be forewarned, if the
World Cup is on, there's a $20 cover
charge. Open 24 hours with graveyard-
shift food specials.

Double Down Saloon

(702-791-5755; www.doubledownsaloon
.com; 4640 Paradise Road) Though the
Double Down has received a lot of press in
recent years, it deserves credit for being a
cool bar before everyone knew it was a cool
bar. The jukebox is better stocked than any
alternative radio station. The folks here are
a pretty eclectic mix of hippies, punks,
rockabillies, Goths, lots of young women
with Bettie Page's bangs, and samples of
various other subcultures. When it gets
busy, this tiny bar can really pack 'em in.
All in all, it's a friendly, albeit rough-and-
ready, crowd. Most nights, there's a band
onstage and no cover charge. If you go for
no other reason, go for the Bacon Martini
and to stare at the psychedelic wall murals
and video screens. 24 hours.

The Griffin

(702-382-0577; www.thegriffinlounge.com;
511 Fremont Street) Sitting down at the bar
in the Griffin for the first time doesn't feel
new at all. That's because it's just right. Just
the right mixture of all walks of life—the old-
timer curmudgeon crowd mixed in with the
new tragically hip crowd; add just a splash of
people who, without even trying, just know
what's hip before anyone else does. The
décor is just right, too, with layered flagstone
that isn't just for effect and a superb fireplace. The atmosphere is perfect: action in
spots here and there but a calm chilled vibe
as well. There's a fire pit with plenty of seating to keep the vibe going. The jukebox has a
bit of everything from Johnny Cash to serious modern punk.

The Griffin kept what was best about the old and added the best of the new including a great jukebox.

Charo Burke

Hookah Lounge at Paymon's

(702-731-6030; www.hookahlounge.com; 4147 South Maryland Parkway) For those unfamiliar with the smoking of the hookah, it may not be what you think it is. It's a serene atmosphere and a relaxing activity but not about the negative connotations that cigarettes or cigars conjure up. At Paymon's there can be a Hookah Man who will guide you through the 20 flavors available and help to decide which would best satisfy. Otherwise, you'll have to rely on your server. This can be very helpful when in a group that can't agree on which flavor to choose. The room is dark with comfortable low seating and jewel-toned Mediterranean décor, of course. The Babylon Spice drink made with fresh ginger, coconut milk, rum, and mango juice was featured on Rachael Ray's $40 a Day.

One Six Sky Lounge

(702-856-5300; www.eastsidecannery .com; Eastside Cannery Hotel and Casino; 5525 Boulder Highway) What ever happened to nice but within reach clubs? You're nicely dressed and couldn't care less about being where the beautiful people are. All you'd like is a swanky-looking club, a friendly bar, and a dance floor you can actually dance on. Is this too much to ask for in Las Vegas? Thanks to One Six Sky Lounge, it isn't. The Eastside Cannery is a nice locals casino in a working-class neighborhood. The modern club is on the 16th floor with floor-to-ceiling windows that provide a superb view, even from the restrooms. Like many other clubs there's a special martini selection, a wine list, and tapas-style food. What this club has that the others don't is realistic prices and zero snobbery. There's even a happy hour going from 5–8 PM. Open Fri. and Sat. until 4 AM

Sand Dollar Blues Lounge

(702-871-6651; www.sanddollarblues .com; 3355 Spring Mountain Road) Las Vegas's ration of residential musicians is staggering. Many are so talented that they can play whatever style pays the bills and possibly provides health insurance—and play it well—and then go play their music of choice around town. The Sand Dollar Blues Lounge is one of those places. Like any good blues bar, it can have its share of nefarious characters hanging out, too, but recent remodeling shooed a lot of them away. It's a bit grimy and the décor is kept to posters and such, but the music, prices, and staff make the place classy in its own way.

O's stage becomes immersed in water repeatedly throughout its layered performances. Courtesy Cirque Du Soleil

6

SHOWS

Las Vegas has always been a draw for entertainment. Singers, dancers, comedians, ventriloquists, magicians, jugglers, animal trainers, acrobats, and every other variety-show-style act has found a home here at some time. And while certain styles of entertainment have had reigns over the showroom throughout the years, there's always something for every visitor. As the entertainment has gotten bigger, so have the ticket prices: they are now similar to Broadway prices. The talent reprising the roles is the best of the best and many have played on Broadway or in London. They're not tired from traveling around the country and the sets are not struck down and rebuilt in the next town. Most headlining acts can carry a high ticket price, but there are no arenas, poor sound systems, or seats miles away from the stage.

There are regular and quick changes in Las Vegas's entertainment offerings. Shows change days, times, and venues. If a specific show is to be seen during your trip, be sure to check the details before leaving and make reservations. Most shows have at least one dark day and many take extended breaks. It would be a shame if it fell on the day you planned to see it.

Try to plan your choice for dinner around the show. This includes time and location. Getting in and out of a large casino resort can take time. Why do it twice? If there's a time limit, let your server know as soon as you can. In a single day, there are dozens of shows with tickets for sale. When a show being considered isn't listed, ask a knowledgeable critic. The servers, bartenders, dealers, front desk clerks, and other employees on the Strip have seen a lot of shows.

> INSIDER TIP: When buying tickets, check with the casino box office or official Web site first. Other Web sites and ticket sellers charge fees for no reason. If there are no tickets available for the date or the seats are not to your liking, then consider the online ticket brokers. If tickets are too good to be true, be sure they're not obstructed.

Carrot Top

702-262-4400
www.luxor.com/entertainment
Luxor
Sun., Mon., Wed.–Fri. 8 PM; Sat. 7 and 9 PM

He's that kid who always disturbed class with his antics. And whether that kid was your classroom chum or not, he more than likely made you laugh more than once. Carrot Top makes his audience laugh a lot more than once. He's best known for his prop comedy, but his show is more topical than that. There are still baby carriers for rednecks, an application for Hooters, and other visual jokes. So many that they fill eight footlockers onstage. There are also jokes about timely celebrity and political news. It's like getting two comedians for the price of one. Because his props collection is extensive, along with his jabs at the news of the day, no two shows are ever exactly alike. This is a straightforward comedy show with no acrobats or extensive body paint or disappearing tigers.

While he's best known for his props, Carrot Top can be topical as well. Courtesy Steve Flynn Public Relations

Fans of Frankie Valli's music will be gleeful during Jersey Boys. Joan Marcus

Jersey Boys

702-414-9000
www.jerseyboysinfo.com/vegas/
The Palazzo
Mon., Thurs., Fri., Sun. 7 PM; Tues., Sat.
6:30 and 9:30 PM
$65–$135

Here's a Tony-Award-winning Broadway show created specifically for those in love with the music of Frankie Valli and the Four Seasons (really the music of Bob Gaudio and the voice of Frankie Valli), not forgetting the foresight and muscle of Tommy DeVito, along with the harmony lessons from Nick Massi. *Jersey Boys* shows the audience that every Season had an influential role. The songs of the Four Seasons are used throughout to highlight the happenings of their career, to and through stardom. Hits like "Sherry," "Big Girls Don't Cry," "Rag Doll," and "Walk Like a Man" are sure to take the audience on a memory lane stroll. But when the band performs on *Ed Sullivan* or *American Bandstand,* the effect of simultaneously showing them on a giant screen in black and white interlaced with original shots of sobbing teenyboppers, the audience is fully immersed in the gloried past. This may appear to be a show good for kids, but the Jersey language with its colorful expletives is used throughout.

KÀ

702-531-3826
www.cirquedusoleil.com
MGM Grand
Tues.–Sat. 6:30 PM and 9:30 PM
Adults $69–$150, Children up to 12 years old $35–$75;

Depending on the preferences of whom you ask, Cirque du Soleil is the best thing to hit the Strip since the showgirl. Although there are multiple Cirque shows, each is unique and designed to appeal to a specific audience. *KÀ* has a definite Asian theme using a fable-like story, a dramatic plot akin to anime movies, fantastical costumes, and sets and music highlighting an Oriental flair. It is also slightly less acrobatic than other Cirque shows. There's also science and fantastic fiction, disdain for the mechanized world, battle scenes, martial arts, and romance. Oh, and a children's story. In fact, *KÀ* is one of the few Cirque shows that has a story line. Sure there are holes in the story, but if viewed like a foreign movie of a little-understood culture, they're forgiven. The tale is of twins (boy and girl) who are trained in martial arts and adored by all. Enter the bad guys, who want to take over with their desire to rule by harnessing firepower. The twins separate, have adventures, and fight their nemeses. Filled with engineering marvels like a rotating battlefield, a ship tossed during a storm, and a sandy shore complete with animal life, *KÀ*'s stage was designed by the same genius responsible for U2 and Rolling Stones tours. If you are weary from enjoy-

Effects like a ship in a violent storm impress at KÀ.
Courtesy Cirque Du Soleil

Lance Burton's honoring of the magicians who inspired him makes for a family-friendly show. Courtesy MGM

ing Las Vegas to the hilt, rest up before going to this show. The comfy seats, melodic score, and darkened stage can lull someone not completely awake. It can feel a little long with "acts" unnecessary to the story line. If you get to choose your seats, don't be convinced that closer is better. Anything closer than seven rows can give neck strain. Is this a kid-friendly show? Yes, but keep the show's length in mind.

Lance Burton: Master Magician
877-386-8224
www.lanceburton.com
Monte Carlo Hotel & Casino
Tues.–Sat. 7 PM; Tues. and Fri. 10 PM
$67–$73

Lance Burton is one of the premier magicians performing on the Las Vegas Strip, and once you see his show you'll understand why. He has appeared (and disappeared, then reappeared) in his own lavishly appointed, custom-built showroom at the Monte Carlo, the Lance Burton Theater, for over 12 years, and his show is one of the most popular in town. During the course of the show, audiences are taken on a "journey through magic," and the illusions that he creates are truly astonishing, ranging from sleight-of-hand tricks he performs alone onstage under a single spotlight to large-scale extravaganzas carried out with the aid of his six stunning assistants. *Lance Burton: Master Magician* is also one of those rare birds on the Las Vegas Strip: a family-friendly show. It was Lance's childhood dream to be a magician, and he clearly relishes the opportunity to share his dream; he brings a child onstage during each show to assist him with an illusion. Book this show well in advance, as it can sell out, especially at holiday times and over three-day weekends.

Liberace Cabaret

702-798-5595
www.liberace.org
1775 East Tropicana Avenue
Days, times, and price vary

Just past the café inside the Liberace Museum is an intimate performance room. Though it's unknown who will be performing here during your trip, it's safe to say that some talented musicians are granted the opportunity to play on one of Liberace's personal pianos. Professional singers make their way to the cabaret as well. Due to a bevy of shows, Las Vegas is well stocked with talented musicians, composers, and singers. But if the bright lights and big costume changes are getting to be too much, check the schedule at the museum. The shows are extremely reasonably priced with the money going into the museum's scholarship fund and are often scheduled for afternoons. At the time of this writing, Broadway pianist and costar of *Jersey Boys* Philip Fortenberry interweaves his musical biography with Liberace's music all the while playing on the infamous mirrored grand piano. An entertainment trifecta in Las Vegas—wonderful talent for a great price that benefits future musicians.

LOVE

702-791-7111
www.cirquedusoleil.com
The Mirage
Thurs.–Mon. 7 PM and 9:30 PM
$99–$150

Taking on the music of the Beatles is an enormous task, even for Cirque du Soleil. Fans of the band can be ardent in their critique of anything having to do with their beloved Fab Four. Anything interpreting the Beatles must be done in admiration and respect for the music, the four musicians, and for the legions of fans the world over. The original desire for the show came from a friendship between the George Harrison and Cirque du Soleil's founder Guy Laliberte. The music has all been remixed and remastered by producers Sir George Martin and his son Giles Martin. The two sifted through years of archived Beatles recordings using fragments from 130 songs and created 26 musical pieces with the aim of getting people to really listen to the music once again. Sir Martin has said that the Beatles were too far ahead of the recording technology at the time. These

LOVE isn't about impersonating the Beatles but rather sharing a version of their influence.
Courtesy Cirque Du Soleil

new recordings are meant to show what they wanted and would have done if possible. For instance, this version of "My Guitar Gently Weeps" is Harrison's first studio demo of the song with an added string arrangement written by Sir Martin. "Goodnight" has the drums from "Lovely Rita." While there are four male characters throughout *LOVE,* they're not impersonators and don't even look like John, Paul, George, and Ringo. It's more like they embody the characteristics that each portrayed to their adoring public—romantic, humorous, mischievous, and witty. The same can be said for many of the performances in the show. They're not strictly dances and acrobatics choreographed to the songs, but rather inspired by the emotions or memories they produce. The opening song "Because" is set to artistic scenes regarding World War II bombing of London. The show does not follow a strict timeline of the Beatles but rather shows how the music was part of the times. One highlight of many is the snippets of the in-studio banter strung together to sound like a conversation about and during the show. It's the reunion that never was. Most likely not every one of your favorite Beatle songs is in the show. And, the interpretations of each song may not what you pictured when you hear it. More important, the show gets the effects and intentions of the band and the music right.

Mac King Comedy Magic Show

702-369-5222
www.mackingshow.com
Harrah's Casino
Tues.–Sat. 1 and 3 PM
$25

The *Mac King Comedy Magic Show* is one of the few family-friendly shows on the Strip, one of the only afternoon shows on the Strip, and a delight from beginning to end. Mac's aw-shucks demeanor belies his quick

Mac King's goofiness adds to the charm of his vintage style magic/comedy act. Courtesy Mac King

wit; his sleight-of-hand skills are nothing short of amazing. A baggy tramp-like plaid suit cloaks a superb magician who's on par with those making Learjets disappear in other casinos. His unusual sense of humor hits exactly the right note for this type of show—it's totally kid-friendly, but with an adult edge so slight that the kids will never notice. Most of Mac's illusions are reliant upon audience participation, and his magician's gift for reading people is apparent in his choice of "assistants" picked from each audience. There are no scantily clad women and no immense props, because he doesn't need them. Even if you're not visiting Vegas with children or your grandma, if you like to be amazed and to laugh until your eyes water, you will enjoy this show. It's also part of a dying breed, a show that's a steal for the quality of entertainment and magic included for the price of a ticket.

MGM Grand's Crazy Horse Paris

866-740-7711
www.mgmgrand.com
MGM Grand
Wed.–Mon. 8 and 10:30 PM
$51–$61

L'art du nu—the art of the nude—is the goal of the original *Crazy Horse in Paris,* France, and the Las Vegas version works toward it as well. The theater is an almost exact match of the French originator. This is a topless/nearly nude show that is erotic and tasteful. It's about being sexy, not dirty. The female nude body has been portrayed in every medium since the inception of art itself. In Crazy Horse Paris, the dancers' bodies are played upon by lights and optical illusions, turning them into "living pictures." The dancers are all professionally trained, as is evident, and some performed at the original location. They are naturally endowed and similar in size and structure. Add the wigs and strategically placed costume props and they resemble Bob Fosse dancers and vintage European film bombshells. Be prepared for the very antisexy side acts though. For example, the poplocking guys, while excellent at their craft, are out of place here. All in all, MGM Grand's Crazy Horse Paris is a stylized peep show with statuesque dancers lip-synching to suggestive music in both French and English. It's well done, but don't be surprised by what it is at its core—proactively titillating.

Mystère
702-392-1999
www.cirquedusoleil.com
TI (Treasure Island Hotel and Casino)
Sat.–Wed. 7 and 9:30 PM
$60–$110

There are many shows on the Strip, even Cirque du Soleil shows, but none of them are like *Mystère*. As one of the longest-running Vegas shows, and the first Cirque show to premiere in Las Vegas, it has thrilled, delighted, and amazed approximately nine million guests since its 1993 opening and it continues to be one of the high points of

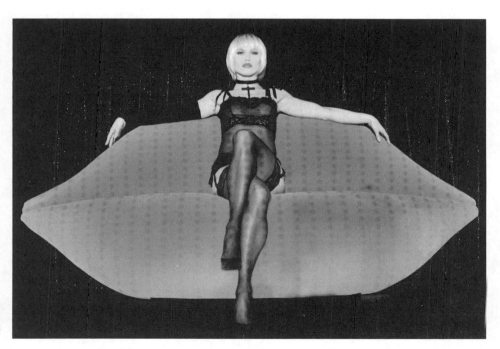

Crazy Horse Paris brings art and sexy together in a sublime understated show that's not for those looking for raucous and raunchy. Courtesy MGM

Vegas entertainment. From the moment you are seated in its huge amphitheater, watercolor blues and purples playing on the walls and stage, a rendering of a Spanish galleon at full sail with pennants flying high above on the ceiling, you are entertained in the inimitable Cirque style—first by a thoroughly mad-looking maître d' "helping" folks to their seats, and later by acrobats, trapeze artists, costumed performers, and clowns performing physical feats that will enchant and astound. The visuals are illusory but the performers' abilities are no illusion: these people are incredibly talented and you will be in awe of them. Every element of the show is an object of play—light, sound, costumes, performers—even the stage itself is used to create the dream that is *Mystère*. To give too many details of this show would be to spoil it, and each person deserves to discover it for themselves; *Mystère* is a must-see for all ages.

Nathan Burton
702-733-3333
www.nathanburton.com
Flamingo Hilton
Tues., Wed., Fri.–Sun. 4 PM
$34, $44

For an afternoon show this one packs a pretty nice punch, especially for the price. The name and face may seem familiar. His best-known trick is an audience favorite on television's *America's Got Talent*. He's the guy who disappears and becomes his own promo poster. The poster is shot out of a cannon, which causes him to reappear. It's an impressive magic trick and this caliber and magnitude isn't usually seen at afternoon shows. Burton doesn't perform with the serious magician expressions and choreography. There is a slight story line, but he's there to make sure the audience has fun, so he doesn't take himself too seriously. Afternoon shows tend to be more conservative compared to many of Las

Vegas's evening shows. The language and costumes are entertaining but not too provocative. It is still a stage show, so there is some skin but no more than at the hotel pool. In fact, these dancers show less. There are few dance numbers, but they're certainly not the focus or the reason to buy tickets. Don't let the time of day lead you astray. This is a real showroom with cocktail waitress and maître d'. The show lasts about 75 minutes.

O
702-693-7722
www.cirquedusoleil.com
Bellagio
Wed.–Sun. 7:30 and 10:30 PM
$94–$150

The first Cirque du Soleil show created exclusively for Las Vegas, O set the standard for their shows on the Strip. As said elsewhere in this chapter, each Cirque show is created around a certain style and therefore appeals to fans of that style. O's style is magical realism, in which a scenario seems illogical but is shown as if it is completely within the realm of the normal. For instance, a man methodically walks onstage bringing with him a simple chair and a folded newspaper. As he sits and reads the paper, it lights on fire. The fire soon spreads to him and engulfs him as he reads. Finished reading, he then calmly stands up, grabs the chair, and exits the stage—all the while still on fire. This isn't presented like a magician's trick with serious eyes and flamboyant hand gestures. Its beauty is in its simplicity and normalcy. Artsy descriptions aside, the show is filled with remarkable beauty, jaw-dropping costumes, and water. Lots and lots of water. The engineers responsible for the design of the stage created one that goes from water to solid and back to water again. The acts that comprise O include the acrobats, trapeze artists, and contortionists traditional in Cirque shows.

The latter use giant lily pads and appear as if in a live Monet painting.

Penn & Teller

702-777-7776
www.riolasvegas.com
Rio Hotel & Casino, 3700 West Flamingo Road
Sat.–Wed. 9 PM
$75, $85

Penn & Teller are among the most imaginative, intellectual performers around, and their show at the Rio is a great showcase for their unique mix of illusion and comedy. They like to keep their show fresh and unpredictable; new bits are introduced all the time, so it's anyone's guess which illusions you'll see when you go. You're likely to see a mix of brand-new things they've cooked up, as well as some of their classics, such as the "Magic Bullet," wherein P & T fire bullets at one another and catch the bullets with their teeth. It's not an elaborately designed show, and there are no Penn & Teller dancers (although the opening act is the swingin' Mike Jones Trio, with their handsome bass player), but if you're seeing their show, you're probably familiar with their amazing range of talents and their penchant for intelligent (and sometimes morbid) comedy. It's a fairly family-friendly show—the adult language is fairly mild and kept at a minimum, but there may be some blood (real and fake) in some of their bits. If you bring kids, age 12 and up is probably a good guideline.

Phantom—The Las Vegas Spectacular

702-414-9000
www.phantomlasvegas.com
The Venetian
Mon. 7 and 9:30 PM; Tues.–Fri. 7 PM; Sat. 7 and 9:30 PM
$69–$150

Why is it called the Las Vegas Spectacular? Diehard *Phantom* fans will notice that this

The chandelier is even more impressive than the original in Las Vegas's version of Phantom.
Courtesy Kirvin Doak Communications

production is only 95 minutes long and not 150 like the original by Andrew Lloyd Webber. But the special effects and custom designed $40 million theater may lessen that sting a bit. And the jewel of the original production, the chandelier, is bigger, better, and well worth the gasps it elicits from the people seated under it. At 5 million dollars to build, it should be. So what's missing? The dialogue providing *Phantom*'s backstory and almost half of "The Point of No Return" song are gone but the story moves along with no plot holes. There was a time when taped music was edging musicians off the Strip, but thanks to shows like this one, live music is back. *Phantom* has a 40-piece orchestra accompanying it. Anthony Crivello stars as the Phantom and plays him as creepy and unnerving, with a slight romantic side. Many are familiar with the original story, whether it be from the book, Webber's musical, or the film. And here it's no different. A young ingénue falls into the trap set by her vocal teacher, the Phantom. But alas, she's in love with her childhood sweetheart. One is young and handsome, the other grotesque and frightening. Who will have heart?

The Rat Pack is Back

702-386-2110
www.ratpackvegas.com
The Plaza Hotel and Casino—downtown
Mon.–Fri. 7:30 PM; Sat. 7:30 and 10:00 PM
$57–$71

Las Vegas was once the place for the hippest and coolest cats to enjoy themselves and let loose. And when Frank Sinatra, Sammy Davis Jr., Dean Martin, and Joey Bishop wanted to have some fun, they took the stage at the Copa Room in the now-extinct Sands. Those longed-for days are gone but not forgotten. Thankfully, the showroom at the Plaza has been spared the modern minimalist or themed décor found elsewhere in town. It has been treasured and remodeled to look like the showrooms once did, with red carpet, big round booths, and sparking chandeliers. In any show that relies on impressions of icons, the concern is can the performer really pull it off? And in this case, the answer is mostly. Let's face it—these are some very talented folks they are imitating. The Dean Martin is basically good—better at the singing than the drunken swagger. The Sammy Davis Jr. seems better at the onstage personality than the singing and dancing. The Frank doesn't so much look like him, but when the lights are down, the voice is pretty

accurate. These three are legends, though. Sinatra behaved like their boss because he was. Sammy Davis Jr. was like no other performer. The best anyone can do is pay a respectful tribute to them. This show does that. There is nothing in the show that isn't done respectfully and with sincerity. Nitpicking about if Sinatra can work the microphone like the Chairman of the Board, or if this Sammy is as adept at the soft-shoe is to be expected. But it won't change the fact that these are great songs and light banter from a lost era and with a live 12-piece orchestra.

Vinnie Favorito

702-733-3333
www.flamingolasvegas.com
The Flamingo
Daily 8 PM
$40–$50

The "Don Rickles" style of insult comedy takes an attentive, kind heart. It's true. A comedian needs to know how to compliment an individual before ripping him or

Vinnie Favorito tells it like it is at multiple casinos on the Strip. Courtesy Vinnie Favorito

her apart. In sketchy lighting, they need to quickly use their powers of perception to decide who can handle the slurring of their looks, status, intelligence, and career choice. Vinnie Favorito has got this talent down to an art. Each show, he picks men and women throughout the crowd and asks them three basic questions. Their name, where they live, and what they do. It sounds like pretty basic stuff that everyone should be able to rattle off without much thought. And maybe that's the issue—simple answers trip people up. If you are highly sensitive to jokes about race, then go elsewhere. Favorito has an archetypal style of making fun of the stereotypes of all nations and states. He believes that if we really laugh at ourselves and each other, then we understand each other better, too. And there isn't a group, gender, job, physical attribute that he can't make fun of. It's as if there's an insult Rolodex in his head. He's got a million of 'em. Each audience is different, so each night is different. After the show, you can buy a CD of what you just experienced. If you or your travel partner is chosen to be skewered with verbal abuse, take the public humiliation home as a souvenir.

Wayne Brady, Making %@it Up

866-641-7469
www.venetian.com
The Venetian
Thurs.–Mon. 9 PM
$55–$165

There are no safe seats at Wayne Brady's show; everyone is fair game. Courtesy Kirvin Doak Communications

You may have seen Wayne Brady on *Whose Line Is It Anyway?*, or on his Fox TV show *Don't Forget the Lyrics*, wowing fans with a mix of music and comedy that's all his own. An extremely talented comedian, singer, and dancer, and he brings it all to his show *Making %@it Up* in the Venetian Showroom. Brady and sidekick Jonathan Mangum have a winning chemistry and infectious energy and they improvise wonderfully with members of the audience brought to the stage to participate in their inspired scenarios. In keeping with the show's classic Vegas Variety show vibe, the Wayne Brady dancers provide glitz and glamour, and Cat Gray and his three-piece band rock the house. Brady performs some of his original material, as well as paying musical tribute to James Brown, Sammy Davis Jr., and Luther Vandross with his impressive impersonation skills. If you like Wayne Brady on television, you will enjoy his live show.

Zumanity is Cirque Du Soleil's zaniest and most provocative adult-oriented show. Courtesy Cirque Du Soleil

Zumanity

702-740-6815
www.zumanity.com
New York–New York
Tues., Wed., Fri.–Sun. 7:30 and 10:30 PM

As said elsewhere in this chapter, there's a Cirque du Soleil show in Las Vegas that suits everyone's taste. This one is for those who enjoy open-minded, risqué humor. From the moment your ticket is taken by a man or woman wearing a provocatively silk-screened T-shirt, to the peep show viewing holes in the lobby, to the Cirque customary preshow, nothing is taboo. Seriously, nothing. These jokes aren't just burlesque-style innuendos, they're outright sexual pranks and gags. Edie, the show's hostess, welcomes all orientations and introduces acts dedicated to titillating fixations. Each act that comes to the stage brings their sensual genre to life. Two young women swim together in a giant champagne glass reminiscent of the classic Playboy cartoon icon. Two men battle it out in a cage Greco-Roman style. There are zaftig sisters, swinging couples, hula hoops, a contortionist, chaps, and baths. And like a Cirque du Soleil show should be, there are also acrobats, gymnasts, dancers, creative costumes, ethereal music, and a sense of leaving the real world behind. This show is strictly for those 18 and over.

7

RESTAURANTS

Steakhouses are Just the Start

For so long, Las Vegas was known as the home of cheap dining. From buffets to 99-cent shrimp cocktails, visitors were fascinated by the prospect of paying $4 for prime rib. And while it wasn't the best prime rib in the city, it was edible. What was the secret to inexpensive buffets and restaurants practically giving away food? Restaurants (and shows) had nothing to do with the resort making a profit. The food was meant to bring customers in or keep them from leaving, but all the restaurant had to do was break even. Then the casinos became corporate owned. If there was money to be made on the food, the prices would reflect it. It started out slowly with prices rising no faster than the tourists would tolerate. Next came the celebrity chefs like Wolfgang Puck, Charlie Trotter, and Mark Miller. At the same time, expensive buffets became a signature of how unique the property was. From Kobe beef to lobster thermidor, buffet offerings represented as much marketing as menu choices. The time of meals at supersteal prices are pretty much gone. As disappointing as this can be for some, dining in Las Vegas is now rated among the best in the United States.

There is one glaring omission in this chapter. There are no buffet listings. There is nothing wrong with a well-executed buffet. There is an enjoyment in a Las Vegas buffet that most the world will never see or understand. But, all buffets are variations on the same themes. They seat large amounts of people, most often have a line, a live carving or omelet station, and a dessert area. So which one should you go to? Figure out which property you like the best and check on their buffet. If the ambience, style, vibe, and theme of the hotel please, then most likely their buffet will, too. If they're not too busy, ask to take a peek at the food before purchasing.

While there are no buffets listed, there are many restaurants that are not located on the Strip. The residents of Las Vegas are getting spoiled. They have become well versed in food and wine but don't want to go to a casino to dine. Would you want to return to work to enjoy a nice meal? Many of the chefs and support staff in local restaurants have left the casino restaurants and bring their experience and knowledge with them. It's worth the drive, walk, or cab ride to eat with the locals.

Las Vegas, because of its large Italian influence, has been home to a multitude of wonderful Italian restaurants in and out of the casinos since the mid-twentieth century. Some are simply family eateries, while some are upscale affairs. In recent decades, however, Las Vegas has seen a surge in Asian cuisine, most of which is located in the "Chinatown" area. Chinatown is a section of Spring Mountain Road that is home to many Chinese as well as

Japanese, Vietnamese, Korean, and Thai restaurants, markets, and businesses. There's also Caribbean, Cuban, South American, Mexican, and many Mediterranean restaurants. The international makeup of the city's residents accounts for some pretty decent international fare. It gets better each year.

When it comes to making dinner reservations in Las Vegas, it is always better to err on the side of caution. Assume reservations are needed and call to make them. Just because it's a Tuesday in February doesn't mean that there isn't a colossal convention in town. This goes for restaurants both on and off the Strip. If reservations are not accepted to any of the listings in this chapter, it is noted in their contact information.

THE STRIP

Aureole
702-632-7401
www.charliepalmer.com
Mandalay Bay Hotel and Casino
Daily 6–10:30 PM
Price: Very expensive

When fine dining is done correctly, you feel pampered but not smothered by the service. When the meal is created correctly, it satiates you with flavors, aromas, and presentation and each course is a separate sensual memory. Charlie Palmer's Steak Aureole brought all this to Las Vegas before many star chefs and gourmet indulgers saw the gastronomical city that it is now. You enter from the casino at Mandalay Bay, but the elevator that takes you down to the dining room leaves the ruckus behind. The dining room is sublime in its decor because aside from the food, the best visual dominates the room. It's a clear glass-and-steel-framed box 42 feet high containing nearly 10,000 bottles of wine in its 46,000 square feet. There are more Austrian wines at Aureole than anywhere else outside of Austria.

The famed Wine Angels can glide up in ten seconds to retrieve the requested bottle. Don't be intimidated by the enormous wine list or the many accolades bestowed upon the collection and sommeliers. The staff is warm and encouraging and no one need feel any question is stupid. For them, it is not about appearances, cost, or ego. It is about the wine and only the wine. Your answers to their questions help them to suggest what your palette may like best for the chosen menu items. From a New Mexican brut rosé at the start of the meal to the 2000 Portuguese port, not one suggestion was incorrect. For the wine connoisseur who wants to peruse and decide on their own, the eWinebook lists all 20,000 plus bottles at Aureole. Just point and click. The dinner menu is seasonal and offers flavors that, while new to some, are presented without ostentation. The pleasure of the genuine French onion soup, rustic and full of slow-cooked flavor, is added to by the addition of foie gras, truffles, and Gruyère

The menu and wine list at Aureole can be intimidating, but the tasting menu, complete with wine pairings, removes any apprehension.
Courtesy Aureole

cheese on top. The presentation of the gazpacho on a plate made of ice has a wow factor and other diners eye it enviously. For the entrées, the roasted Colorado lamb was impeccably cooked and sat atop a summer squash polenta and stuffed piquillo pepper. The Hawaiian swordfish was also roasted and the blood orange salsa with it was a match made in heaven. Room or not, dessert is an absolute must. Megan Romano is a pastry chef extraordinaire, and you'll be doing yourself a disfavor by skipping dessert. If your timing is right, her award-winning early summer grape float with pistachio baklava will be on the seasonal menu. Once you're finished, walk off the dessert by requesting a tour of the kitchen. True foodies will have a very quiet dinner. If you keep waxing on poetically about the food, there will be less time eating.

The Café at Harrah's
800-214-9110
www.harrahslasvegas.com
Harrah's Las Vegas
Open 24 hours
Price: Moderate

A staple of Las Vegas dining culture, the ubiquitous hotel coffee shop has undergone some welcome changes of late. The moniker, for one, has gone from the homey "coffee shop" to the more cosmopolitan "café," and the décor has morphed from the chrome and vinyl of bygone days to the chic and modern. The Café at Harrah's, with its European-flavored décor and soft lighting, is a coffee shop only in the fact that it is open all the time and serves good food at reasonable prices. Breakfast choices include an array of omelets and egg dishes, as well as fresh fruit or French toast and waffles; for lunch you may enjoy a Mile High Deli Sandwich stacked Dagwood-style, or their tasty Silver State chili with chive sour cream and diced sweet onions

served in a sourdough bread bowl. On a lighter note, The Café offers grilled chicken Cobb salad, or as an appetizer, Thai spring rolls with sweet chili sauce. Dinner entrées include crispy-skin salmon with asparagus and grape tomatoes, a surf-and-turf selection of Canadian lobster tail and a beef filet, and pan-seared bluenose bass.

Café Bellagio
702-693-7111
www.bellagio.com
Bellagio
Open 24 hours
No reservations
Price: Moderate

Located next to the Conservatory inside the Bellagio, Café Bellagio is open 24 hours a day and offers casual dining in an upscale environment—it's the always luxe Bellagio's version of the Vegas hotel coffee shop, even offering outdoor dining with great views of its beautiful pool and grounds. Generous portions are the order of the day, and their gelato is said to be some of the best outside Italy itself, but know going in that the menu prices are higher than the usual coffee shop: you can spend anywhere from $7.50 to $18.00 for a breakfast item alone. Breakfast, lunch, and dinner are served all day, and don't forget dessert—their tiramisu is only $8.50, large enough to share, and absolutely to die for. Breakfast dishes include the Bellagio omelet (lobster, asparagus, tomatoes, and cheddar), eggs benedict, and huevos rancheros. For lunch, try the tandoori chicken wraps or the French onion soup, and dinner selections include chicken piccata and filet mignon. Reservations aren't usually necessary, but be aware that Café Bellagio can fill up quickly when shows and events within the hotel let out.

Carnegie Delicatessen

702-791-7223
www.mirage.com
The Mirage
Daily 7 AM–2 AM
Price: Moderate

There's no fanfare here. There's no aged beef, modern décor, or Tolstoy-book-sized wine lists. There is, however, potato pancakes, matzoh ball soup, and sandwiches so high they should come with rappelling equipment. Splitting a sandwich makes complete sense even if the $3 charge to do so doesn't, especially tacked on to one already costing $16 to $20. This is also a great spot for breakfast. Without walls, the restaurant can get pretty loud, but in the morning the sports book and slot machines are peacefully quiet. While this location doesn't have the history or ambience of the original, it is one of only four in the nation. The line to sit down can be long, but takeout is available.

Chin Chin

702-740-6300
www.chinchin.com
New York–New York Hotel & Casino
Daily 8 AM–11 PM
Price: Inexpensive

Chin Chin is the right kind of place when blue jeans are the uniform for the day. Not a traditional Chinese restaurant, Chin Chin is styled like a neighborhood café with hints of Los Angeles sassiness. It just never took off like other L.A. popular eateries. In the early '90s, their Chinese chicken salad was talked about on television's evening dramas and daytime talk shows. Like wood-fired pizza and focaccia, the dish is now passé, but Chin Chin may have been the originator. Their trick was a dressing made with a specific kind of pickled ginger. To avoid oily lettuce, order the dressing light with extra on the side. Easily accessible and versatile Chinese food means that the dim sum is ordered off a menu and not a rolling steam cart. It can take some of the fun away, but it's also reassuring. The Szechuan dumplings come with a garlic cilantro sauce that can be addictive. The same sauce is also on Anthony's Special Noodles. The pot stickers are mediocre, as is the shui mai. For the roasted meats, the Hunan chicken and sliced barbecue pork are moist. Staples like orange chicken, minced chicken in lettuce cups, and beef chow fun are dependable here. All in all, it's an inexpensive, casual, quick meal for lunch or dinner.

Charlie Palmer's Steak

702-632-5123
www.charliepalmer.com
The Four Seasons Hotel (at Mandalay Bay)
Daily 5–10:30 PM
Price: Very expensive

Nestled inside the Four Seasons Hotel is a cavernous, carnivorous cocoon. Charlie Palmer's Steak is what steakhouses used to aspire to. Quality meats aged 28 days, cooked flawlessly, then served succinctly by an attentive, unimposing staff in a quiet, cozy dining room decorated with wood grains and leather. There are surprises, though. The young staff is energetic and their eagerness to do things correctly is clear. Like the staff and décor, the menu is classic without being dowdy. From the appetizers, the buffalo milk ricotta tortellini has much more flavor than similar dishes served elsewhere. The hazelnut pesto and firm texture help to set it apart. Two things are needed for a great steak: above-par beef and a perfect temperature. Both are found at Charlie Palmer's Steak. For sides, the brussels sprouts with pancetta has the ability to convert anyone to vegetable lover. The truffle baked potato, while not displeasing, didn't match up to expectations. A classic steak dinner should end with a classic dessert, like the cinnamon apple

Dining at Company American Bistro can include entrance to the hot club LAX. Courtesy MGM

cartouflis with paper-thin apple chips served on a dense brown cake. If there's no room, take one to go for the next morning's coffee. The subdued and quiet bar provides a relaxing spot for a before- or after-dinner drink. The entrance to the Four Seasons Hotel and Charlie Palmer's Steak are south of the Mandalay Bay entrance. Using the valet at Mandalay Bay will leave you with quite a hike.

Company American Bistro

702-262-4702
www.luxor.com/dining
Luxor
Mon.–Thurs. 5–10:30 PM; Fri. and Sat. 5–11:30 PM
Price: Inexpensive to Moderate

Agreeing on what type of food to eat can be difficult. Not everyone wants steak or Mexican or sandwiches. Maybe someone is starving and the other would like a light snack. And what's really needed is something before heading out to the club scene. Company American Bistro is a rare commodity. This is a restaurant with a menu that offers an eclectic variety. The plates are designed to be shared, and, at these prices, ordering multiple dishes is worry free. The menu is divided into five sections—Brew Buddies, In the Raw, A Little Bit, Goes a Long Way, A Little Bit More. Each contains dishes derived from the title. For instance, crispy house-made ranch chips—served in a miniature frying baskets—can be found under Brew Buddies, while the Salisbury steak meatballs are under A Little Bit. A daily special can be found under In the Raw but the chilled sliced yellowtail is a nice-sized portion and very fresh. Also enjoyable is the miso-glazed eggplant, which has been flash fried. The wine selection is plentiful with an unobtrusive display, but what shines here are the beer choices. The beer choices are varied and unusual on

The Strip. A rich dark beer from San Miguel pairs ideally with a nicely cooked salmon. The fish was nice, but the beer made it better. The Asahi Black would work well with the yellowtail sashimi. Beer for dessert? There's Young's Double Chocolate or a Belgian raspberry beer to end the meal. The end of the meal can be significant at American Company Bistro. Dinner guests are eligible for a VIP entry into LAX nightclub next door, making for a smooth transition from dining to dancing.

Cypress Street Marketplace

Caesars Palace
Daily 11 AM—11 PM
Price: Inexpensive

Most, if not all, Las Vegas resorts have a food court or something close. Some have better selection than others. Some have nationally recognized chains like Nathan's Hot Dogs and others cater to the cultural makeup of their clientele. The Cypress Street Marketplace at Caesars Palace is hands down the best food court on the boulevard. Free of any national chains, this comfortable and casual spot features food that tastes genuine. Caesars refers to the area as the Napa-style picnic in the park and has included cypress trees as an indoor sunshade and more importantly, a dining value with variety. Choose from tossed-to-order salads, hand-carved rotisserie sandwiches, Chinese food, barbecue, wraps, and pizza.

Dos Caminos

702-577-9600
www.brguestrestaurants.com
The Palazzo
Daily 11 AM—11 PM
Price: Moderate

Mexican food means many things to many people. It should always mean distinct flavors, a variety of ingredients, and some spice. Dos Caminos is the fourth of its kind. The other three are located in New York City. At first glance, the décor may lead one to believe that this Mexican food will not meet the aforementioned criteria. The chocolate browns, chrome, and modern light fixtures are misleading. A longer look reveals that the light fixtures are designed to resemble the magical glow of luminaria, the "wallpaper" print is taken from old Mexican film posters, and the bumpy and completely white wall is an art piece signifying Dias de los Meurtos. The restaurant is hip, attractive, and comfortable. The menu offers many recognizable dishes, as well as those lesser known by some. If the heat outside is in full force, start with one of the wine and Spanish brandy sangrias. The red version uses peach, mango, and orange, while the white has yellow watermelon, grapefruit, and golden raspberries. Along with being refreshing, they're also not so sickly sweet as some make them. With the customary tortilla chips come the three best salsas on

Like the rest of the Dos Caminos menu, the spicy Cajita Sundae is about Mexican comfort food with a twist. Crystal Wood

the Strip. The roasted plantain empanadas are a subtly sweet appetizer filled with black beans and fresh Requesón. The chipotle-braised beef brisket taquitos are crisp and somehow not too oily. Luckily, these come with the house-made pinto beans, since not all entrées do. They're worth asking for. For something more filling, the turkey picadillo burrito has a smoky sweet taste. Although picadillo traditionally uses beef, the turkey gives it a cleaner taste. For dessert, the cajeta sundae puts in one glass salty, sweet, and spicy. Along with vanilla and roasted banana ice creams are chocolate sauce, spicy cascabel peanuts, and two types of syrup called cajeta. It's a combination that more desserts should aspire to. The lounge has a late-night menu and is more relaxing than the many clubs on the Strip. It's common to pick up your drink and move to the lounge instead of traipsing all over the Strip. Odd as it may seem, be sure to check out the décor in the restrooms—very kitschy cool, like a velvet painting of a Mayan ritual.

Earl of Sandwich

702-463-0259
www.earlofsandwichusa.com
Planet Hollywood
Price: Inexpensive
Sun.–Thurs. 6 AM to midnight; Fri.–Sat. 6 AM to 2 AM

Whether it's due to dinner reservations that night and just a nosh will do or needing some power carbs after or before imbibing of alcohol to the full extent, Earl of Sandwich is the perfect place. The sandwiches are made on terrific bread and with choice ingredients. The tuna melt has ardent fans, as does the Original 1762 with its moist roasted-in-house beef and horseradish sauce. Though it's mostly sandwiches here, there's a nice selection of salads, and a creamy tomato soup shares the menu as well. Breakfast sandwiches are surprisingly disappointing.

Florida Café

702-385-3013
www.floridacafecuban.com
1401 Las Vegas Boulevard South
Daily 7 AM–10 PM
Price: Inexpensive

According to the Cuban American and Floridian population of Las Vegas, this is authentic. Tucked away in an inconspicuous Howard Johnson lobby is the Florida Café. It isn't visited by Hollywood's elite and no one in the kitchen has had a television show or published a cookbook. This is just purely good food. Go hungry and with no plans for dancing that night. Arroz con Pollo is an enormous comfort food dish with yellow rice, peas, carrots, plantains, and a lot of chicken. The Cuban sandwich and Florida sandwich a la locura use Cuban-style bread, which is slightly different than Miami style. The Bistec de Palomilla is a pounded thin steak cooked with mojo, a marinade made of onions, garlic, and lime. Often it can be overcooked, but here it is juicy and tender. A decidedly tasty side dish is the tostones—plantains that are fried, flattened, fried again, and salted.

Gallagher's

702-740-6450
www.nynyhotelcasino.com
New York–New York Casino
Sun.–Thurs. 4–11 PM; Fri. and Sat. 4 PM–12 AM
Price: Expensive

At the New York–New York Hotel and Casino, they tried to re-create a Disney-fied version of NYC. For some it's too cute in a good way and for others it's a bad way. The theme helped to bring a Gallagher's out to the west coast. The original has been a beacon of beef in Manhattan's theater district since 1927. Gallagher's serves choice beef house sirloin aged 21 days. The evidence of the aging process is on display for all to see in the windowed case near the entrance. Think of it as a peep show for meat lovers. The prime rib, porterhouse, and rib eye are generous portions and definitely pleasing to carnivores. The surprisingly delicious items are the seafood dishes. Lobster and king crab legs can be risky at many steakhouses but not at Gallagher's. If the bone-in king cut of prime rib is ordered for the main entrée, consider the hot or chilled seafood appetizer platters. Even the shrimp cocktail and New England–style clam chowder are something special. The side dishes are ordered separately and some, like the four-cheese macaroni, Yukon gold mashed potatoes, and seasonal mushrooms, are more worthy than others. For dessert, go for the classics—sticky English toffee pudding or one of the daily crème brûlée flavors. The tables here are close together and, with a lot of hard wood surfaces, the din of the crowd can be deafening. This is no place to enjoy a steak in peaceful surroundings.

Grand Lux Café

702-414-3888
www.grandluxcafe.com
The Venetian
Open 24 hours
No reservations
Price: Moderate

A sister restaurant of the ever-popular Cheesecake Factory, the Grand Lux Café offers a similar experience as its predecessor. Thankfully the menu isn't a novel, though it offers chicken pot pie, shrimp jambalaya, and other Cheesecake Factory familiars. The atmosphere is slightly more upscale, but the murals, colors, and overall design look like you-know-where. Sandwiches, burgers, and salads here are always fresh and well made. The pasta dishes tend to be nothing too original, but are a safe bet. For dessert, a few cheesecakes can be found, but overall it's pies, cakes, and very tasty roasted pineapple upside-down cake with macadamias. Be sure to order it early, as it takes 30 minutes to prepare. The Grand Lux Café is a good spot for lunch and for a bite before a show but not for a quiet or romantic meal.

Kahunaville Island Restaurant and Party Bar

702-894-7111
www.kahunaville.com
TI (Treasure Island)
Mon.–Thurs. 11 AM–10 PM; Fri.–Sun. 11 AM–11 PM
Price: Inexpensive

Located next to the Mystère showroom, Kahunaville is both a lively party bar and a Polynesian-themed restaurant, which combine in a very Vegas way. Team Kahuna, Kahunaville's world-class flair bartenders, showcase their talent nightly in a display of shaker-spinning, bottle-juggling prowess. Multiple screens are sure to be showing sports of all kinds, and of course, the fun lasts until very, very late. If the bar scene isn't your thing, but creatively presented food is, then head past the party crowd down into Kahunaville's Oasis Dining Room, and sample their extensive bill of fare. Breakfast offerings are fairly standard, like the Fruit Platter, a variety of seasonal and exotic fruits served with a strawberry yogurt dipping sauce, and the Kahuna omelet, which comes stuffed with chorizo sausage, mozzarella and provolone cheese, and onions and peppers. For lunch, try the Makai Crab Cake Sandwich, a seared jumbo crab cake served with lemon caper aioli on a soft Kahuna bun, or the Ahi tuna salad, tossed with their house Caesar dressing. Dinner entrées include Hawaiian pork tournedos, which are pan-seared pork filets nestled in bacon and served with a coconut curry sauce, and miso salmon, served with fresh veggies and jasmine rice. And even though you're not in the bar, there's still live entertainment—a large waterfall takes up one whole side of the dining room, and every hour it puts on a different water show, complete with lights and dancing water fountains.

Mix

702-632-9500
www.chinagrillmgt.com
THEhotel at Mandalay Bay
Daily 6–10:30 PM
Price: Very expensive

On the 43rd floor, 400 feet up, Mix commands stellar views of Las Vegas and The Strip. The city tends to look more and more like a *Blade Runner* cityscape, and from this perch it's unmistakable. The view is shared by every table in the house, not just those guests with the right title, job, or pedigree. If the weather is cooperating, ask for a seat on the balcony when making a reservation. Should the twinkling neon get wearisome, look up to the 24-foot chandelier made of 1,500 hand-blown Murano glass spheres and daydream. Alain Ducasse is a chef of many accolades, including Michelin stars at multiple restaurants. However like any other celebrity chef, he's not here every day. When a world-famous chef has places to be, he can't be everywhere at once. The menu is changed whenever the season or item freshness or availability dictates. The snap in the refreshing crunchy lobster salad is due to the fresh, sweet cucumbers. On the seafood menu, the New Zealand John Dory with aromatic herb butter and baby bok choy is not an everyday fish, and it's not on the menu every day. But it is worth the splurge. If ordering the bison tenderloin au poivre, the diner must not only like pepper, but love it. Even pepper fans may think this is too much, especially on such a lovely cut of meat. Lovers of baba au rhum will not be disappointed by Mix's. Ducasse is famous for his rendition, which is a small cake served with a pot of rum and another of crème. The server constructs it according to your specifications. The meal is capped off with warm madeleine cookies with warm Nutella, another Ducasse signature dessert. No matter how stuffed you are, these are an absolute must-try. Anyone who fears heights should be prepared for the glass elevator ride up to the restaurant. Once again, modern décor and an open kitchen do not lend themselves to tranquil dinners. All those hard surfaces can make for a very noisy evening. The patio is much quieter. Diners of the restaurant will not have to pay the $25 cover charge to enter the lounge side, but that patio is for bottle service only.

Pampas Brazilian Grille

702-737-4748
www.pampasusa.com
Miracle Mile Shops
Daily 11 AM–10 PM
Price: Moderate

Pampas Brazilian Grille, which recently opened its Las Vegas restaurant inside the Miracle Mile Shops at Planet Hollywood, is a "churrascaria," a Brazilian steakhouse that specializes in rotisserie-grilled meats and seafood served rodizio-style: servers bring a variety of grilled meats to your table, still on the spit, and you may partake of as much as you like of each. When you're seated, your server leaves a marker at your table with which you signal when you're ready to be served the next meat course. Green means "Next course, please!" and red means "Still enjoying the last course," and when you're ready for your next course, you just turn your marker to green.

Churrascaro or rodizio-style dining is coming into its own in the United States, and Pampas Brazilian Grille is an excellent place to acquaint yourself with it. As if the many succulent cuts of meat brought straight from the grill to your table weren't

The Peppermill Restaurant has been a Las Vegas mainstay for decades Leah Koepp

enough, there is another benefit of dining rodizio-style—you can set the pace of your own meal, and rodizio is, by definition, all you can eat. If you are brought a course you don't like, then you don't order it again; once you've tried everything, you can order more of what you like. Pampas' menu features three different types of rodizio: Ultimate Meat, Ultimate Seafood, and Ultimate Surf & Turf, a blend of the two. The real star here is the Ultimate Meat, which includes grilled seasoned chicken thigh, lamb grilled to perfection, and bacon-wrapped filet mignon, to name but a few.

If rodizio isn't your thing, their menu includes such traditional favorites as rib eye and New York steaks, or if you're in the mood for something a bit more exotic, they serve a wonderful Brazilian bouillabaisse served over linguine.

In addition to the wide variety of meats and seafood they serve, Pampas also has an extensive salad bar that features forty different items, all of them made fresh each day, and unlike many churrascaria, they also offer a few kid-friendly dishes, making it a great place to take the family.

Payard Pâtisserie & Bistro

877-346-4642
www.payard.com/lasvegas.php
Caesars Palace
Daily 6:30 AM–3 PM
Price: Moderate

Tucked away near the front door of Payard Pâtisserie is the attached bistro. Petite and sweetly elegant, it looks as if Audrey Hepburn should have dined here. The round chandeliers, white leather booths, and gold walls could be a set in a lavish film from yesteryear. For breakfast, try the vanilla waffle with fresh berries. The vanilla adds more taste than expected and, yes, that is fresh, high-quality, whipped cream. Payard is a third-generation French pastry chef, so any item, breakfast or lunch, that includes a baked good is sure to please. The eggs Florentine are flawlessly made, but the buttery croissant makes the dish superb. The continental breakfast buffet takes something so simple and perfects it. The juice, coffee, fruit, made-in-house smoked salmon, and, of course, the pastries are all so ideal and you can eat as many as you like. The service is proper yet friendly. This is appreciated because the entrées, sweets, and décor can give a giddy feeling, like being in Paris again.

Peppermill Inn

702-735-4177
www.peppermilllasvegas.com
2985 Las Vegas Boulevard
Open 24 hours
Price: Moderate

Ah, the Peppermill Inn. This star of television and film (*CSI: Las Vegas, Casino, Showgirls*) is one of the few places that the cool old Vegas still exists. The foliage is fake and the portions enormous and many residents have fond memories of this goofy place. The food? This is a coffee shop, after all, so the menu has all the standard fare—breakfast 24 hours a day, burgers, sandwiches, salads—plus a few "exotic" dishes that are best left alone. Will this be the best meal you have in Las Vegas? Doubtful, but it will be the most colorful. The cherry blossom trees, fairy-light-lit booths and plethora of mirrored surfaces can't be beat for kitschy fun. And, it may be the biggest portions seen, too. The pancakes could be used to flag down passing ships. A simple Cobb salad is the size of a basketball. Either consider sharing or taking leftovers back to the room. Before you leave, take a quick peek into the Fireside Lounge. If there's time and alcohol is needed, order a scorpion. And again, best to share. Once you've ordered, get the camera ready because the drink, replete with gobs of fruit and elongated straws, is a scenic photo opportunity.

SushiSamba

702-607-0700
www.sushisamba.com
The Venetian
Daily 11:30 AM to 4 PM; Sun.–Wed. 5 PM to 1 AM; Thurs.–Sat. 5 PM to 2 AM
Price: Expensive

Outside of Japan, Brazil has the largest Japanese population worldwide. The immigration started just over a century ago as a result of labor needed for coffee farming.

Get courageous with Japanese/Brazilian fusion at SushiSamba. Courtesy SushiSamba

Tacos & Tequila works as an inexpensive meal or snack, before or after a show. Courtesy T&T

This would explain how SushiSamba gets away with serving ceviche and sushi, surrounded by São Paulo graffiti pop art and traditional Japanese images, while Brazilian beats play loudly. This isn't just hip fusion food, it's how new styles of food are created. While the style of food has substance, the restaurant is hip, cheeky, and a place to be seen. However, none of this makes the atmosphere unfriendly or unwelcoming. Servers are happy to suggest items and drinks by asking questions on what you do and don't enjoy eating. They'll then construct your order based on your answers and their knowledge of the food. Trusting a chef in a Japanese restaurant is referred to as omakase, or "entrusting," and it means that you are allowing the chef to pick the best items in the kitchen on that day. SushiSamba provides two types of omakase meals, traditional or signature. Whichever is chosen, it's sure to be a dining mystery tour. If ordering from the menu is your preference, there is an assortment to choose from. Truffles possess their own siren song. Served with tempura green beans, the truffle oil creates an appetizer worth crashing the boat into the rocks.

From Small Plates, the tuna tataki (Japanese for pounded) is layered with white asparagus, fresh heart of palm and avocado, then drizzled with citrus oil. The yellowtail seviche taquitos come with a spicy aji panca sauce, which is best suited to those seeking a kick in the taste buds. Continuing with seafood, the rockfish à la plancha is, as the name says, grilled on a metal plate and topped with charred asparagus and grapefruit. The robata grill options are plentiful, including, beef, poultry, and vegetables. The duck breast has a strong smoky flavor and comes with a peppy sancho pepper vinaigrette. Many of the dishes have their own custom sauce, exclusive to SushiSamba. Imagine a California roll, but instead of the expected ingredients it's filled with far superior ones, like king crab and Asian pear. That's the Pacific roll, and it dominates its inane precursor. Along with the Brazilian and Japanese food, SushiSamba is known for libations from both cultures. Their sake list is one of the largest on the West Coast, with more than 120 options, including many not found around Las Vegas and a few not seen elsewhere in North America. There are many mixed cocktails to choose from, but there are three made only at this SushiSamba location. They include the Parisian Geisha, with vodka, sake, mint, and lemongrass; the Figo with spiced wine, fig liquor, pear juice, and lime; and the Bushido, which brings together shochu, plum sake, and daikon beer. There are six other SushiSamba restaurants worldwide.

T&T, Tacos & Tequila

702-262-5225
www.tacosandtequilalv.com
Luxor Hotel and Casino
Daily 11 AM to 11 PM
Price: Inexpensive

This is a very casual laid-back hip restaurant serving modern traditional Mexican cuisine with classic rock playing loudly. It's got a trendy vibe with scantily clad waitresses—attentive and helpful servers and not just a pleasure to behold. With tequila in the name, you can be sure they serve a lot of it. There are more than 70 to choose from, including those fused with pineapple and other flavors.

The mango margarita is sweet and tangy and does its job. The Lifesaver sweet shrimp citrus ceviche was very fresh, but the tacos were most definitely the highlight of our visit. The beef tacos had a smoky bacon in them that made an incredible combination with the red blended salsa served alongside. This may sound a bit odd to enjoyers of the standard taco, but it's the way they should all be served. Open until the wee hours, Tacos & Tequila offers a break from the standard coffee shop before finally heading back to your room. Because the restaurant is located right by the entrance to Carrot Top's show, consider eating here once the show has started. After the show, it could be very busy.

EAST

Egg Works

702-873-3447
www.theeggworks.com
2490 East Sunset Road
Daily 6 AM–3 PM
No Reservations
Price: Inexpensive

Not all breakfasts are created equal. There are those restaurants that make breakfast the most important meal but prefer their lunch crowd. There are those that put their better staff on the dinner shift. And then there's Egg Works. This place cares about breakfast and it shows. These aren't breakfasts made with brandy poached pears or exotic cheeses. They're made with hearty ingredients found in any well-stocked grocery store.

Throughout the menu are items that feature the restaurant's namesake, like Works Veggie Bennie, Works Omelette, Works Skillet, Works Scramble, and the Works Crepe. This last one is stuffed with vegetables, cheese, three meats, and poppy-seed dressing. This gives it an updated syrup-on-sausage taste. On top of great breakfasts, the staff is always efficient and pleasant. If there's a problem, it's fixed. It seems like someone is always cleaning or picking up. And you lose track of how many cups of coffee you drank because the staff is always working to keep your cup full. Astonishingly, some people aren't breakfast people or don't want it for lunch. For them there are salads, soups, Cincinnati chili, plus hot and cold sandwiches. Tucked away in a combination strip mall/industrial complex, the location can be difficult to spot from the street. However, the location is superbly situated to McCarren Airport, the airport car rental garage, and Sunset Park. Don't be intimidated by driving from the Strip. Especially from the south end, it's a pretty straightforward trip with just a few turns.

Hofbrauhaus Las Vegas

702-853-2337
www.hofbrauhauslasvegas.com
4510 Paradise Road, Las Vegas
Mon.–Thurs. 11 AM–11 PM; Fri.–Sat. 11
AM–midnight
Price: Moderate

Remember that trip to Germany where you
learned about the beauty of beer and
sausage? Or perhaps the itinerary of a dream
German vacation would have a visit to the
famous Hofbrauhaus of Munich. Whether
you've been to or dreamed of the original,
this one can help satiate. Built as the only
authentic replica of the original
Hofbrauhaus, the building incorporates a
beer hall, indoor beer garden, towers, tur-
rets, and long family-style tables with open
party-like atmosphere. A quiet dinner may
be very difficult to find here. Adding to the
genuine Bavarian revelry are the bands.
Every four weeks, a new band is flown to
Las Vegas from Germany. The accuracy is
evident from the accordion players to their
lederhosen. Once they start playing, the
toasting, stomping, or pounding on the table
can happen at any moment. If legitimate
Bavarian beer produced with only barley,
hops, and water is sought, this is a must
stop. Along with the original, dunkel (dark),
lager, and hefeweizen, seasonal brews are
also available. All the beers are imported
directly from the breweries in Munich. The
sausages cannot be exported legally, so
they've brought the recipes and hand-
selected four purveyors nationwide to produce them. A fine sausage must be cooked
correctly, so most of the cooks are also
imported. There's schnitzel, sauerbraten,
schweinebraten, imported mustards, and a
giant pretzel that could take on and beat
most others in any culinary contest. This is
true comfort food. The Jagerschnitzel is a
juicy and tender pork cutlet topped with a
creamy mushroom bacon sauce and served
over spätzle, a German noodle. Finish it all
off with a shot of apple schnapps for dessert.

*The lobby at Lawry's The Prime Rib matches the
menu—classic and succulent.* Courtesy Lawry's Restaurants

The ambience is uplifting, the food is satisfying, and the beer gratifying. While technically this restaurant is east of the Strip, it's
only a scant two miles distant.

Lawry's The Prime Rib

702-893-2223
www.lawrysonline.com
4043 Howard Hughes Parkway
Mon.–Fri. 11:30 AM–2 PM; Sun.–Thurs. 5–10
PM; Fri.–Sat. 5–11 PM
Price: Expensive

In the past, Americans could eat prime rib
and feel privileged, not guilty. Thankfully,
eating prime rib at Lawry's brings back that
time. The décor is a mix of a few periods
with art deco lines combined with rich
jewel tones and a multitude of hardwoods.
Not only does the meshing of decades work,
it adds to the feeling of heading back in
time. Your female food server wears the
uniform of the period, right down to the
artfully pinned hat. As pleasant and comforting as the look of the restaurant and

staff is, it can't be eaten. If mothers could make a spinning salad like the food servers at Lawry's do, every kid would wolf theirs gladly. It's a show in itself. The bowl sits on crushed ice, the special dressing is added from way up high, the bowl is spun like a carnival ride. The succulent prime rib is wheeled tableside in a stainless-steel cart designed by one of the original founders. While you watch and your mouth waters, the prime rib is cut to your specific order by a properly trained carving chef. Yorkshire pudding should be just like theirs, firm and perfect for sopping up jus. The creamed corn has been known to change the minds of those who dislike the dish. Do your best to save room for dessert. The banana cream pie has a toasted coconut crust that is delectable. Because the pie travels well, consider taking a piece back to the room. The restaurant does serve lunch, but it is not the same menu, or even really a small variation of it. Called the Ale and Sandwich Bar, there is a carver for prime rib, roast turkey, and other meats, but it's done buffet style, no nifty carts. There are also a couple salads, meal platters, and those famous sides, like creamed corn and creamed spinach. Lawry's is located just one mile east of the Strip, taking East Flamingo.

Lindo Michoacan

702-735-6828
2665 East Desert Inn Road
Daily 11 AM–11 PM
Price: Inexpensive

You can watch the corn tortillas being made by hand. That sentence alone should elicit a journey to Lindo Michoacan. While the art of making tortillas is commonplace in some areas of the country, it's nonexistent in others. This festive, loud, busy, and friendly restaurant is perfect for both the Mexican food novice and expert, which is why it's been voted the best in Las Vegas for numerous years. When the restaurant suffered a debilitating fire, it felt like forever until it reopened. The seafood dishes are the crowning jewel from the Chiles Rellenos de Camarones to the Tostada de Ceviche. The recipes are all made with immense pride. The more traditional Birria de Chivo is made of fresh goat, cooked with chiles and beer (no water) and served with cilantro and raw onions. The service may be so good because they're confident in what is served. The one group that won't be too happy here are strict vegetarians.

Mr. Lucky's 24-7

702-693-5000
www.hardrockhotel.com
Hard Rock Hotel
4455 Paradise Road
Open 24 hours
Price: Inexpensive

The Las Vegas casino coffee shop has changed dramatically over the decades. They used to rely on the repeat business of locals to get through the slow season. Now there is no slow season and many coffee shops need only provide sustenance rather than true food. There are exceptions, though, and Lucky 7 can be one. The food is dependable and worthy. Offerings like French toast, milk shakes, ribs with watermelon barbecue sauce, and chicken noodle soup won't win the originality award, but this is a coffee shop. Since it is open to the casino floor in the Hard Rock Hotel, it can get very loud, especially when an event or concert lets out. The least dependable thing at Lucky 7 is the service. They can be attentive or take little notice of you. It's a crapshoot.

Marssa

702-567-6125
www.marssalv.com
101 Montelago Boulevard, Henderson
Loews Lake Las Vegas Resort
Tues.–Thurs. 6–10 PM; Fri. and Sat. 6–11 PM
Price: Expensive

Considering it's a six-hour drive from the nearest ocean, there is a lot of sushi in Las Vegas these days. But there is only one properly trained master sushi chef in all of those restaurants, and he's at Marssa. Chef Osama "Fuji" Fujita's training in Japan lasted 20 years. For three years, he worked exclusively on rice and cutting vegetables, just waiting for someone to see him as ready for more. Now he creates sushi that is unique, beautiful, and delectable. When the rose made of Hawaiian tuna arrives, it's like ingesting art. Not kitschy like radishes cut into flowers but sculptured fauna that melts as you enjoy it. Sushi connoisseurs will relish the textures brought together in the Osaka style Marssa Box. It is distinguished by not only the layers of tuna, smelt roe, crab and wasabi caviar but also their order, along with the omission of any seaweed. Marssa also has a menu of items that aren't sushi. There is of course a lot of seafood, like spicy lobster, but there are also tempuras, Kobe short ribs, and a few steak entrées. But it would be a waste to be in the restaurant of the only chef in America to earn the All Japan Chefs Association's recognition of achievement in 2007 and not at least try his sushi. Whether sake wine is a new taste or not, the sake selection at Marssa offers opportunities for experiencing it in a myriad of ways. They have both hot and cold sake, of course, but the one recommended for those eating and drinking adventurously through their vacation is crème de sake. Referred to as nigori, this type of sake is only coarsely filtered and the rice solids left behind, giving it a milky appearance. There are 15 other sakes to choose from and a sake flight sampler that includes the nigori and three others. Kampai!

Montesano's Eateria

702-870-3287
www.montesanos.com
9905 South Eastern
Mon.–Sat. 11 AM–9 PM
Price: Inexpensive

Owned by the Montesano brothers, this restaurant definitely has a friendly, family feel. A small Italian eatery, complete with red-and-white checkered plastic cloths on the tables and photos of Frank Sinatra on the wall, Montesano's Eateria delivers on its promise of delicious, casual dining. Wear your comfortable clothes and elastic-waistband pants because Montesano's provides extremely generous portions of all of its entrées and its pizza, too. It's a tough choice between the pasta or the pizza, but both choices are definite winners. Garlic knots, which are served to each table with any regular pasta entrée, are warm and dripping in butter and garlic and are not to be missed. Montessano's also offers other excellent menu options, including stromboli, calzones, hot and cold hero sandwiches, pasta fagiole soup, and stracciatella soup. Leave room for dessert, or at least be

Chef Fujita's sushi is well worth the drive to Lake Las Vegas. Courtesy Loews Resort

prepared to take some sweet treats to go, as a bakery filled with freshly made Italian pastries such as cannoli, tiramisu, zeppla, napoleons, and cheesecake can make any dieter's eyes dazzle. But, if you're truly not in the mood for treats, at least peruse the deli full of meats and cheeses that can be taken with you.

Paymon's Mediterranean Café

702-731-6030
www.paymons.com
4147 South Maryland Parkway
Daily 11 AM—1 AM
Price: Inexpensive

Paymon's (once known as the Mediterranean Café) has always been adept at keeping up with the times. What was once a place for inexpensive lunches in a neighborhood laden with fast food chains has expanded, gussied itself up a bit, and increased its size. While at one time there was an attached Mediterranean grocery, there is now a hip, college student hookah bar. The most important aspect has always remained the same—friendly but not intimidating food. Ethnic comfort food, perhaps? When you've had enough buffets, steaks, lobster, and themed restaurants, Paymon's offers a no-nonsense menu for those who enjoy couscous and feta as part of a regular diet. The staples are all here, including baba ganosh, bourrani, moussaka, an assortment of kabobs, and pita sandwiches. A personal favorite is fesenjan, a chicken dish with a tangy pomegranate and crushed walnut sauce. It's not too sweet and the walnuts give it a hearty texture. The restaurant is located in a small, nondescript strip mall that is an easy short drive from the Strip. It can get busy during special events for UNLV, located about a block away. While the décor isn't posh, they do try to whisk you away from the strip mall with some murals, silk trees, and a gurgling fountain.

Rick's Café

101 Montelago Boulevard
Loews Lake Las Vegas Resort
Daily 6 AM—10 PM
Price: Moderate

Enjoying the day at Lake Las Vegas is easy to do, but settling down for lunch or dinner is best done in Rick's Café inside the posh Loews hotel. The menu, food, and service are of a finer quality than anticipated in hotel casual restaurants. Dining is available outside as well. The roasted eggplant is stuffed with Israeli couscous and tofu. Vegan dishes are rare in Las Vegas dining. This one not only fits the bill but is full of flavor, too. If the heat is making it difficult to eat an entire meal, the dates stuffed with Maytag blue cheese and pancetta are delicious and light. Due to the hotel's Moroccan theme, the menu features appropriate items like a Mediterranean seafood chowder, lamb chops with pomegranate molasses, and two types of tajine. The gracious service, calm surroundings, and eclectic menu are a welcome relief from casino restaurants.

Shuck's Tavern and Oyster Bar

702-255-4890
www.shuckstavern.com
9338 West Flamingo Road
24 hours
Price: Moderate

Some people think it is hard to get fresh, high-quality seafood in the desert, and in many instances that is true, but Shuck's is the exception. It serves three different kinds of crab—snow, Dungeness, and Alaskan King—as well as a variety of oyster, shrimp, ceviche, calamari, and even clambake selections. Seafood fans couldn't ask for more. Also listed on the menu are gumbo, jambalaya, Seafood Louie, crab cakes, po'boys, tuna steak, mahimahi, halibut, swordfish, salmon, catfish, and tilapia, as well as traditional bar food delectables such as nachos, chicken wings, and the like. But who wants to go to Shuck's for a burger? The true beauty of Shuck's is not just that every seafood item is delicious and surprisingly fresh and reasonably priced, but that it is available 24 hours a day at two additional locations around town (2090 E. Serene Ave. and 7155 N. Durango Road), served outside a casino in an extremely casual atmosphere, and does not require the use of fine linens or hifalutin attire. Did we mention that you can play a few slots and drink a cold one down at the bar as you dine? Shuck's is still considered to be a hidden gem even by many of the locals, but it's worth a stop if you're off the Strip and need a great meal.

The Tillerman

702-731-4036
www.tillerman.com
2245 East Flamingo Road
Daily 5 PM–10 PM
Price: Expensive

The Tillerman Restaurant, a Las Vegas favorite for more than 20 years, is an excellent choice for an intimate night out or a gathering of friends. Close enough to be accessible to any Strip hotel, yet far enough away to be a respite from flashing lights and clanging bells, the Tillerman blends unique décor with excellent food and service. Request seating in the center dining room and you won't be disappointed—it's filled with lush foliage and features a large round stained-glass window and a skylight, which floods the dining room with natural light in the spring and summer. The skylight is retractable and is opened when weather permits. Your meal begins with the Tillerman's signature tableside Lazy Susan salad bar, which features an array of homemade dressings along with assorted vegetables and croutons. Don't fill up on salad—the meal portions are more than satisfactory, and there are many wonderful

choices on the bill of fare. Start with the crispy fried crab cake or Classic Oysters Tillerman, and move on to the Atlantic swordfish or the Chilean sea bass, which is always delightful. They do their steaks to perfection as well, offering cuts of aged beef. For dessert, try the chocolate éclair—heaven on earth. The Tillerman also offers an extensive and varied (and pricey) wine list, with many served by the glass.

WEST

Agave

702-214-3500
www.agavelasvegas.com
10820 West Charleston Boulevard
Daily 11 AM–11 PM
Price: Moderate

When it comes to Mexican food, Las Vegas is no different than anywhere else in the country. As the food has become more popular and understood, the variety available has increased as well. Real Mexican food and true tequila are the niches that Agave is looking to fill. It starts inside and outside the restaurant with the décor and art. The lights above the tables are hand made for the restaurant by artisans of Guadalajara. They're truly astonishing and it's hard not to stare at them. On the walls is a collection of Mexican folk art that's worth strolling

Get to know real sipping tequilas at Agave.
Courtesy Agave

The Bagel Cafe in northwest Las Vegas is more than just great bagels .　Leah Koepp

around to look at. Pay close attention to the atypical margarita glassware; it was designed exclusively for Agave. With the rising status of tequila from college parties to a sipping enjoyment that can be compared to whiskey or brandy, Agave is the spot to learn what the drink truly is, how it got here, and what to look for. The warm and informative staff will walk you through Aficionado Flights, a sampler of three different tequilas from the 89 they carry. You can choose or have your server/bartender assist you. You'll be given a "map" of your choices to keep; after all, once you return home you can't be expected to remember that Canicas Anejo smelled of butterscotch. There are other restaurants that offer similar services in the valley, but this one is better priced and more educational. So the art is real, so is the tequila, but what about the food? Let's just say that the turkey mole enchiladas actually taste like mole, as opposed to just "brown." And the braised birria-style short ribs not only fall off the bone but also are chockful of flavor. The portabella mushroom tamal may prompt meat lovers to try a vegetarian meal or at least a meatless appetizer.

The Bagel Café

702-255-3444
www.thebagelcafelv.com
301 North Buffalo Drive
Mon. 6:30 AM–5 PM; Tues.–Fri. 6:30 AM–8 PM; Sat. and Sun. 7 AM–5 PM
Price: Inexpensive

The key to The Bagel Café's success is its use of fresh ingredients. All bagels, more than twenty varieties, are prepared daily the traditional way—boiled and then baked and made completely by scratch on-site. The bagel and lox is deliciously salty—classic and highly recommended. Top your bagels with your choice of ten whipped and airy cream cheeses ranging from traditional plain to cinnamon raisin walnut for the sweet tooth, or spread them with your choice of meats. Meats such as brisket, salami, pastrami, bologna, lox, sable, sturgeon, kishka, and countless others are available either in an overstuffed sandwich noted on the menu or by the pound to take with you. But the bagel café has more to offer than bagels and meat. All the soups, including the delightful chicken noodle, and salads are homemade. Even the large-portioned cakes, pies, cookies, pastries, and even sliced breads, more than 100 for you to select from, are also freshly made on the premises. Peruse these hard-to-resist beauties in the glass cases up front and plan on taking some with you. The bustling atmosphere of the Bagel Café is a perfect setting for lively lunchtime conversation with your friends or a grab-and-go visit to their bakery for a loaf of sweet challah bread and a latte.

The student and professor chefs at Cafe Bleu cook up a Las Vegas steak-dining bargain.
Courtesy of Café Bleu

Café Bleu

702-851-5322
www.vegasculinary.com
1451 Center Crossing Road
Tues.–Fri. 11 AM–12:30 PM and 6–7:30 PM
Price: Moderate

No matter how famous they are now, all the celebrity chefs had to start out somewhere. Some were taught by a treasured family member, but many just delighted in cooking and went to school to learn more. Le Cordon Bleu is one of those schools. The Las Vegas location has a 10,000-square-foot restaurant on campus, and it's one of the best dining bargains in town. While technically it's a classroom, it is also a stylishly decorated restaurant with modern lines and minimalist décor. The students working in this on-campus café are in their final weeks of school before heading out to their externship. They work the front and back of the house under the watchful eyes of their instructors. All gra-

tuities are added to the school's scholarship fund. The menu and hours are diminutive due to the restaurant's being staffed by students, but the food is considered one of the best budget deals in town. For the students, this is their final exam, so they are playing close attention to your meal from start to finish. The wine list is more extensive than one would expect at a school and is reasonably priced. The red wines are almost entirely from California. The white wine list is scarcely a dozen long but has wines from other locales as well. Dessert and sparkling wines are also available. Be sure to ask about the school's own merlot, Red Wine & Bleu. The students and instructors were responsible for the wine from the choosing of the grapes to the aging. Even the label was the winning design of a student. Because the school cannot sell this wine, samples are given to interested diners. Available menu items change frequently. On one visit, a crab salad with lump crab and a generous dollop of crème fraîche started the meal. The salmon dinner was moist and the New York strip steak was accompanied by a tangy red-wine reduction. The dessert menu is seasonal and featured a pumpkin cheesecake that was not too sweet. Before you finish dinner, ask your server to request a tour of the classroom kitchen before dessert.

Capo's Italian Steakhouse

702-364-2276
www.caposrestaurant.com
5675 West Sahara Ave.
Sun.–Thurs. 5–11 PM; Fri.–Sat. 5 PM–1 AM
Price: Moderate to Expensive

There's no password needed to enter through the "secret" door into the sleek under world of this speakeasy themed Italian restaurant. Once inside the joint, overstuffed red high back chairs and circular booths, chandeliers, and baby grand piano complete with crooner give a feeling of the deceptive debauchery of the old days. The menu is ruled by dishes classic to Italian food in America and most are named using mob slang and vernacular. The Bust a Cap appetizer is mushrooms stuffed with Italian ham, olives, roasted red peppers, and topped with cheese. They're traditional and flavorful, as is the veal Goodfellas piccatta and multiple pasta dishes. For dessert, skip the usual and order a tiramisu martini or one of the other strong and sweet specialty martinis. Each night a singer croons the songs of Sinatra, Dean Martin, and other artists. When you happen upon a portrait of Al Capone, ask to see the Roulette Room hidden behind the boss's picture. For a more masculine evening, there's the Card Room, which looks like what it sounds like. This is a great spot for bachelor parties or gambling enthusiasts. Once plentiful in Las Vegas, cigar rooms are becoming harder and harder to come by. At Capo's the area is a dimly lit enclosed patio with comfy leather couches.

Finding the front door can be tricky at the speakeasy-themed Capos. Courtesy Capos

Hash House A-Go-Go

702-804-4646

www.hashhouseagogo.com

6800 West Sahara Ave

Daily 7:30 AM–2:30 PM; Mon.–Thurs. 5–9 PM; Fri. and Sat. 5–10 PM

Price: Moderate

The restaurant founders call this "twisted farm food" and once the entrée is on the table, their reasoning is clear. The dishes are made with fresh ingredients, the menus are based on good ol' fashioned meals, and the portions are sized for those home from plowing the fields. The "twist" comes from fried leeks atop the fried chicken and bacon waffle, or a pork tenderloin benedict with yellow tomatoes. Then there's also the tuna melt made with Ahi. Breakfast fans can give thanks for the seven choices of hashes, including meatloaf. Sandwich connoisseurs should try the crispy pork tenderloin or apple-smoked bacon and mashed-potato-stuffed burger. Gems on the dinner menu include chili-crusted maple duck breasts and a stuffed meatloaf. Nothing like Mom ever made, this twisted dish has spinach, roasted red peppers, mozzarella, and cream sauce. What's surprising here is that having giant plates of food is not the first aim of the restaurant. First come ingredients and flavor. Second is the efficient and friendly service. Third are the portions. Fourth should be where to take a nap to sleep off a food coma.

Jamms

702-877-0749

www.jammsrestaurant.com

1029 South Rainbow Boulevard

Daily 7 AM–3 PM

Price: Inexpensive

Breakfast is the most important meal of the day at Jamm's, and it comes with bread in a little flowerpot, too. Yep, that's right, the home-baked popover served in a small planting pot comes with all egg dishes. It's warm, tasty and just like the restaurant, rather charming. At breakfast and lunch, generous portions are served while they're hot by an efficient and friendly server who never skimps on the coffee refills. There are 20 omelets to choose from, including the White Castle, Tigerlily, and Reuben. The latter has sauerkraut, corned beef, and Swiss cheese. For those interested in other breakfast fare, there's a half-dozen benedicts, two skillets, all the basic egg and meat combos, excellent breakfast sandwiches, and potato pancake smothered in ham, bell peppers, green onions, and cheddar cheese (aptly named the Denver potato pancake). For lunch, there are more sandwich choices and they can be served with sweet potato fries. The décor is down home, just like the food and service.

J.C. Wooloughan's Irish Pub

702-869-7725

www.jwlasvegasresort.com

JW Marriott Las Vegas Resort & Spa, 221 North Rampart Boulevard

Sun.–Thurs. 11 AM–1 AM; Fri.–Sat. 11 AM–2 AM

Price: Inexpensive to Moderate

Céad Míle Fáilte, or one hundred thousand welcomes, to you! This is one of the best and most authentic Irish taverns in Las Vegas. J. C. Wooloughan, a born-and-bred Irishman, felt a little homesick for his native land and re-created a little bit of Ireland in the desert. Designed outside Dublin, the pub's wooden interior was pieced together and shipped to the United States, where it was reassembled by the same Irish craftsmen. Inside are open areas for dancing and socializing, bar areas for intimate chats, and crannies for cozy conversation and dining. Have a pint or two of Guinness, Harp, or a shot of your favorite whiskey to go with your bangers and mash, shepherd's pie, Irish sausage rolls, fish and chips, or corned beef and cabbage. The toughest choice you'll have to make in this fun and lively pub is to choose between the sticky toffee pudding or chocolate whiskey cake as your dessert. Our recommendation? Have both! Live music is featured each evening from Wednesdays through Saturdays and patrons are encouraged to chime in or even dance along.

LBS: A Burger Joint

702-835-9393
www.lbsburger.com
Red Rock Casino Resort
Daily 11:30 AM–11 PM
No reservations
Price: Inexpensive

You can get a burger anywhere, but at LBS: A Burger Joint, inside the Red Rock Hotel and Casino, you get a burger experience. They serve only the best dry-aged, organic beef that is ground fresh daily as well as all-natural veggie patties made with more than 22 vegetables and grains. The buzzword at LBS is "fresh"—every beef, turkey, and veggie burger is hand made from fresh (never frozen) ingredients in-house every day. In addition, the menu features homemade

The formula for the Perfect Burger at LBS. Crystal Wood

ketchup and pickles, and the French fries are hand cut. Even the sauces that top these fantastic burgers are made by hand daily in the LBS kitchen. Start with an order of the potato twisters, delicate curlicues of fried potato cut with a special machine and garnished with their one-of-a-kind fry sauce, or the unique and tasty fried bread-and-butter pickles with herb mayonnaise. Ever wonder what the Perfect Burger is? LBS has it, and it comes grilled to order and topped with oven-roasted tomato, Gruyère cheese, and their own red onion marmalade on a sweet egg bun. Come ready to eat, because the décor isn't the only thing Texas-style in this joint. The portions are extremely generous, and the burgers will more than satisfy the heartiest appetite. While you enjoy your meal, check out some of the unique design elements in their intimate urban-loft-meets-steakhouse dining room, like the red neon steer skull and the American flag collage made from 3,000 license plates hanging above the grand, saloon-style bar. Unlike some restaurants in Las Vegas, this is a very family-friendly place.

Mary's Hash House

702-873-9479
www.hashhouse.net
2605 South Decatur #105
Daily 6 AM–2 PM
Price: Inexpensive

There's something about owner Mary's mismatched coffee mugs. They're not just different colors or sizes—some have hot rods, others kittens. Take a look around and you may spot a variety of Christmas mugs. This is part of the charm of Hash House. While most restaurants in town have decorators and themes, this one has clocks with varnished pictures of galloping horses. Along with all this charm, they also make six homemade different breakfast hashes to order, including corned beef, ham, roast beef, and chicken. There's the

Super Hash, which is a mixture of these, and Party Hash with added jalapeños and mushrooms. For lunch, soups are made each day and the triple-decker melts are scrumptious. Mary describes her food as Midwestern-style breakfast and lunch. The atmosphere is friendly and casual and she knows many of her customers by name.

Metro Pizza

702-362-7896
metropizza.com
4001 South Decatur Boulevard
No reservations
Sun.–Thurs. 11 AM–10 PM; Fri. and Sat. 11 AM–11 PM
Price: Inexpensive

While the décor desperately needs some updating, thankfully the menu has mostly been left alone. Now and again something is added or removed but not the standbys. The decadent Steinbrenner calzone has the required gooey cheese and red sauce, then is filled to the hilt with eggplant parmesan. For thick-crust lovers, most pizza can be ordered "Metro" style. It takes longer to cook due to the hand-tossed girth but is well worth the wait. The Chicago is one of six stuffed pizzas on the menu. It's filled with two layers of cheese and spinach between two layers of crust with the sauce put on top after it's out of the oven. The buffalo wings are crispy and dripping with sauce. Metro's food is accessible and satisfying like all pizzas should be. There are also locations on the east side, near UNLV (702-736-1955) and southeast, in the suburb of Green Valley (702-458-4769).

Nora's Cuisine

702-873-8990
www.norascuisine.com
6020 West Flamingo Road #10
Mon.–Fri. 11 AM–2:30 PM; Mon.–Thurs. 4:30–10 PM, Sat. and Sun. 4:30 PM–1:00 AM
Price: Moderate to Expensive

Run by Nora Mauro and husband Gino and their sons, this local favorite is the place to go for off-the-Strip Italian cuisine. Seating can be hard to come by, but the wait is worthwhile, especially if that means giving yourself time to cozy up to the full bar for a drink, complete with soft candlelight glittering in the backdrop. At the bar, you'll find an extensive cocktail menu and long list of grappa, port, cordial, liqueur, and brandy choices served by Nora's own mixologist, bartender extraordinaire Gaston Martinez. Know that the wine list, itself, is over seven pages long, and you are bound to find something to drink for everyone in your dinner party. Once you arrive at the table, you'll find that the menu contains both unique and traditional fare such as chicken marsala, veal scaloppini, fettuccini alfredo, spaghetti and meatballs, and even pizza. But don't be fooled by the label "traditional." These entrées come with fresh ingredients and rich and robust sauces that cannot be duplicated. The portions are also quite generous, so plan on having leftovers to take with you. Make sure to order the mozzarella caprese appetizer. The staff is fast and friendly, and everyone on duty is likely to be related to one another. The result is a sense of pride and ownership in the food being served and a family affection that can be felt wafting through the air.

Nora's Wine Bar and Osteria

702-940-6672
www.noraswinebar.com
1031 South Rampart Boulevard
Sun.–Thurs. 11 AM–10 PM; Fri. and Sat. 11 AM–11 PM
Price: Moderate to Expensive

The Mauro family, having enjoyed the ongoing success of their first restaurant, Nora's Italian Cuisine, opened Nora's Wine Bar and Osteria in the Summerlin area of Las Vegas in 2006. It too has been extremely popular with the local crowd; it has the same neighborhood bistro vibe as its older cousin, but has an outdoor dining area that is lovely on those warm desert nights. The menu at Nora's Wine Bar and Osteria features Italian and Sicilian favorites with a hip upscale feel—family-style and small plates are the order of the day, as are wine and food pairings. Your server will bring you a selection of three olive oils and three types of salt to sample, along with fresh bread. You may start your meal with a selection of artisanal meats and cheeses, or you may be intrigued by their cicchetti, or "small bites," a kind of Italian amuse-bouche—the Arancini, balls of homemade risotto stuffed with peas, mozzarella, and meat sauce, are a local favorite. Other highlights of the menu include the pappardella alla Luisa, pappardelle pasta in a delightful cream sauce with leeks, sausage, and sun-dried tomatoes, and the pork Siciliana, breaded pork tenderloin served with roasted tomatoes and arugula tossed with lemon vinaigrette. Nora's Wine Bar also features (you guessed it) wines, and a lot of them. Many of Nora's wines can be sampled using the Enomatic system, which dispenses wines in increments of one, three, and six ounces, depending on the guests' preference. In addition to its automated wine system, Nora's pours about 60 wines by the glass and has more than 350 wines on its wine list.

Osaka Japanese Bistro

702-876-4988
www.lasvegas-sushi.com
4205 West Sahara
Mon.–Sat. 5 PM–1 AM; Sun. 5–10 PM
Price: Moderate

Osaka Japanese Bistro opened as Las Vegas's first Japanese restaurant in 1967 with a sushi bar, teppanyaki grill, and private tatami rooms. The menu boasts traditional fish choices, as well as exotics typically found only in Japan, such as awabi

(live abalone), sayori (halfbeak), aoyagi (live surf clams), and kanpachi (rudder-fish) in a range of sushi rolls or sashimi choices. For those of you who opt out of sushi but still want delectable seafood choices, you can choose among South American lobster tail, jumbo sea scallops, Alaskan king salmon steaks, Chilean sea bass steaks, and more. There are also plenty of menu options for land lovers, including selections of hard-to-find Kobe beef, filet mignon, rib eye steaks, chicken, sausage, and pork specialties. Regardless of your entrée selection, you will find a large variety of imported Japanese liquors, rice wines, beers, and flavored sakes to complement any meal. Make sure to leave room for the red bean ice cream at the end. Dinner preparation almost always includes a show from a staff of lively chefs making sushi rolls at the bar or grilled onion volcanoes and shooting flames, complete with spatulas wildly cutting through the air at the teppan grill—either way, you are guaranteed a good laugh, full belly, and a memorable dining experience. Osaka Japanese Bistro has a second location at 10920 S. Eastern Avenue in Henderson (702-616-3788). This location, though farther away from the Strip, does offer lunch service and live entertainment.

Raku

702-367-3511
5030 Spring Mountain Road #2
Mon.–Sat. 6 PM–3 AM
Price: Moderate

Get to Raku soon or you may be too late. It won't have disappeared. On the contrary, everyone will have found it. This is a tiny little restaurant that seats about 35 people, including the counter. Yes, the food is worth sitting at the counter for. The portions are tapas-sized. The prices reflect the quality of ingredients used. Don't be concerned with ordering the entire meal in one go. Ask the server for suggestions and start with a few items. The tofu is made fresh on the premises and may create unrealistic expectations for any other tofu in your dining future. The fried tofu came in a slightly sweet dark broth with diminutive mushrooms that melted more than they were chewed. The pork cheeks skewers are juicy and tender and may prompt an immediate repeat order. The duck is grilled just right, then drizzled with balsamic soy sauce. Corn stuffed with potato is just as it reads, but the corn kernel is gently cut from the cob and yet still remains attached to the other kernels. The corn is then wrapped around a mashed potato; it's uncomplicated yet addictive. For the more adventurous eater, there's pig ear, and—for the really daring diner—cow tongue served sashimi style. The desserts change often, but if the green tea crème brûlée with green tea ice cream is available, give it a try. After a decade of crème brûlée being offered at almost every restaurant, it's refreshing to taste a different version. Raku is located in a far corner of a nondescript older strip mall. It is easy to drive past it. Be sure to check out the restroom for a good laugh.

Roma Deli and Restaurant

702-871-5577
www.romalv.com
5755 Spring Mountain Road
Mon.–Thurs. 10 AM–9 PM; Fri. and Sat. 10 AM–10 PM; Sun. 11 AM–8 PM
Price: Moderate

Roma Deli and Restaurant is an authentic Italian deli and café located in the Spring Valley area of southwest Las Vegas. You'll find all your favorite Italian dishes represented on their lunch menu, such as penne, ravioli, spaghetti, and linguine paired with marinara and meat sauces, along with chicken and eggplant parmigiana. They also offer a full board of tasty hot and cold sandwiches, made fresh to order. For dinner, you may be tempted by the salmon meu-

niere, saltinbocca di pollo, their pork chops Milanese, or one of their house specialties, penne con broccoli aglio e olio, penne pasta tossed with broccoli and virgin olive oil, or rigatoni boscaiola, rigatoni smothered in a tomato wine sauce and served with your choice of Italian sausage or chicken and mushrooms. The wine list is chockful of wonderful wines from Italy, sold by the bottle. Roma Deli offers traditional tableside dinner service, but their lunch service is more casual: you seat yourself, and you order your meal from a posted menu at one of two counters. If ordering hot food and/or salad, you order at the counter in the rear, under the Roma Deli awning, and a server brings your order to your table. If ordering a sandwich or meat or cheese, you order at the deli counter and take your food with you to your table; you can also order their authentic Italian deli meats by the pound to go, or browse their selection of pastas, sauces, and Italian grocery items.

Twin Creeks

702-263-7777
www.silvertoncasino.com
Silverton Casino Lodge
3333 Blue Diamond Road
Tues.–Thurs. 5–9 PM; Fri.–Sat. 5–10 PM
Price: Expensive

When you dine at Twin Creeks, you may be surrounded by locals. This means they serve good food at a price locals will pay. Start the evening with a cocktail first. While this may sound old-fashioned, but Twin Creeks has the number-2-rated cocktail in the nation according to Condé Nast *Traveler* magazine. The New World Cocktail has a blend of rum, two liqueurs, fresh lemon sour, and caramelized orange zest. There are many other specially designed cocktails at Twin Creeks, many with Vegas-themed names. If you prefer to sip your before-dinner drink, the bar at Twin Creeks is known for their menu of boutique bourbons. The décor is subdued and features

Get a bit off the Strip and eat steak with locals at Twin Creeks. Courtesy Silverton Lodge

natural materials, including flagstone-covered walls. The varied seating options include high tabletops and chairs, as well as traditional booths. If this style of chair is uncomfortable for you, make mention of it when making a reservation. To start the meal, consider having the chop chop salad. While it's not enormous, there is enough for two to enjoy it without filling up. Tossed with a creamy white balsamic, the salad is fairly classic, except that the unique bacon pieces make for a nice blend of textures. The filet mignon is not over– or under seasoned and the temperature is spot on. There are more expensive filets in town, but they're not necessarily better. The sides to choose from are standard. The macaroni and cheese was nothing to write home about, although the poached asparagus was very nice. The coffee is served in a French press, which is appreciated and rarer in Las Vegas than it should be. Twin Creeks comes

across as somewhat hip but without the attitude. Though the Silverton Lodge is less than one mile west of the Strip, it is at the southern tip of Las Vegas Boulevard.

Vintner Grill

702-214-5590
www.vglasvegas.com
10100 West Charleston Boulevard Suite 150
Sun.–Thurs. 11 AM–10 PM; Fri. and Sat. 11 AM–11 PM
Price: Expensive

The greatest compliment a Las Vegan can give to a local restaurant is that it blends perfectly the old and the new Vegas. In the Vegas that once was, seeing acquaintances when out for dinner was almost assured and waiters knew their customers by name. Everyone just knew about the place, about the menu, and about who else ate there. The new Vegas brings enlightening meals, celebrity chefs, and professional décor. Vintner Grill has almost all of both versions of Vegas. That's because Chef Matthew Silverman isn't a celebrity, yet. He doesn't seem to have the gregarious personality that most of them do, but his creations have their own personae. A member of the Wisconsin Cheese Board, Silverman has access to cheeses that range from difficult to find to impossible to get. On any night, you may find more than 30 cheeses to choose from. From starters to desserts, from soft to firm, and from Wisconsin to Spain, the cheese menu has the power to demonstrate to a *fromage* novice why Europeans take cheese so seriously. The servers and management are more than delighted to share their knowledge and preferences with you. The difference in taste and texture between a Pleasant Ridge Reserve cheese that was aged one year and one aged for six years is most notable and remarkable. The latter is not available for purchase in any store. It's delicate with a slight lingering spice and has naturally occurring crystals of salt. It turns to cream with little chewing.

The menu at Vintner Grill is seasonal. The roasted parsnip soup with candied pecans was subtle, with fresh grated nutmeg and feta calling for attention. Lobster cannelloni can be found all over town, but it's often flavorless or overly rich. Here the truffled cauliflower cream sauce served on top isn't just for appearances but is perfectly paired for flavor. The lobster is allowed to shine by not being overly shredded. The spicy Moroccan tuna is soft as butter and served appropriately rare. It came with a seriously salted grilled baby asparagus. If each bite of tuna includes the vegetable, they blend like magic as they were designed to. When it comes to desserts, Las Vegas restaurants tend to repeat themselves. Must they all have tiramisu? After eating the dessert over and over elsewhere, Vintner Grill's version is a welcome reprieve.

Finding the Vintner Grill can be a bit tricky. It's located in an office building that conjures memories of medical appointments. But don't be fooled. Once you enter the restaurant, those memories drift away. The décor can be described as Southern modern chic with loads of comfy Marrakech-style pillows. Outside is one of the better dining patios in town. There are a few cabanas if you're seeking a more romantic atmosphere. They can be requested with a reservation but are not guaranteed. One final nod to the coolness of this restaurant: black-and-white films starring Humphrey Bogart play without sound on small screens in the dining room.

NORTH
Bob Taylor's Original Ranch House and Supper Club

702-645-1399
www.bobtaylorsranchhouse.com
6250 Rio Vista Street
Daily 11 AM–10 PM
Price: Expensive

Saddle up and gallop in to the oldie-but-goodie steakhouse that reminds diners that Las Vegas really was part of the Wild West. Once in the outskirts of town, Bob Taylor's Original Ranch House and Supper Club has been a steakhouse staple since its opening in 1955. It has a welcoming view on its tree-lined path and five acres that makes even city slickers reminisce about the old cowboy era. Lined with old-fashioned, authentic cowboy memorabilia on its walls and featuring plain wooden tables and chairs, this place has steaks and smoked prime rib that will make you holler "Yee-haw!" Not intended for the delicate eater, the menu offers hefty portions of filet mignon, porterhouse steak, prime rib, New York steak, top sirloin, rack of lamb, beef brochettes, and even barbecue chicken prepared over mesquite wood and charcoal grill for the meat-and-potatoes lover in you—all at reasonable prices. The adventurous are encouraged to try the sautéed chicken livers appetizer or the Diamond Jim Brady, a 32-ounce New York steak; diners who down the whole piece of meat earn a free dessert.

It's best to reserve the patio cabanas at Vintner Grill well in advance. Courtesy Vintner Grill

Country Café

702-644-4811

3603 North Las Vegas Boulevard

Mon.–Sat. 7 AM–8:30 PM; Sun. 7 AM–3 PM

Price: Inexpensive

For those heading out to Valley of Fire, Las Vegas Motor Speedway, or to Utah, Country Café is a family-owned hole-in-the-wall joint that has served hearty breakfasts and hot coffee with pleasant down-home service for more than 20 years. The décor is kitschy country with replica tin signs and flowered curtains, but it is spick-and-span. The strip mall where it is located may not appeal to everyone, but the owners try to keep their front area neat and welcoming. The specialty of the house is eggs with a rib eye steak in a choice of 6-, 10- and 16-ounce sizes. Lunch is served here, too, with homemade potato chips.

The Inn at Silk Purse Ranch

702-395-9111

8101 Racel St

Thurs.-Sat. 5 PM –10 PM; Sun. 4 PM–9 PM

Price: Expensive

The Inn at Silk Purse Ranch is in the far north end of town and away from the bright lights of the casinos. Once a horse ranch and private home, the restaurant is a conversion of the original house that sits amid grassy lands surrounded by fruit trees covered in twinkle lights. Before you dine, soak up the soft and romantic atmosphere, listen to the trickling water of the pond, and even sneak a kiss from your sweetie under the gazebo. Enjoy the candlelit glow of the intimate dining room and savor the cheese-and-cracker tray and the warm bread brought to every table. Try either the Beef Wellington or the duck in berry sauce—they're both heavenly. Order salad with mandarin oranges and Craisins, with garlic mashed potatoes as your side, and your taste buds will thank you. Wash it all down with a glass of wine from the inn's wine menu. Known as a place where locals go for chic dining, the prices reflect the elegance of the locale. Reservations are recommended, and please be quiet when first entering the grounds, as weddings are sometimes held at the facility.

Mount Charleston Lodge

702-872-5408

www.mtcharlestonlodge.com

1200 Old Park Road

Mon.–Fri. 8 AM to 9 PM; Fri. and Sat. 8 AM–10 PM

Price: Expensive

Just 35 minutes from the Las Vegas Strip and at the end of Highway 157 is the Mount Charleston Lodge. Known as the "old lodge," which should not be confused with the "new lodge" in the lower elevations, the Mount Charleston Lodge, surrounded by 23 cabins rentable for extended stays, is a welcome respite from the hustle and weather extremes of the desert. Often covered in snow in the winter months and soft cooling breezes during the summer months, the lodge is definitely the place to go for atmosphere. While the overall menu is decent, there are some gems hidden within it. Anything served for breakfast is delicious, but the elk burger and the buffalo burgers are the tops. Whether you come for breakfast, lunch, dinner, or even cocktails, sit inside and warm up by the fire or sit outside on the patio deck and relish the fresh pine air. The lodge boasts a lounge with a full bar, a long wine list, and a menu of coffee specialty drinks. If you're a big fan of dessert, save room for the deep-fried cheesecake. Ask the barkeep about horse-drawn sleigh rides through the snow during the winter months.

FOOD PURVEYORS

British Foods, Inc.

702-579-7777
www.britishgrocer.com
375 South Decatur Boulevard, #11
Daily 10 AM–6 PM

Supposing it's true that Cadbury chocolate in England is different from the Cadbury sold here in the States, then there is one for sure reason to visit British Foods. And if that's not enough, their stock is full of snacks, kippers, Devon cream, teas, and jams from throughout the Commonwealth nations. Play close attention to the dates stamped on the items. All told, this itty-bitty storefront carries more than 750 different imported foods. Need haggis for a dare? It's here.

Capriotti's

702-474-0229
www.capriottis.com
324 West Sahara Avenue
Mon.–Thurs. 11 AM–8 PM; Fri. and Sat. 11 AM–9 PM; Sun. 11 AM–6 PM

Hankering for a sandwich? Then the place to go is Capriotti's. It's not fancy or themed or even decorated, but just serves honest-to-goodness sandwiches. At last count, there are more than 25 locations in and around Las Vegas. The address listed above is closest to the Strip, but look around—you never know where one will appear. There's even one inside the Red Rock Casino Resort, which makes it a perfect location for stocking a picnic lunch before heading to Red Rock Canyon. Though they started in Delaware, the home office is now in Las Vegas, too. For those from Las Vegas who leave for other destinations, this is one of those joints that must be visited while back home. For the price, its sandwiches can't be beat. All beef and turkey is roasted on the spot, and there are high-quality cold cuts. Don't be misled by the sizing. The large is a 20-inch sandwich that could easily feed two. Not bad for $10. Which is the best? That's a heated debate, but usually it's between the Bobby with turkey, stuffing, and cranberry sauce and the Slaw B. Joe with roast beef, coleslaw and Russian dressing.

Chocolate Swan

702-632-7777
Mandalay Bay Place
Daily 8 AM–10 PM

A piece of seven-layer carrot cake, a glass of sauvignon blanc, and a view. Perfect as it seems, it gets better when you have a first bite of the carrot cake with cream cheese frosting and fresh roasted Georgia pecans. The éclairs come in three sizes and are made with homemade pâte à choux pastry dough. If giant cakes and pastries seem like too much, try the namesake Chocolate Swan. Purchased individually, it's a picture-perfect raspberry dipped in dark or milk chocolate. A handful of those should do nicely. The wine list is about 40 strong and comes with suggested dessert pairings. The original is located in Elk Grove, Wisconsin, and this is their only other location.

Espressamente illy

702-869-2233
www.illy.com
The Palazzo Shoppes
Sun.–Thurs. 6 AM–midnight; Fri. and Sat. 6 AM–1 AM

There are more than 200 of these coffee shops in 32 countries on five continents, but this is the first one in America. Finally, we are truly a coffee-crazed nation. Along with superior coffee and espresso, you'll find pastries, panini, soup, European truffles and bonbons, made-to-order dessert crepes, and 54 flavors of gelato. Seating here is spacious and decorated in illy's signature red, white, and chrome—not a coffeehouse look at all, but rather a sleek, fresh contemporary café. It's estimated that 6 million cups of illy coffee are made each day. If you'd like to add one more from your kitchen, the accessories for making a illy espresso or cappuccino at home are available for purchase here.

Ethel's Chocolate Lounge

702-796-6662
www.ethelschocolate.com
3200 Las Vegas Boulevard
Mon.–Sat. 10 AM–9 PM; Sun. 11 AM–6 PM

Created in 1981 by Forrest Mars Senior (yes, of that famous candy bar company), Ethel M Chocolates was originally named to honor his mother and use her methods and recipes. The factory was built just 20 minutes from the Strip and Las Vegas's hometown chocolates were born. Recently, chocolate is undergoing a transformation in this country. Because of that, Ethel M became Ethel's Chocolate Lounge and the look got sleeker and more refined. The chocolates are still very good and can come in a box with a lid collaged in photos of recognizable Las Vegas spots. There are eight other locations throughout Las Vegas and Henderson, including the Flamingo Hilton and McCarren Airport. The factory has a self-guided tour and cactus garden.

Freed's Bakery

866-933-5253
www.freedsbakery.com
4780 South Eastern Avenue
Mon.–Thurs. 10 AM–5:30 PM; Fri. and Sat. 9 AM–6:30 PM; Sun. 10 AM–3 PM

Freed's Bakery has been a staple in Las Vegas for nearly 50 years. Every kid in Las Vegas dreamt that their birthday cake would come from the place that made the best rugelach cookies in town. The well-known cakes are also made for superstar celebrations, such as Ozzy Osbourne's 60th birthday and scores of other celebrity celebrations held in Las Vegas. After years of love from locals, Freed's Bakery started to get notice from the big names in food—*Bon Appetit*, Food Network, *Martha Stewart Weddings* and *Condé Nast Traveler,* to name a few. All of this notice caused them to add a second location, but not much else has changed. The cookie and pastry choices vary from day to day, but you can always count on flavors that remind you of childhood. Cake lovers can rejoice, too. Slices are available, including Rachael Ray's favorite Wedding Cake filled with Bavarian cream and strawberries.

There's almost always a line at In-N-Out Burger.
Charo Burke

In-N-Out Burger
www.in-n-out.com
4888 Dean Martin Drive
4705 South Maryland Parkway
Sun.–Thurs. 10:30–1 AM; Fri.–Sat.
10:30–1:30 AM

There are more than 150 In-N-Out Burger stands now, but unless you're from California or Arizona, there's good reason to have one fast food meal in Las Vegas. Just to be clear, there are no onion rings, chicken sandwiches, salads, or anything else besides burgers, shakes made with real ice cream, and fresh-cut fries. The burgers come with American cheese, tomato, hand leafed lettuce, spread, and onions, grilled or raw. They are very happy to hold any of those but there is no avocado, barbecue sauce, jalapeños, or any other burger condiments. The reason for listing what they don't have is because listing what they do have is too succinct—fresh fries, juicy burgers, and creamy shakes. The two addresses above are for the locations closest to the Strip. There are six others in Las Vegas and one in Henderson. If you're out and about, just ask someone. They'll know where the nearest location is.

Italcream
702-873-2214
3871 South Valley View Boulevard

Giovanni Parente has the quintessential Las Vegas history. Born in Naples, Italy, Parente had to immigrate at a young age. After living in Australia, then working at the famous Copacabana in New York, he arrived in Las Vegas. For 31 years he worked for the sadly demolished Dunes Hotel. From there, he became the personal maître d' for Debbie Reynolds and started to work on perfecting gelato. And undoubtedly he has reached his goal. If his story doesn't pique your interest, maybe some of the flavors will: amaretto, cherries jubilee, crunchy rum, green tea, stracciatella, and zabaglione. There's over a dozen varieties of sorbetto for those avoiding dairy and a half dozen or more surprisingly tasty sugar-free gelatos. Altogether there can be over 50 flavors to choose from, though they are only available by the pint and gallon. There is no seating available, just a buy-and-go storefront. The price of a pint of Italcream's delectable concoctions is cheaper than a tiny scoop of their same product at one of the area resorts.

Luv-It Frozen Custard
702-384-6452
www.luvitfrozencustard.com
505 East Oakey Boulevard
Open: Sun.–Thurs. 1–10 PM; Fri. and Sat. 1–11 PM
Cash Only

Luv-It's Frozen Custard has been a summer staple for nearly four decades. Charo Burke

When it's over 100 degrees, a cool treat is of the utmost necessity. For the last 35 years, for residents and especially for kids living in the oppressive heat, Luv-It Frozen Custard has been the true oasis. Frozen custard is just what it seems, custard made with eggs and vanilla, then frozen. It has less air and fewer calories than traditional ice cream. Flavors always include vanilla, chocolate, and strawberry, plus two seasonal offerings like cinnamon, lemon, raspberry, malt cream, and butter pecan. All seasonal flavors are listed by date available on the Web site. Be warned that, while the treats are sweet, the neighborhood is . . . not so much, but the area surrounding the business is well lit. This is one of those establishments that you have to hear about to find. On summer nights expect a line that can be up to half an hour long.

Payard Pâtisserie
702-731-7849
www.payard.com/lasvegas
Caesars Palace
Daily 6:30 AM–11 PM

What a gift breakfast pastries are for all breakfast adorers! How else can you justifiably start the day with dessert? Thanks to the storybook-like Payard Pâtisserie, dessert for breakfast and a giant truffle-dispensing clock have left the fairy-tale world and become a reality. The magical clock is 13 feet high, displays nine different time zones, and dispenses complimentary chocolate truffles at varied intervals. The windows built into the clock show the inside workings designed to mimic the six-step process of truffle making. Delectable pastries in the morning lead to chocolates and sweets throughout the day. Payard Pâtisserie in Manhattan was named one of the top 101 restaurants in NYC. If you can't make it there, then I'm sure that these fresh baked macaroons and superb coffee at this location will do.

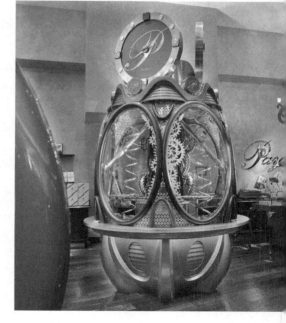

Las Vegas is the perfect spot for something as decadent as Payard Pâtisserie's truffle clock.
Courtesy Caesars Palace

There are more than 50 golf courses to choose from in Las Vegas. Las Vegas News Bureau

8

RECREATION

Away from the Neon

The Las Vegas Valley features some of the best weather and desert scenery in the world, and the combination of the two can be the backdrop for some truly outstanding outdoor experiences. With both Lake Mead and Mount Charleston less than an hour's drive from the Strip, this area has charms to excite every kind of outdoor enthusiast, from hiking and horseback riding to skiing and snowboarding, from boating to rock climbing. In the heat of the summer it may be tempting to stay in the cool of the casino, but during the rest of the year the moderate temperatures and sunny days make playing outside almost irresistible. Go on, get out of the recycled casino air. Just don't forget the water bottle and sunscreen!

BICYCLING

Cycling is not one's best bet for getting around Las Vegas. Most major thoroughfares do not feature bike paths, the city's sprawl is so great as to be pedal-prohibitive, and traffic is often unforgiving to those on two wheels. Even on the Strip, where the distance between places is relatively short, the traffic congestion is such that riding a bicycle is not as pleasant an experience as one would anticipate. However, there are options for those looking to take in the desert's beauty by bicycle away from the hubbub and honking of the city streets. Nevada law does not require a helmet while riding, but it's just good sense, and tour guides will require their use. It cannot be overstated: Water is an absolute must. The summer heat is brutal and even other times of year can see relatively high temperatures. Always make sure to have plenty of water along. For those adventurous souls who brave the busy streets but may decide here and there to hop on a city bus, all public transit vehicles are equipped with racks able to accommodate two or three bikes and there is no additional fee to bring a bike on board. Check the Regional Transportation Commission of Southern Nevada's Web site at www.rtcsouthernnevada.com for a map of all bike routes in the Greater Las Vegas area.

Road Biking

West Charleston Boulevard to Red Rock Canyon (6 miles west of the edge of town on West Charleston Boulevard to the entrance of Red Rock Canyon NCA) It's a beautiful ride up to Red Rock Canyon from the outskirts of Las Vegas. Park your vehicle at one of the shopping centers along West Charleston Boulevard (the last one is called Vista Commons; it's on the north side of West Charleston about 1 mile west of the 215 freeway) and pedal the six or so miles up to the canyon. The road is paved all the way, with some gradual up- and downhill climbs, and the approach to Red Rock is always breathtaking. As you ride up, you'll see the red and orange of the canyon ahead in stark relief against the brown of the mountain foothills. In spring wildflowers are in bloom, lending even more beauty to the already stunning scenery.

Red Rock Canyon National Conservation Area (www.redrockcanyonlv.org; from Las Vegas Boulevard, drive west on Charleston Boulevard [State Route 159] about 17 miles, entrance on the right) This protected area, located 17 miles west of the Las Vegas Strip, is an excellent place to take in the desert's beauty while on two wheels. Designated a National Conservation Area in 1990, the incredible sight of the red, orange, and even pink cliffs of Red Rock Canyon rising from the ancient sea floor have welcomed many visitors to its roads and trails. Featuring steep climbs and jaw-dropping views, the 15-mile, one-way Red Rock Scenic Loop is a must-ride for the experienced cyclist. There are a few places to pull out and take in the vistas (and some water); worth special note is the overlook at the loop's summit at 4,800 feet. Beautiful sandstone cliffs, striking shadowed canyons, and the Las Vegas skyline are all visible from here. No water is available on the loop, however, so be sure to bring some along. Guided tours and bicycle rentals are available through **McGhies Ski, Bike, and Board** (702-252-8077) and **Las Vegas Cyclery** (702-596-2953).

No matter how cute they are, be sure to keep your distance; wild burros kick and bite. Las Vegas News Bureau

Red Rock Visitors Center Entrance to Blue Diamond and back (State Route 159, about eight miles each way) If you drive far enough west on Charleston Boulevard, it becomes State Route 159, and if you keep following it, you'll ride through some of the most incredible mountainous terrain to be seen in the Las Vegas area. Park your car at the entrance to the Red Rock Visitors Center and Scenic Loop and ride from there to the tiny town of Blue Diamond, nestled in the foothills of the Spring Range. You're sure to spot some burros along the road (you may be tempted to feed them, but please don't) and scads of yucca trees. The mountain colors are truly awesome to behold. The gently curving road (two lanes in some places, four lanes in others) is paved with a climb of about 500 feet and you'll share it with general highway traffic (some of it going quite fast), so be on your game. Appropriate for moderately experienced to experienced riders.

Points North, East, West, and South: It is possible when visiting Las Vegas to bicycle within surrounding recreation areas like Lake Mead National Recreation Area (about 35 miles to the east), Mount Charleston (about 35 miles northwest), and Valley of Fire (about 50 miles northeast), and to outlying towns such as Pahrump (about 40 miles to the west) and Boulder City (about 43 miles to the south). As stated earlier, Nevada roads are not all bike-friendly; bike lane availability will vary, and you can check Southern Nevada road conditions at www.nevadadot.com/traveler/roads.

Mountain Biking

The intrepid mountain biker will only have to look around to find a place to take a bike off the road in the Las Vegas Valley. Drive far enough in any direction and you'll find open desert, rocks, and sand—enough to excite any fan of off-road cycling. For those who prefer to ride established trails, there are some options.

Bootleg Canyon Mountain Bike Park (US 93 south to Boulder City, left on Yucca Street, follow Yucca until it becomes a dirt road to the parking area at the entrance to Bootleg Canyon) Disneyland for the advanced mountain bike enthusiast. Twenty-four different trails totaling about 35 miles have been carved out of the rock, sand, and sage of Bootleg Canyon; fifteen of them are cross-country and nine of them are downhill. Sporting names like Armageddon, Reaper, and P.O.W., Bootleg Canyon's mountain bike trails have been designated by the International Mountain Biking Association as an "epic ride."

Also epic are the views of Lake Mead, Las Vegas, and the surrounding mountains!

Cottonwood Valley (Head west on Charleston Boulevard, which turns into Highway 159, past Red Rock entrance, road changes direction, turn right at Highway 160 for 4.7 miles to two parking lots) The only mountain biking area allowed in Red Rock Canyon is Cottonwood Valley. There are 125 miles of interconnecting single track, six suggested trail loops, and an 11-mile NORBA (National Off Road Bicycle Association) race loop here. Portions of the many trails may have been created by the families of wild burros here. Finding your way isn't too difficult as the mountains are due west, but maps are available at the Red Rock Canyon Visitor Center.

BOWLING

Bowling in the Entertainment Capital of the World? For some, the glitz and the glamour of Las Vegas can wear thin. When it's time to get real and live like a normal person, Las Vegas has fantastic bowling centers. Many of them are open 24 hours. Las Vegas's popular bowl-

Desert Dangers

The desert is a place of exquisite beauty, and experiencing it brings a sense of freedom and wonderment. Before you go out into the great wide open, however, be aware of and prepared for the serious hazards that lurk out under that beautiful blue sky.

Dehydration: Perhaps the easiest desert danger to avoid, but the most insidious. Don't let the dry heat fool you. Though it evaporates quickly, you are sweating; you do need water and lots of it, more than you may be accustomed to drinking throughout the day. The relative humidity rarely rises above 50 percent in the Las Vegas area, and in the summer months, it can stay as low as 5–10 percent. In these conditions, dehydration can set in after only about 30 minutes of exercise, especially when it's hot, and one often does not realize that they are becoming dehydrated. Early symptoms of dehydration include thirst, flushed skin, headache, and overall weakness. As dehydration progresses, muscle cramps, confusion, dry mouth and tongue,

When you explore the desert, it's important to bring lots of water. Charo Burke

nausea, and loss of consciousness can occur. If this stage is reached, emergency medical attention is needed. Beyond dehydration is heatstroke, another extremely dire condition and one that can be deadly. How can you avoid dehydration and heat illness? **If you're planning outdoor activities, bring plenty of water.** Your water regimen should begin before you take off for your desert excursion. Due to their diuretic nature, your morning coffee or tea don't count. It is recommended that you drink about 8 ounces of water for every fifteen minutes of athletic activity, and that includes walking or hiking in the desert. Bring enough water to satisfy this requirement, and then bring more than that. And while you're at it, bring an extra gallon of water for your vehicle. The desert heat can be as hard on your ride as it is on your body, and having extra water along is a really good idea. Another smart idea is wearing sunscreen. The sun shines about 325 days a year in these parts, and on a typical late spring, summer, or early fall day the UV index is 11, which means that without protection, your skin will begin to burn within mere minutes. As we've all had the misfortune to learn at some point in our lives, nothing can ruin a vacation like a bad sunburn, and you can get sunburned here in a heartbeat.

Dangerous Critters: Looking out across the open desert, it appears that nothing lives here besides the sage and yucca, but there's an incredible variety of fauna that make their home here. Many desert denizens are harmless, but some of that wildlife should be avoided at all cost. The wild burros come right up to the road. They're not timid and they know that humans usually have food. And, yes, the babies are adorable, but the adults with them can bite and kick with no provoking. It's fine to take their pictures, but keep your distance, and, for heaven's sake, do not feed them. Rattlesnakes are common, as are scorpions and poisonous spiders such as the black widow and brown recluse. The best way to avoid these animals is not to disturb their homes. When hiking in the desert, always wear sturdy hiking shoes or boots and watch your step—don't stick your feet into brush or holes. If you sit down, be careful where you plant your backside. Nothing spoils the fun like fire ants in the pants. And although they're not often spotted, mountain lions can be found in the desert; as humans encroach on their homes, they are more often seen as they hunt and protect their young. When it comes to dangerous animals, be watchful and be prepared to move out quickly if you spot them.

Abandoned Mines: Many of the intrepid folks that settled this area came here for one reason: money. And the way they made that money was mining the precious metals found in the remote areas of the West. These days, mountain foothills are rife with their abandoned mines, some well over a hundred years old. **If you come across one of these mines, STAY AWAY. NEVER go into an abandoned mine;** there may be dangerous gases, hazardous rocks, and drop-offs inside, and the risk of cave-in is very, very high. Many people die every year in accidents in abandoned mines, because the mines have been abandoned for a long time (and were never safe to begin with), and because they are in such remote areas that when accidents do happen, rescuers either cannot reach them in time or simply can't get into the mine to help them because it's too dangerous.

Weather: Monsoon season in the desert stretches from mid-June through early September. At this time of year, the days usually begin sunny, hot, and humid, but come late afternoon, towering cumulonimbus rule the sky and conditions can deteriorate very quickly. The danger from summer pop-up storms is twofold: lightning and heavy rain that can result in flash floods. If you're outdoors when a storm comes up, take shelter indoors if possible; if you're away from buildings, take shelter in your vehicle. If you're away from your vehicle, DO NOT take shelter under trees. Hunker down close to the ground and keep a low profile, as lightning tends to strike the highest part of the landscape. If you're planning to camp in and/or hike through canyons or washes, keep an eye on the skies all year round, but especially during monsoon season. Floodwaters rage through canyons and washes during and after storms, often coming down from many miles upstream, and when you're below ground level in a canyon, you usually can't tell it's happening until it's too late. If dark clouds gather upstream, stay out of canyons and washes. Also, don't try to cross flooded roadways either in vehicles or on foot. A good rule of thumb is, "Turn around, don't drown."

ing movement can be attributed to Midwest transplants, oppressive summer heat, the fact that not all Las Vegans gamble, and people who work nontraditional hours seeking activities at 2 AM that aren't club related. For those who feel a slight tremble if the distance from the card tables is too great, these are located in casinos. The popularity of bowling in Las Vegas has given rise to a vast amount of leagues. Call the bowling center of your choice before you go and make sure there are lanes open for nonleague play.

Gold Coast Hotel and Casino (702-367-7111; www.goldcoastcasino.com; 4000 West Flamingo Road) Voted Best of Las Vegas Bowling Alley from 1989 to 1996, 1998, and 2004 by the Las Vegas Review-Journal, so you know it's got the pro shop, arcade, and snack bar. This one's got 72 lanes and 2,000 lockers in which you can keep your treasures. At night, this joint gets loud. There's a live DJ who needs to learn microphone volume control. If cigarette smoke bothers you, stay far away.

Orleans Hotel & Casino (702-365-7111; 4500 West Tropicana Ave) Winner of the Las Vegas Review-Journal's 2006 Reader's Choice Best of Award, the staff is key here. Not that the 70 lanes, full-service pro shop, snack bar, a lounge, bar and arcade aren't cool, too. It's just that the staff is known to go that extra distance, especially for those who haven't bowled in a while.

Sam's Town Bowling Center (Sam's Town Casino; 5111 Boulder Highway; 702-456-7777) Having all the bowling center amenities, plus a day care center, makes this the most family-friendly spot—sometimes too family friendly, but with 72 lanes, there's room to try and get away. After midnight on the weekends, Extreme Bowling takes over with disco music and fog machines creating an amusement-park ambience.

Strike Zone (702-547-7777; www.sunsetstation.com; Sunset Station Hotel Casino; 1301 West Sunset)

The 72 Brunswick Pro Anvil Lanes and a 24-hour schedule of the Strike Zone once again demonstrate how Station Casinos do things right. If you're not familiar with the Anvil lanes, don't fret, just enjoy them. There are 42-inch plasma televisions between each lane, the carpet glows in the dark, and the lights are hand-blown glass. Now this is Vegas bowling! Like the rest of the city, the lights come up at night at these bowling lanes. It's called Cosmic Bowling and features far-out tunes and laser light show graphics. Call ahead for schedule. Don't worry if you're wearing sandals when you get here. Each shoe rental includes a free pair of new socks.

CAMPING

Beautiful weather year-round makes for some excellent camping in the wilderness and recreation areas around Las Vegas. There is something for everyone—whether you prefer mountain cool, desert heat, or lakeside leisure, it's all here.

Lake Mead National Recreation Area
Spring and autumn are the best times to camp in the desert, when the days are warm and the nights are pleasantly cool. Temperatures at Lake Mead are usually 10–15 degrees warmer than in Vegas, so plan accordingly, especially in summer, when the heat can be dangerous. Always have plenty of water on hand and bring your own shade. Each of the following campgrounds are open year-round and feature grills, running water, and restrooms, and allow trailers, RVs, and tents. Fees are $10.00 per site, and there are no reservations. Call the **Lake Mead Visitor Center** at 702-293-8990 for additional information.

For backcountry camping, Lake Mead has hundreds of miles of shoreline and wilderness area, and much of it can be accessed on foot, and by boat or vehicle. Primitive and backcountry camping is permitted unless marked with signs, and there are limits to how long one may camp. A rundown of all restrictions and maps to the backcountry is available at www.nps.gov/lame/planyourvisit. Low water levels due to drought have closed some launch ramps. You can check for the latest level at www.nps.gov.

Boulder Beach: Located in the Boulder Basin area, this is one of the most popular camping spots in the region. The shoreline is just 150 feet from the camping sites. There are 154 sites available with a 30-day limit. A developed trailer village with full recreational facilities, RV sites available with full hookups (sewage, water, electric). Contact Lake Mead RV Village (702-293-2540).

Callville Bay: Boulder Basin area. Full camping accommodations, propane, self-service laundry, and houseboat rentals available. Contact Callville Bay Resort (702-565-8958) for RV reservations. 80 sites available with a 30-day limit with full hookups (sewage, water, electric).

Echo Bay: Located in the Overton Arm area on the western shore of Lake Mead, there are boating, fishing and marina here. Houseboats are available for rent. 166 sites available with a 30-day limit. Contact Echo Bay Resort (702-394-4000) for RV reservations.

Las Vegas Bay: Located on the western shore of Lake Mead in the Boulder Basin area with boating and waterskiing. Fishing includes rainbow trout, largemouth bass, bluegill, and

There's plenty of room for windsurfing on Lake Mead, the largest man-made reservoir in the United States. Las Vegas News Bureau

crappie. Contact Lake Mead Recreation (702-293-8907). 89 sites with a 30-day limit.

Mount Charleston/Spring Mountains National Recreation Area

It's hard to believe that there is a high-country haven among the bristlecone and ponderosa pines less than an hour's drive from the lights and excitement of the Strip. Pinch yourselves, people, because it's true. Within the Toiyabe National Forest, Mount Charleston, Kyle Canyon, and Lee Canyon is where locals and visitors go to hike, bike, picnic, climb rocks— even ski and snowboard. The summer camping here is especially popular, as daytime temperatures rarely exceed the low 80s and nights are pleasant, staying in the 50s and 60s. The six developed campgrounds listed offer drinking water, picnic tables, toilets, and fire rings or grates; water is available from Memorial Day through Labor Day each year. Reservations for all campgrounds can be made at www.recreation.gov, or by calling the National Reservation Service at 827-444-6777. All fees given are for peak season.

McWilliams: (Lee Canyon area) Some shade from ponderosa pine, white fir, and others. An attractive setting, but there is little privacy between campsites. Most sites enjoy a view of Mummy Mountain but rocks can make pitching a tent a challenge. Open year-round, 40 campsites available. Flush and vault toilets. Fees $19–$34.

Dolomite: (Lee Canyon area) Winds up the north side of the canyon with many sites terraced above or below another site. Though fewer trees for shade, the curvy design and wide separation between sites offers decent privacy in comparison to McWilliams. It's not as rocky, either. Open May to October, 30 campsites available. Flush toilets. Fee $19.

Hilltop: (Deer Creek area) The best and most panoramic views of Spring Mountains, Sheep Mountains, Mercury Test Site, and lights of Las Vegas. Site placement offers decent privacy. Open May to October, 35 campsites available. Only showers in the area. No trailers over 25 feet. Fees $19–$47.

Fletcher View: (Kyle Canyon area) This spot stretches along Kyle Canyon, along a wash, beside State Route 157. One of the better sites for spotting wildlife, including foxes and deer. Most sites have tent pads. Open year-round, 11 campsites available. Showers, campfire pits, pedestal grills, flush toilets, electrical hookup available. Fees, $19–$38.

Kyle Canyon: (Kyle Canyon area) Also along the wash and State Route 157 but sites are tucked in among Gambel oak, ponderosa pine and mountain mahogany. The manzanita and wild roses between sites provide excellent privacy. Three local stone bridges add charm and most sites have a view of Kyle Canyon's north wall. One negative aspect is the traffic noise that can be heard throughout the campground. Open year-round, 25 campsites available. Vault toilets. Fees, $19–$34.

Red Rock Canyon

Formerly known as 13-mile Campground, **Red Rock Canyon Campground** (from West Charleston Boulevard [State Route 159], turn left onto Moenkopi Road and travel one mile) has 71 individual campsites and 5 group campsites. The only developed campground in the Red Rock NCA, this campground is open from September through late May. Campsites are available on a first-come, first-served basis, and there is a campground host on-site. Although improvements are expected within the next few years, this campground offers a fairly rugged camping experience. The roads leading out to this site are unpaved. There are no electrical, water, or sewage hookups, nor are there any dump stations for RVs, showers, or shade. Water faucets for drinking water do exist, and firewood is for sale through the campground host.

DISC GOLF

Fans of disc golf are a dedicated sort and used to flying a bit under the radar. Theirs is not a sport advertised in glossy travel magazines or on flashy cable programs. Disc golf is accessible, family friendly, and inexpensive. All Las Vegas courses are playable free of charge unless there's a tournament going on and then there may be a small registration fee. It's also great for traveling, as the necessary equipment doesn't take up much space in packed luggage. Those used to playing with a lot of foliage and hills will be taken aback by the lack of trees and flatness, but the Vegas Valley wind can play havoc with a shot. Should you get to Las Vegas and discover that your discs are back at home, the offices for **Baskethead Disc Golf** (702-373-8178; www.baskethead.com) will sell their disc golf supplies in person. Or stop by Sin City Disc Golf (702-423-8300; 8974 Lanta Island Ave.) Check out www.lvbagtag.com for upcoming events and competitions.

Freedom Park (From the Strip: I-15 North to US 95 South to Exit 73 Eastern Ave., north 0.25 mile to a right on Bonanza, half mile to left on Mojave. Park is 0.25 mile on right) At the time of this writing, Freedom Park was closed for major renovations. The course and park were in desperate need of revitalizing. It is in a part of town that was ignored in the past when it came to the new exciting things that were happening due to suburban growth elsewhere in the valley. It is expected to reopen spring 2010, with a planned 3,960-foot, par-33, 9-hole disc golf course.

Mountain Crest Park (I-15 North to US 95 North, exit #85 [Craig Road], head west on Craig, make a right/head north on Durango Road, Mountain Crest will be on your left) Redesigned in 2003, the 18-hole, 5,254-foot course now has new tee pads. Depending on preference, the out-of-bounds pins may be a bit tight.

Sunset Park (Take East Tropicana 2.5 miles to South Eastern, turn right) Possibly the seventh-oldest disc golf course in the nation (1978), this park holds a lot of memories for children who grew up in the area before the population explosion. With a whopping 24 holes, the course is 8,775 feet long. Park between the pool and the ballpark to be closest to the first tee. This course has its own pro/designer, Vince Gardner. He's responsible for the planting of the trees on the course and disc golf players say he's done a bang-up job.

EXTREME SPORTS

Thrill seekers haven't far to look to find chances to get the adrenaline pumping in and around Las Vegas, and we're not talking about the gaming tables. Something about the desert must bring out the daredevil in people, because opportunities to get your hair blown back abound.

Glider Tours

If you've ever dreamed of riding the breeze like the birds, then a glider flight may be your thing. Pilot and owner Thierry Maioli of **Motorglider Tours of Las Vegas** (702-290-3892; www.motorglidertourslasvegas.com) takes off from the North Las Vegas airport, flying passengers (one person at a time) to a height of 8,000 feet, then cuts the engine and glides back to the airport. Maioli offers aerial tours of Red Rock Canyon, Mount Charleston, Valley of Fire, and Hoover Dam—call for additional tours offered. The Red Rock tour lasts approximately an hour and costs $160. The glider wing can fly as close as 200 feet to the face of a cliff at Red Rock Canyon. Pilot instruction also available. Free hotel pickup available and tours can be scheduled seven days a week. Passengers must weigh less than 240 pounds, but there is no age limit. **The Soaring Center** (702-874-1010; www.soaringcenter.net; Exit 12 off Interstate 15 in Jean, NV), which operates out of the Jean Airport Sport Aviation Center, offers glider and aerobatic flights for up two passengers at a time. Their combined weight must be less than 350 pounds. The single-person flight lasts 30 to 45 minutes and costs $175. For two people, the cost is $249. An aerobatic thrill flight for one is $199. Transportation from the Las Vegas Strip is available.

Ziplines

Ever feel like zipping down a mountain at 50 miles per hour with nothing but a harness between you and the desert one thousand feet below? Located in Bootleg Canyon high above Boulder City, **Bootleg Canyon Flightlines** (702-293-6885; www.bcflightlines.com; 1512 Industrial Road, Boulder City) offers you the chance to take in the view zipline-style. Basically this means you sit on a paragliding harness that's suspended from cables. If you can keep from screaming on the ride down, the quietness of the desert is as stunning as the view. The experience lasts about two and a half hours, and includes your orientation, harness fitting, and practice run on a small zipline. Once you've been granted clearance from your guide, you'll be good to go to the top of Red Mountain (a half-hour hike) and "fly" the canyon. There are four runs total, the last being the fastest. There are no age restrictions, but they don't recommend children under 12 riding the ziplines. Each individual must weigh between 75 and 250 pounds. Appropriate dress is necessary, so no flip-flops, sandals, or cowboy boots. Rides to Bootleg Canyon can be provided one hour before your scheduled flight but only from Excalibur and Bally's resorts. Bootleg Canyon Flightlines is open seven days a week; $149, the last flight of the day is $169.

Rock Climbing (Indoor and Outdoor)

When considering where the best outdoor rock climbing in the Las Vegas area is, most people look to **Red Rock Canyon**. One can scramble over boulders with their tennies as their only equipment, or rappel down sheer rock faces hundreds of feet high. There are wind- and water-scoured canyons and crannies to explore, and amazing views from high above it all. Red Rock boasts some 2,000 climbing routes, many accessed by trails; it is a world-class rock-climbing destination, visited by around 100,000 climbers per year. Permits are required for overnight climbs and late exits from the **Conservation Area**, and must be secured seven days in advance; call 702-515-5050 to obtain a permit. Call the climbing rangers at 702-515-5138 or 702-515-5042 for more information on specific climbs. A detailed climbing inventory, along with some excellent maps, can be found at the Bureau of Land Management's Red Rock canyon Web site at www.blm.gov/nv/st/en/fo/lvfo/blm_programs/blm_special_areas/red_rock_nca.html—click on the "Red Rock Climbing Inventory" link. Guided rock climbing in Red Rock Canyon is available through the **Red Rock Climbing Center Outdoor Guide Service** (702-254-5604; 8201 West Charleston Boulevard Suite 150; www.redrockclimbingcenter.com), **American Alpine Institute** (360-671-1505; www.aai.cc), **Jackson Hole Mountain Guides** (800-239-7642; www.jhmg.com), and **Mountain Skills Rock Climbing Adventures** (575-776-2222; www.climbingschoolusa .com). **Valley of Fire State Park** and the **Spring Mountains NRA** also boast many wilderness areas in which to climb; however, no guided rock climbing tours are available, and most climbing routes are accessible only by trail. See their respective Web sites, www.parks.nv.gov/vf.htm (Valley of Fire) and www.fs.fed.us/r4/htnf/districts/smnra (Spring Mountains NRA) for more information about climbing in these areas. If you want to get your climb climate-controlled style, there is an indoor option also. **Red Rock Climbing Center** (702-254-5604; www.redrockclimbingcenter.com; 8201 West Charleston Boulevard, Suite 150) has more than 8,000 square feet of climbing terrain, including a 35-foot-high lead wall and over 50 top-rope and lead routes. They also let the kids get in on the fun, with specified Kids Climb times, two hours at a time, five days a week.

Skateboard Parks

Skateboarding is as popular in Las Vegas as it is all over the world. And while there are 24 skate parks throughout the valley, listed here are the ones that are the skaters' top favorites—private and public.

Anthem Skatepark (2256 North Reunion Drive, Henderson) Designed by the legendary Site Design Groups and constructed by Site Skate Parks, this park was designed for all ages and abilities. It has a street-style flow-course and various pockets of depth and radii featuring two big volcanoes, tall extensions, and rollers. There is also a small kidney pool.

Area 702 Indoor Skate Park (702-870-7588; 3040 Simmons Street, Suite #104) The newest indoor park, Area 702 offers a vert ramp, huge wooden bowl with 12-foot cradle, eight-stair granite ledges for grinding, and a plethora of rails. Well-stocked shop for all your skateboard needs. Mon.–Thurs. 10 AM–8 PM; Fri.–Sat. 10 AM–10 PM; Sun. 12 PM–8 PM.

Skate City (702-433-5544; www.skatecity.info; 4915 Steptoe St. Ste. 600) A 7,000-square-foot indoor skate park designed for all levels, though the lines are a bit tight. The hours are short, because the park is also used by BMX riders. To keep things interesting, the layout is changed every now and then. Schedule listed is for skateboarding only. Tues.–Fri. 3 PM–8 PM; Sat. and Sun. noon–4 PM; One hour $6, two hours $10, all day $15.

Hollywood Skate/BMX Park (702-455-0566; 1650 South Hollywood) This 29,000-square-foot park was designed for the advanced skater and features a snake run, 11-foot-deep kidney bowl, and an 18-foot full pipe. Hollywood Skate/BMX Park requires helmets to be worn by all participants. All participants ages 12 and under must be accompanied by an adult who remains on-site. All participants must have a signed waiver on file before entering the park. Call for seasonal and special event schedule. Fees are $5 per person, per day. Helmet and pad rentals are available for $1 a day.

Skydiving

Who can understand why some people love jumping out of perfectly good airplanes? They do, and there are a few outfits in Vegas that specialize in flying you up and letting you out—at thousands of feet above the ground! **Skydive Las Vegas** (800-875-9348: www.skydive lasvegas.com; 1401 Airport Road, Boulder City) is the oldest skydive school in Nevada and specializes in giving first-time jumpers the thrill of a lifetime. Each of Skydive Las Vegas's instructors and its Jumpmaster have received the highest rankings awarded by the U.S. Parachute Association and have more than 1,000 jumps each under their belts. Daily free round-trip shuttle transportation from a central location on the Strip is available, as are online reservations. See Web site for age/weight restrictions. Fees start at $149.

Vegas Extreme Skydiving (866-398-5867; www.vegasextremeskydiving.com; Jean Airport, exit 12 off I-15) offers tandem skydiving for beginners and solo skydiving for experienced jumpers, with a team of highly trained instructors licensed and rated by the United States Parachute Association. Want to take the plunge with your significant other—literally? Vegas Extreme Skydiving offers a skydiving wedding package, which includes a DVD, flowers, and a champagne glass with the Vegas Extreme Skydiving logo. Transportation from the Strip is available. See Web site for age/weight restrictions. Tandem jumps start at $199.

Also located about 20 minutes down I-15 in Jean is **Sin City Skydiving** (877-727-5827; www.sincityskydiving.com; 23600 South Las Vegas Boulevard, in Jean, NV). A group member of the United States Parachute Association, Sin City Skydiving caters to experienced skydivers, as well as the novice jumper. They provide free round-trip shuttle service from the Strip to their jump site, and offer group, local, and military discounts and a free T-shirt with every Internet reservation. See Web site for age/weight restrictions. Weekday jumps start at $249.

Indoor Skydiving

Yearning for the sensation and thrill of skydiving but not eager to bail out of an airplane at 4,000 feet? **Vegas Indoor Skydiving** (702-731-4768; www.vegasindoorskydiving.com; 200 Convention Center Drive, Las Vegas) can help you satisfy your curiosity while keeping your feet (somewhat) planted on the ground. Built in 1982 and operating for years under the name Flyaway, Vegas Indoor Skydiving is the oldest indoor skydiving facility in the United States. Vertical wind tunnel technology (along with a special flight suit) is used to simulate the rush of free fall, and the chamber is foam padded from floor to ceiling for your protection. See Web site for weight restrictions and guidelines; there is no age restriction, but guests must weigh a minimum of 40 pounds, and minors must be accompanied by a parent or guardian.

FAMILY FUN

Whether or not you consider Las Vegas a family destination probably depends on what kind of a family you have; most of the "toys" and "playgrounds" here are for adults only, but there are quite a few places for the under-21 set to have fun, take in a ball game, drive a go-kart, and check out some underwater wonders. You just have to know where to look! This is not a cumulative list of all that is family friendly in Las Vegas. Throughout this book, other things to do and see that are family friendly are listed.

Excalibur Hotel and Casino (702-597-7777; www.excalibur.com; 3850 Las Vegas Boulevard South, Las Vegas) They all scoffed when Circus Circus opened the Excalibur back in 1990; admittedly, the idea of an Arthurian-themed hotel on the Las Vegas Strip seemed utterly surreal. But almost twenty years later, in a climate where so many properties have ditched their family-friendly themes, the Excalibur is still flying pennants from its spires, and still getting medieval on its visitors like it was 1199. The midway offers carnival-style games as well as many arcade favorites and a SpongeBob SquarePants 4-D motion ride. The Excalibur also boasts one of the only shows on the Las Vegas Strip with true family appeal, the Tournament of Kings, wherein knights from several different countries joust against one another in King Arthur's Arena while being lustily cheered on by the crowd. Dinner is served during the show, hands-on style—no utensils provided, which delights children to no end. Adults, dress accordingly. It's an extremely entertaining night, one the little kids (and the big kids) won't soon forget. Showtimes Wed.–Mon. 6 PM and 8:30 PM.

Gameworks (702-432-4263; www.wegotfamily.com; 3785 Las Vegas Boulevard South, Suite 010;) What better place for a multistory arcade than right on the Strip? In fact, with over 55,000 square feet of attractions, Gameworks is not your typical arcade—it's a lot like a casino for kids, but there's plenty here for both kids and adults alike. Among the approximately 200 interactive games at Gameworks is an eight-person virtual Indy racing game and a "bowling alley"—a bowling experience in which players throw a real ball down a lane, then watch as it knocks down virtual pins. There's even a lounge area, just like in a real bowling alley, to cheer on your friends while enjoying a snack or beverage. The arcade attractions at Gameworks run the gamut from the newest and most advanced games around to the classic favorites like Pac-Man, Space Invaders, Centipede, and of course, air hockey and pinball machines. Upstairs on the second floor is the Loft, where adults 21 and over can sample specialty cocktails and signature martinis away from the lights and noise of the arcade. Open Sun.–Thurs. 10:00 AM to midnight; Fri. and Sat. 10 AM–1 AM.

King Putt Mini Golf (702-541-6807; www.kingputtlv.com; 9230 South Eastern Avenue, Suite 140) Tucked away in a shopping center in the eastside Green Valley suburb of Las Vegas is King Putt Mini Golf. Mini golf courses seem to come and go in Vegas, but one thing that is around in Vegas more often than not is the heat, and that may be the reason for the lack of family-oriented outdoor attractions. At King Putt, you can play an 18-hole mini golf course without breaking a sweat, because it's indoors, a beautiful thing when the temps are in the triple digits. The charm of King Putt is in its glow-in-the-dark Egyptian décor, complete with hieroglyphics, sphinxes, and pyramids. A kitschy good time! A new location but with a classic jungle theme is now open at 7230 West Lake Mead Boulevard Mon.–Thurs. 2 PM–10 PM, Fri. 12 PM–1 AM; Sat. and Sun. 10 AM–10 PM, extended hours when school's out. Play one round for $8.50, second round on same day is $4.

Las Vegas 51s Baseball Club at Cashman Field (702-386-7200; www.lv51.com; 850 Las Vegas Boulevard North, Las Vegas) The Cashman Field Complex opened in 1983 and seats more than 9,000 spectators. For many years it was the home of the AAA Pacific Coast League Las Vegas Stars, the San Diego Padres' farm team. These days the affiliation and team name has changed, but the charm has not—the home team is now the 51s, and they're the AAA farm club of the Toronto Blue Jays. Changes notwithstanding, this park is just as friendly as always, and spending an evening under the stars (it's way too hot out there during the day, in most cases) in this cozy little ballpark with your beverage of choice and a hot dog is just this side of heaven. Seats are inexpensive, as are concessions, and never hard to get; the games that draw the largest crowds are usually ones that feature fireworks displays directly after the game (and for good reason—the fireworks are top-notch, every time). The season starts in April with a couple of exhibition games from major-league teams and then the 51s take it from there, playing through August and into the very start of September. A special aspect of this team is their team logos and mascot. The logos feature the classic big-eyed alien or nuclear insignia, which, when placed with the team's name has a fun quality. The mascot is very similar to a certain Star Wars character most fans would rather forget. Oh yes, there's a bobble head. Many nights feature promotional giveaways, so even if you don't pony up at the souvenir shop, the kids are bound to leave with a little something.

Las Vegas Mini Gran Prix (702-259-7000; www.lvmgp.com; 1401 North Rainbow Boulevard, Las Vegas) What began as a couple of go-kart tracks on the edge of town has become, over the last ten years or so, a mini–amusement park in the growing Summerlin area of northwest Las Vegas. These days, the park includes an airplane ride called the Dive Bomber, the Dragon, a small coaster, the Tornado Twister, and the 90-foot-long Super Fun Slide, as well as a decent-sized arcade and the aforementioned go-kart tracks, four of them, with different skill levels; the easiest, Kiddie Karts, is designed for children age 4 and up, and the most difficult (but still not too difficult), the Adult Gran Prix, requires a driver's license to ride. Throw in a large restaurant serving all the requisite pizza-place goodies and you've got a place to take the kids when they've seen enough white tigers and volcanoes. All karts and rides are accessed by a ticket system. Tickets cost $6.50. If five or more are purchased the price goes down to $6.00 each. Mostly the rides are half a ticket each and the carts are one ticket. Wristbands are available at $18 an hour. Party and group packages available. Sun.–Thurs. 10 AM–10 PM; Fri.–Sat. 10 AM–11 PM

Pole Position Raceway (702-227-7223; www.polepositionraceway.com; 4175 South Arville) Do you feel the need, the need for speed? Will 45 mph do? At Pole Position Raceway, the Italian electric karts are cool, the quarter mile track is indoors, and because the concept was designed by race car drivers, it's a real racing thrill. Besides hitting 45 mph, the karts emit no exhaust, so being inside won't kill your lungs. There's hairpin turns, screeching wheels, and a big screen so everyone knows who's winning and who's not. Pole Position Raceway was brought to Las Vegas with the help of NASCAR champion Kurt Busch and seven-time AMA Supercross champion Jeremy McGrath. With names like that backing it up, it's really about the racing. Anyone who won't be racing can watch the race from the second floor, where there's also an arcade. Racing memorabilia is scattered around, including the racing suit of Dale Earnhardt Sr. and one of Kurt Busch's race cars. There are adult and junior versions of the carts and races. A complimentary shuttle service is offered and stops at many of the casinos. Call or check the Web site for current details. Adults $25 (at least 56 inches tall), juniors $22 (at least 48 inches tall). Sun.–Thurs. 11 AM–11 PM; Fri.–Sat. 11 AM–midnight.

Shark Reef at Mandalay Bay (702-632-4555; www.sharkreef.com; 3950 Las Vegas Boulevard South) Where else but Vegas can you spend a few hours by the pool and then visit the ruins of an underwater temple and its fascinating denizens? At the Shark Reef at Mandalay Bay, you'll find sunken treasure of a different kind—this unique attraction, which is accredited by the American Zoo and Aquarium Association. The exhibit, which houses around 1,200 different species, including reptiles, sharks, rays, and even a piranha tank, is split into three parts: the sunken temple, where you will find moray eels, a water monitor, and the only golden crocodiles in the New World. It's quite lush and humid in this area of the Shark Reef, and they've done a wonderful job of creating a tropical feel. There are benches throughout, so you can pause and enjoy the atmosphere. Beyond this area lies the touch pool area, where people of all ages can get a much closer look at and even touch two or three different varieties of rays, sea stars, horseshoe crabs, and Port Jackson sharks.

Enjoy golf near celebrity villas at Lake Las Vegas. Las Vegas News Bureau

Also in this section of the Shark Reef is a beautiful circular jellyfish display that shouldn't be missed. The third section is the most impressive of all—you find yourself in the wrecked hull of a sunken ship, surrounded on all sides (there are even windows in the floor!) by tiger sharks, manta rays, sea turtles, and tropical fish of every stripe. Just off the galleon area is an underwater tunnel, where one is almost as close as can be to some of the most exotic underwater wildlife anywhere. There is a staff of naturalists throughout the exhibit to answer your questions and provide extra information, and audio wands are distributed at the beginning of the self-guided tour, which takes 1–11/2 hours to complete. If the Shark Reef is your only plan for Mandalay Bay that day, park in the lot at the far south end (convention center parking). The entrance here is much closer to the aquarium than the parking garage. However, if it's summer, this is uncovered parking and your car will become scorching hot. Sun.–Thurs. 10 AM–8 PM, (last admission at 7 PM); Fri.–Sat. 10 AM–10 PM (last admission at 9 PM). Adults $16.95, children 12 years old and younger $10.95, children 4 and younger admitted free.

GOLF

Las Vegas has become a premier golf destination over the last ten years, hosting many major events and tournaments at courses all over the Las Vegas Valley. There are many excellent options for the avid golfer in and around Las Vegas. This list of some of the most popular public courses in town, along with contact information, represents a variety of price ranges; some hotels provide transportation to and from both public and private golf courses for their guests. Check with your front desk or concierge for more information. Most courses and clubs offer online reservations and enforce a dress code.

Aliante Golf Club (877-399-4888; www.aliantegolf.com; 3100 East Elkhorn, North Las Vegas) Complimentary transportation for groups and tournaments aboard either their motor coach or shuttle bus.

Angel Park Las Vegas (888-446-5358; www.angelpark.com; 100 South Rampart Boulevard, Las Vegas) The Mountain Course is a par 71 that is for those who like a challenge and has amazing views. The Palm Course is kinder to beginners and intermediate players at a par 70. Voted Best of Las Vegas numerous times.

The Arroyo Golf Club at Red Rock (866-934-4653; www.thearroyogolfclub.com; 2250C Red Springs Drive, Las Vegas) Arroyo Golf Club is a fair but challenging course where every different level of player can choose a tee that is suited to their abilities.

Badlands Golf Club (877-257-1001; www.badlandsGC.com; 9119 Alta Drive, Las Vegas) Designed by Johnny Miller with consultation from two-time Las Vegas Senior Classic winner Chi Chi Rodriguez, Badlands Golf Club features three nine-hole courses and focuses on accurate ball striking.

Bali Hai Golf Club (888-427-6678; www.balihaigolfcub.com; 5160 Las Vegas Boulevard South, Las Vegas) The only public course on the Strip, it has some airport noise. Most holes are open and there is no out-of-bounds.

Bear's Best (702-804-8500; www.clubcorp.com; 11111 West Flamingo Road) World champion golfer Jack Nicklaus has selected his favorite 18 holes from the more than 200 courses he's created. The holes come from such courses as Cabo Del Sol, PGA West, Castle Pines, and Bear Creek.

Black Mountain Golf & Country Club (702-565-7933; www.golfblackmountain.com; 500 Greenway Road, Henderson) One of the oldest courses in the area, Black Mountain Golf Club recently celebrated its 50th anniversary.

Callaway Golf Center (702-897-9500; www.cgclv.com; 673 Las Vegas Boulevard South, Las Vegas) Callaway Golf Center is located on the Strip and is famous for its lighted par course, the Divine Nine, and 110-stall driving range. It is also home to the St. Andrews Golf Shop.

Desert Pines Golf Club (888-427-6678; www.waltersgolf.com; 3415 East Bonanza Road, Las Vegas) In fall of 2007, Desert Pines underwent a major renovation including 18 new greens. The four lakes bring water into play on nine holes. The climate-controlled practice center is 20,000 square feet.

Desert Rose Golf Course (702-431-4653; 5483 Club House Drive, Las Vegas) Designed by Dick Wilson and Joe Lee, this county course is managed by American Golf Corporation and is only 7.5 miles east of the Strip. The forgiving layout and affordable play make this a good course for all levels.

Las Vegas Paiute Golf Resort (800-711-2833; www.lvpaiutegolf.com; 10325 Nu-Wav Kaiv Boulevard, Las Vegas) This resort has three different Pete Dye–designed courses—Snow Mountain, Sun Mountain, and Wolf. Snow has no parallel fairways, seven water hazards, and a spacious putting green. Sun has an especially picturesque front nine and four sets of tee boxes that measure between 5,465 and 7,112 yards. Wolf is the longest course in Nevada at over 7,600 yards and was designed for tournament play.

Legacy Golf Club (888-446-5358; www.thelegacygc.com; 130 Par Excellence Drive, Henderson) Legacy is the annual spot of U.S Open qualifying and is an early Arthur Hills design using some of the more interesting holes in the valley.

Painted Desert Golf Club (702-645-2570; www.painteddesertgc.com; 5555 Painted Mirage Drive, Las Vegas) The first desert course in the Las Vegas valley, Painted Desert has holes shaped by the desert areas and many bunkers. A former site for the American Open, this course offers a true test of golfing skills.

Revere Golf Club (877-273-8373; www.reveregolf.com; 2600 Hampton Road, Henderson) The Revere has two courses—Concord and Lexington. With rolling fairways, elevation changes and tight design make the latter one of the most challenging in the valley. The Concord offers generous fairways and more landing area.

Rhodes Ranch Golf Club (702-740-4114; www.rhodesranchgolf.com; 20 Rhodes Ranch Parkway, Las Vegas) A 6,909-yard course designed by Ted Robinson, who considers these par threes as his best ever. Three of the four feature considerable water hazards.

Royal Links Golf Club (888-427-6678; www.royallinksgolfclub.com; 5995 East Vegas Valley Drive, Las Vegas) All 18 holes are designed to mimic holes from the courses in rotation in the British Open. Throughout the course, monuments and markers are dedicated to the history of the game.

Shadow Creek (1-866-260-0069; www.shadowcreek.com; 3 Shadow Creek Drive, North Las Vegas) One of Golf Digest's regular Top Ten. Recently built a world-class short-game area with multiple greens.

Siena Golf Club (888-689-6469; www.sienagolfclub.com; 10575 Siena Monte Avenue, Las Vegas) The Schmidt-Curly design features 95 white sand bunkers and is popular with the locals, so book early.

Silverstone Golf Club (877-888-2127; www.silverstonegolfclub.com; 8600 Cupp Drive, Las Vegas) Siverstone is one of the few 27-hole courses in the area. Designed by Robert Cupp, the course received $2 million worth of enhancements in 2007. One of the area's best practice facilities.

Tournament Players Club Las Vegas (702-256-2500; www.tpc.com; 9851 Canyon Run Drive; Las Vegas) A Bobby Weed and Raymond Floyd course designed for the PGA tour. The course is challenging but is playable by all levels.

Tuscany Golf Club (702-951-1500; www.tuscanygolfclub.com; 901 Olivia Parkway, Henderson) A great golf value with upscale conditioning and facilities. The course is fair yet challenging, especially for the price.

Wildhorse Golf Club (702-434-9000; www.golfwildhorse.com; 2100 Warm Springs Road, Henderson) Municipally operated.

Boulder City Golf Course (702-293-9236; 1 Clubhouse Drive, Boulder City; www.bouldercitygolf.com) As an older course, there are hundreds of mature trees and large greens. Walking is allowed.

Boulder Creek Golf Club (702-294-6534; www.bouldercreekgc.com; 1501 Veterans Memorial Drive, Boulder City) Though it's 30 minutes from the Strip, this course is a golf value. Boulder Creek consists of three 9-hole courses, Desert Hawke, Coyote Run, and Eldorado.

HIKING AND BACKPACKING

It is said that Las Vegas is one of the best cities to visit if you're looking to take a hike, and it's easy to see why. Feasibly, one could drive in any direction until the road turns to dirt, park the car, and hit the trail. Well, maybe not an *established* trail, however, and therein rests the problem. There are thousands of square miles of desert around Vegas to get lost in, but that's probably exactly what you'd get—lost. Instead of taking a chance out in the great unknown, why not try some of the well-worn, mapped trails in the Las Vegas Valley and its surrounding recreation areas, and save your risk-taking for the tables instead? The following is a sampling of some of the finest hiking found in Las Vegas, and indeed in all the Southwest. Happy trails!

Red Rock Canyon

Several trailheads of varying distances and degrees of difficulty are located on the Red Rock Scenic Loop Drive—23 in all. What follows is a sampling of some of the trails found in Red Rock Canyon, but a complete, descriptive list of trail names, lengths, and degrees of difficulty is available at www.redrockcanyonlv.org. One of the easiest and shortest trails begins at the first trailhead you come to, the **Moenkopi** trail. At 2 miles long, it's about an hour and a half round trip, with views of the Spring Mountains, Calico Hills, and Wilson Cliffs. Further up the road, the **Keystone Thrust** trail is a moderately difficult hike of 2.2 miles that should also be about an hour and a half round trip. Along this trail, you'll visit the Keystone Thrust, an area where older rock was thrust over newer rock about 65–70 million years ago, creating spectacular red, orange, and pink sandstone formations. The most difficult hike of this group is the **Turtlehead Peak** hike, so named because this trek, at five miles long and gaining over its course 2,000 feet of altitude, takes you from Sandstone Quarry to the top of Turtlehead Peak, at 6,324 feet. By all accounts, it's a hike that can be tricky in places, especially near the summit, but a popular one among local hikers for its brilliant views of the Spring Range and the Las Vegas Valley.

> INSIDER TIP: The Red Rock Canyon Scenic Drive and its hiking trails attract many visitors—weekends are extremely busy, parking tends to be at a premium, and you'll have lots of company on the trail. Holiday weekends are even worse. Come on a weekday for a more relaxed visit and an easier time finding a parking spot.

Spring Mountains National Recreation Area

The Spring Mountains offer some fantastic places to hike away from the heat and hectic pace of Las Vegas—limestone peaks tower above while bristlecone and ponderosa pines sigh in the mountain breeze, and all you'll hear is the crunch of gravel and pine needles under your boots. Several trails of varying degrees of difficulty can be accessed, and some of the more popular of these trails include the **Mary Jane Falls Trail**, a moderately strenuous trek on a well-used trail that culminates at the base of Mary Jane Falls; the **Fletcher Canyon Trail**, an easy hike that features a gain in elevation of only about 850 feet and takes you down a dry streambed and some gorgeous mountain flora; and the **Mummy Springs Trail**, a three-mile hike on which you can visit the "Raintree," a bristlecone pine tree that is said to be the oldest living thing in Nevada. Consult www.fs.fed.us/r4/htnf/districts for a complete list of trails maintained by the U.S. Forest Service in the Spring Mountains NRA, including maps, descriptions, and traverse times.

Whether you are in a car, on foot, or riding a horse or bike, Red Rock Canyon provides Las Vegas's finest outdoor recreation. Las Vegas News Bureau

HORSEBACK RIDING

Here's an activity that points directly to the lightning speed growth of Las Vegas's urban sprawl. Until the early 1980s, horseback riding could be found in neighborhoods on the outskirts of the more populated areas. Now, equine enthusiasts have to head out of town for fun. There are many tour groups that offer horseback rides as well. But since not all of them can be checked on for horse health, the two most trusted are listed.

Cowboy Trail Rides (702-387-2457; www.cowboytrailrides.com) (Take West Charleston past the Red Rock Resort, continue west for 8 miles. It's the only left.) Six different tours are offered ranging from one hour to five. This is a perfect way to see Redrock Canyon as longtime locals do. If you don't bring water or soda, they're available for purchase before and after rides. Reservations are strongly recommended, as holidays, weather, and conventions can increase the number of interested riders. Children over 8 years of age are welcome. Those thirteen and under will be required to wear a provided helmet. Transportation can be provided; call ahead for details. Tour costs: $89 to $390

Mount Charleston Riding Stables (702-872-7009; Mt. Charleston Restaurant and Lodge; US 95 north 6 miles past the Santa Fe to state route 157. Turn left and travel 18 miles to the Mt. Charleston Lodge.) The 3.5-hour trail ride takes you into Fletcher Canyon with aspen trees singing in the wind. Overnight wilderness rides are available, too. A short 38 miles from downtown, the ride is $60 prepaid and prereserved, the 25-minute rides are $8 adults, $6 children 3–6, and free for the little ones under 3.

PARKS

Parks in Las Vegas are a newer idea, especially when compared to cities around the country, for a number of reasons, one of the most important being a lack of precipitation. It takes a long time for trees to get large here, and as water is more precious than gold in the desert, trees and grass are also quite expensive. Over the past 15 years, city planners and housing developers have created parks that work better in an arid environment while helping to foster an area of community and family fun. The parks below are listed for those who are visiting from cold or wet or gloomy places where sunshine is the sought-after commodity. Las Vegas residents can spot you a mile away because you're wearing shorts in December and sitting out by the pool, even though it's been closed since September. If it's the dead of summer, don't be surprised by parks with little to offer in the way of shade trees. You've been warned.

Centennial Hills Park

(7101 North Buffalo Drive) Centennial Hills Park has an informative fossil wall and giant steel sculptures of prehistoric animals that once roamed the area. During the warmer months the colorful playground turns on a splash pad. There are also soccer fields, dog runs, horseshoe pits, and a jogging/walking path. The outdoor grass amphitheater with seating capacity for 3,500 hosts family films and plays. Near the amphitheater is the first fully Americans with Disabilities Act (ADA)-compliant playground in Las Vegas. This playground allows children of all abilities to play together and is accessible for children with disabilities, with ramps and plays areas designed specifically to allow wheelchair access. The playground is challenging for fully able children as well. It is built into a hillside with three levels accessible via ramps and bridges, and offers activity features conducive to those with disabilities.

Tennis players rejoice at the more than 20 courts in the Darling Tennis Center. Charo Burke

Charlie Kellogg and Joe Zaher Sports Complex

(7901 West Washington Avenue, between Buffalo and Durango) Tennis and soccer fans rejoice, because Las Vegas has got you covered. This 110-acre park has 23 tennis courts, including one that seats 2,800 spectators, and 11 lighted soccer fields—seven artificial turf and four natural. There are three dog-only areas split up by canine size, a 2.5-mile walking/jogging path that surrounds the park, and two playgrounds. UNLV men's and women's soccer teams play some of their home games here—for the current schedule check www.unlvrebels.cstv.com. Tennis court fees at the complex's **Darling Tennis Center** (702-229-2100) are $3.50 an hour (ages 19–49). Free play hours are Mon. through Thurs. Noon–2 PM. Hours can change due to special events. Otherwise they are Mon.–Fri. 9 AM–5 PM, Sat. 7 AM–7 PM and Sun. 7 AM–5 PM.

Dog Parks

Give your dog a chance to get to know Las Vegas, too. Dog parks here can get very busy. Please be sure that your dog is okay with a lot of doggy attention before venturing to one. In Clark County, dog owners are expected to pick up after their dogs not only because it's the nice thing to do but also because it's the law.

Silverado Ranch Park Dog Park (9855 South Gillespie) Silverado Ranch dog runs include: benches, lights, water. Two runs are available.

Sunset Park Dog Park (2601 East Sunset Rd.) There are two dog runs on the south side of Sunset Lake for large and small pets with benches, tables, and water taps. The closest parking is off Eastern Ave. between Sunset and Warm Springs roads.

Desert Breeze (8425 West Spring Mountain Rd.) The three dog runs are divided by size small, medium, and large (over 30 pounds). If you have a big dog (especially an older one) who prefers little ones as playmates, ask the dog owners present if your pup can join in on the fun. The dog runs are located on the south side of the park off the park road and is accessible from either Durango or Spring Mountain. Water taps are available for dogs.

Molasky Park—Dog Run (1065 East Twain) Dog runs are located off Katie Rd. and include sitting areas and water taps. There are three dog runs at this 10-acre park.

Shadow Rock Park—Dog Park (2650 Los Feliz) The dog run is located east of park area toward the mountain, which provides a beautiful and relaxing environment to exercise your pets. The facility also includes trees, two shade shelters, benches, and water taps.

Firefighters Memorial Park
(West Oakey at Redwood) Those looking to pay tribute to the firefighters who gave their lives on 9/11 in helping those that needed them most that day will want to stop by this memorial park. The names of the fallen are etched in a stone tablet that is part of a nearly 10-foot-tall sculpture designed by artist and firefighter John Banks. There are also picnic areas and two playgrounds.

Floyd Lamb Park
(About 20 miles from the Strip; take Highway 95 north past Ann Road, follow the signs. Entrance is on right.) While Las Vegas may be new, this area has been visited since prehistoric times. When Southern Nevada had more rain and cooler temperatures, mammals

Peacocks at Floyd Lamb Park. Charo Burke

would gather here to drink from what is now called Tule Springs. Fossils of mammoths and giant sloths have been found here. Then came the Indians of the area, followed by prospectors. Eventually, a dude ranch was built so that those waiting for their divorce could stay the required six weeks here. At the time, this was the shortest required residency in the country. About 100 acres was also a working ranch, Tule Springs Ranch, for raising cattle and growing alfalfa. The ranch buildings are still there and show the early Las Vegas lifestyle. Since 1964, it had been a state park but was recently transferred to the city. Today the more than 680-acre park hosts four stocked ponds, scenic paths, volleyball courts, and horseshoe areas. Open year round May–August, 8 AM to 8 PM, September–April, 9 AM–5 PM. Fees are $6 per car or $1 per person, whichever is greater. Cash only.

ICE SKATING

Ice skating in the desert may seem like an oxymoron, but we do have many athletic folks from all over the world performing in our many shows. Thanks to the many Cirque du Soleil employees living in the valley, ice skating can be pretty popular.

Fiesta Rancho Casino Ice Arena (702-631-7000 2400; www.fiestarancholasvegas.com/entertainment/ice/; North Rancho Drive, North Las Vegas) An NHL regulation-size, 31,000-square-foot ice rink located inside the property.

Las Vegas Ice Center (702-320-7777; www.lasvegasice.com; 9295 West Flamingo Road, Las Vegas) Home of the AAA Nevada Stars. Adults: $9; Youth (5–18 yrs): $8; Child (under 5 yrs): $7. All prices include skates.

MonteLago Village Ice Skating Rink (888-387-1234; Lake Las Vegas Resort, 30 Strada di Villagio, Henderson) One of the first floating ice rinks in the country, at 40 by 80 feet it can hold up to 60 skaters at a time. Open Thanksgiving week through mid-February. Public skate sessions daily noon–9 PM. Closed Christmas Eve. Public skating 3 PM–9 PM on Christmas Day; Noon–9 PM on New Year's Eve; Noon–9 PM on New Year's Day. All-day pass $12.

RUNNING

Runners living in a cold and wet weather climate can get very antsy during the winter. So vacations to warmer, drier locales are a must. Feel free to join the No Whining Wednesdays running group at a well-stocked one-stop running shop, **Red Rock Running Company** located at 7350 West Cheyenne (702-870-4786). Starting promptly at 5:30 PM, regardless of the weather, this group isn't about chatting but about serious running for 6 to 8 miles. Be on time, because they don't wait for stragglers. If that day doesn't work for you and you don't want to run alone, check out the Web site for the Las Vegas Track Club (www.lvtc.org).

Bootleg Canyon (1021 Yucca Street, Boulder City) Although it's about 45 minutes southeast of Las Vegas, Bootleg Canyon has 15 challenging trails. Located in charming Boulder City, the canyon is also home to a world-famous mountain biking park. The River Mountain Hiking Trail, which leads from the St. Jude's parking lot to the summit of Black Mountain Overlook, is closed to biking and is dedicated to runners and hikers exclusively.

Las Vegas Boulevard Rising in the wee hours may be the only way you'll get to run the Strip. But, there's something to be said for being on one of the most recognizable streets in the world before the action gets started. It's surreal. Tourists from far-off places are trying to adjust to the time zone, employees cleaning up from the night before, and casino workers heading home make up most of the population. From the Sahara to Mandalay Bay and back is almost 7.5 miles.

Las Vegas Hilton Complimentary running path circling the perimeter of the hotel. You need not be a guest of the hotel. There are some curves and minor slopes, but the material used on most of the track makes it a comfortable run.

Red Rock Canyon There just can't be enough said about the splendor that is Red Rock Canyon. It's one of the things of which Las Vegans are most proud. Enjoy it every way possible and you'll agree. The Moenkopi Loop starts at the visitor center. A few minutes there will let you know what you are gaping at. The loop ends back at the center and is two miles. The main trail at the rock climbing area is about 3.5 miles.

University UNLV Campus Track Head east on either East Tropicana or East Flamingo for nearly two miles to arrive at the campus. The track is located near the center of campus near the softball field. Be sure to pay close attention to where you park. Citations can be given for parking outside Guest Parking areas.

SKIING/SNOWBOARDING

Snow in Las Vegas is a true rarity. And although it can happen, it doesn't last. If it does, run out of the casino quickly and get a picture. Snow and The Strip are one of those once-in-a-lifetime photos that will make the folks back home go "huh?" That being said, Las Vegas is 75 miles from Utah. But there is one ski resort you can get to for the day.

Las Vegas Ski and Snowboard Resort (Take U.S. Highway 95 north approx. 30 miles to Highway 156, Lee Canyon. Follow Highway 156 for 17 miles) Only ski resort in Southern Nevada. Ski and snowboard rentals available. Bib and jacket rental, too. Snowboard and skiing lessons for children (6–12) and adults (group and private). Average annual snowfall, 120 in. Eleven trails, four lifts, longest run 3,000 feet. Darkside Terrain Park offers a variety of terrain features including tabletop jumps, assorted rails, and 500-foot intermediate half-pipe. The season is roughly Thanksgiving through Easter. Open daily 9 AM–4 PM.

Lee Canyon is an easy drive from the city.
Las Vegas News Bureau

Palazzo Shops: many high-end shopping choices and smaller crowds. Courtesy Shoppes at Palazzo

9

Shopping

Better Bring an Extra Suitcase

First Las Vegas was known for fast divorces, then gambling, next came entertainment, which was followed by family-driven fun. And although the theme parks have long been paved over, the other Las Vegas draws have remained successful. Over the last 20 years, Las Vegas has become an international shopping destination. It started with the Fashion Show mall. the first full-fledged shopping center on the Strip, and it hasn't showed any signs of stopping.

Contrary to the stereotypes, Las Vegas residents do not wear sequins unless they're onstage. Those that do have moved here from elsewhere and were fans of the bedazzled look long before they arrived. Residents also don't tend to wear items with gambling designs emblazoned all over. The shirts with poker suits and slot machines done in puffy paint are worn by visitors and while they're always welcome, no one should mistake them for a local.

The more than 45 million square feet of retail space assures that there's something here for everyone. Many visitors, domestic and international, pack little to nothing in their luggage so that all their purchases will fit at the trip's end. On average, visitors spend more on shopping than shows and sightseeing combined and say that it is an important factor in deciding their trip. From the enormous international chain stores to the haute couture flagship boutiques, Las Vegas has all that the fashion conscious are seeking.

Most can find what they want in one of the many retail malls or plazas on the Strip. For those looking for something more unique, we've listed stores throughout the Valley. This section includes stores that can only be found in Las Vegas and those that are just unusual enough or specialized for a specific audience.

No matter which hotel you're staying at, there's always shopping nearby. Many hotels have at least a small promenade of shops. Where multiple locations are listed for an outlet, the location nearest to the Strip is first.

ON THE STRIP MALLS

Fashion Show Las Vegas (702-784-7000; www.thefashionshow.com; 3200 Las Vegas Boulevard South) When the Fashion Show Mall opened on the Las Vegas Strip in the early 1980s, it ushered in the era of high-end Vegas shopping for the masses. Upscale shops have always had a presence at most major strip properties, but they generally were the bailiwick of moneyed tourists; The Fashion Show, with major anchors **Saks Fifth Avenue**

and **Neiman Marcus,** brought in as many locals as it did visitors and quickly became one of the premier shopping destinations in Las Vegas. Fashion Show Las Vegas has since undergone a massive renovation; in 2004, a four-year project expanded the mall to more than twice its previous size (it's now almost 2 million square feet and one of the largest malls in America) and added new design elements, such as The Great Hall and the Plaza, and, towering above the mall out on Las Vegas Boulevard, the Cloud, a 480-foot long, 128-foot high (at its highest point) canopy on which four huge video screens play images day and night. Fashion Show Las Vegas, in addition to its over 250 shops and restaurants, hosts free runway shows three days a week and as many as seven times daily in the Great Hall on an 80-foot long runway that rises out of the floor to a height of about four feet. At one end of the runway is the Box, a staging area for the runway shows. It's actually a huge elevator in which the models dress and prepare for shows, and then ride up to the runway—the rear of the box is the changing room, the front of the box all that's visible to the audience and is designed specifically for each show—and it rises out of the floor along with the runway, at the start of each show. It's really something to see—when visiting the Fashion Show mall, don't miss it. Extensive concierge services are available at Fashion Show Las Vegas, including package checking and delivery (your purchases can be checked and then brought directly to your car after your shopping excursion), restaurant reservations, photocopies and faxing, Las Vegas visitor information, and for an extra charge, car detailing while you shop. As is usually the case in Vegas, free parking at the mall is extensive, both covered and uncovered.

The Forum Shops 702-893-4800; Caesars Palace) The Forum Shops at Caesars, with its opening in 1992, started the trend of resort-centered shopping malls. With 634,000 square feet of shopping space spread throughout more than 160 boutiques, shops, specialty stores, and restaurants, the Forum Shops still remains the premium casino-based destination mall on the Strip. Designed to reflect the greatness of the Roman Empire, the mall is lavishly decorated with cobblestone walkways, Ionic columns, and replicas of the Trevi and Triton Fountains. It's by far the most pleasant mall to just walk through and enjoy. The ceiling is painted with a sky and goes from dawn to dusk about each hour. This can throw your body clock off a little bit if you spend a whole day here. Stores vary widely from the amazing **Houdini's Magic Shop** and **Playboy** for your own set of Bunny gear; to top-name luxury stores such as the internationally renowned **Burberry,** noted for its check-patterned scarves, jackets, and other goods; high-fashion apparel retailers **Christian Dior, Fendi, Gianni Versace, Roberto Cavalli, Salvatore Ferragamo,** and **Valentino;** leather goods and accessory giants **Gucci, Louis Vuitton,** and **Coach,** and exclusive jewelers to the stars and to the wealthy, **Harry Winston** and **Bulgari.** Though there are **Victoria's Secret** lingerie stores in every major city, there isn't one like the one here. This location has different décor, divided boutiques, and an "adults only" area. Need to recharge your batteries after such amazing shopping? Take a breather and dine in one of the sixteen restaurants. Have a bottle of wine at Wolfgang Puck's restaurants: **Spago** for American food and **Chinois** for Asian cuisine; or have some sweets at the **The Cheesecake Factory** or a hearty meal at **BOA Steakhouse.** Make sure to catch both the Festival Fountain and the Fall of Atlantis fountain shows at the top of every hour from 10 AM to 11 PM. Watch the special effects and animatronic figures as the Festival Fountain statues come alive to celebrate the history of the Roman Empire, and the figures at the Fall of Atlantis Fountain retell the story of Atlantis's demise. After the show, continue walking through the mall and ponder the over 100 species of tropical puffers, sharks, flounder, and other sea creatures in a 50,000-gallon saltwater aquarium. Feedings are each day at 1:15 and 5:15 PM. Specific common areas of The Forum Shops are open 24 hours a day and the wee hours can allow for some unencumbered window-shopping of stores in this vicinity.

Grand Canal Shoppes (702-414-4525; www.grandcanalshoppes.com; The Venetian) Upscale shops, live "street" performers and gondola rides are intended to give that Italian galleria feeling. It's estimated that 20 million visitors come through here each year. Even if the stores are not your preference or style, it's a cool stroll when it's unbearable outside. Although when the foot traffic is plenty, the path can become somewhat claustrophobic each time it crosses over the canal. The canal is one quarter mile long, indoors and out. The gondola rides with singing gondoliers are available for same-day reservations only and are on a first-come, first-served basis (702-414-4908). Stores in Grand Canal Shoppes are mostly upscale but are varied; some here are making their Las Vegas or American debut. If want the toothbrush that Oprah has, you'll need to visit **Acca Kappa**. This Italian bath and beauty company has been manufacturing their products since 1869 and this is their only store in the states. **Ancient Creations** carries one-of-a-kind jewelry made from ancient coins from throughout the Old World, including Greece, Asia, and medieval Europe. Carrying all those shopping bags can build up an appetite. Good thing there's no shortness of eating establishments in Grand Canal Shoppes. From fresh seafood and a water-encased wine cellar at **AquaKnox**, to Italian food and an imported 40-foot-high bar at Zeffirino, there are choices here for almost every palate. If dining takes away from precious shopping time, there are casual eateries, too. Add zip to your shopping energy with coffee and gelato at Cocolini or bulk up on protein and carbs with burgers and fries at Johnny Rockets. If eating is simply out of the question, stop by the oxygen bar, **Breathe**, to inhale some pep into your step.

Miracle Mile Shops (702-866-0703; www.miraclemileshopslv.com; Planet Hollywood) Miracle Mile shops have undergone a lot of recent construction. What was once Desert Passage in what was once the Aladdin is now Miracle Mile at Planet Hollywood. The 1.2 miles of storefronts in Miracle Mile are geared a bit more toward shoppers looking for something special as opposed to the "if you're looking for a price tag, it's out of your price range" shops. Along with sleeker modern décor are 170 shops, 15 restaurants, free rain-storm fountain show, and two live performance theaters. In Miracle Mile there are the only Las Vegas locations of fashion stalwarts **GUESS? Accessories**, athletic attire from **Volcom**, **TOUS of Barcelona**, and local darlings **Vegas Royalty**. The only locations of Las Vegas microbrewer **Sin City Brewing Company** and 1950s-inspired **Bettie Page** can be found here. Don't let the mile length be too intimidating. It's a circular mile, keeping you from having to walk to one end and back again. The entertainment contained within goes from the family friendly to the hubba-hubba. There's bizarre magic and comedy from **the Amazing Jonathan**, a Beatles live tribute from **Fab Four**, and the sounds of Motown in **Hitzville**. Kids will love **Popovich Comedy Pet Theater**. Adults might prefer the educational **Stripper 101**.

> INSIDER TIP: Check mall Web sites for packages, discounts, and offers on specific retail shops. These range from free gifts with purchase to discounts via the Web only. Packages can include treatments at health and beauty stores.

Pick up a complimentary map to avoid walking in unnecessary circles at Miracle Mile. Courtesy Miracle Mile

MonteLago Village (702-564-4700; www.montelagovillage.com; Lake Las Vegas; 30 Strada di Villaggio, Henderson) MonteLago Village at Lake Las Vegas calls to mind a quaint Italian village, replete with winding cobblestone streets, restaurants, a waterfront, and boutiques. Its architectural style is chic Mediterranean, and its shops are varied. **Moonbeams** features gifts for women, after which you may want to stop at **Splash Bath and Body** to further pamper the lady in your life. At **Tesoro,** you'll find interesting gifts from far-off places, and at **Sunset and Vines** there's something for every wine lover, including uncommon selections. Stop into **Flights of Fancy** and check out their colorful kites, wind socks, banners, and garden accessories—if it dances on the wind, they have it. MonteLago Village also often hosts art and craft shows, which set up along the streets in good weather. Seasonal activities are offered as well—in the winter there is a floating ice rink that is open to the public, and on certain summer nights the ice rink is a floating stage on which the "Stars On The Lake" concert series is presented.

The Fashion Show Mall was the first on the Strip for serious shoppers. Courtesy Fashion Show Mall

The Shoppes at Palazzo (702-414-4525; www.theshoppesatpalazzo.com; The Palazzo) Palazzo Shoppes doesn't have a Disney-like theme, but it does have more than 60 exclusive stores and boutiques, along with 10 restaurants and the most whimsical complimentary entertainment on the Strip—the Living Garden. Nearly half of the stores are firsts for Las Vegas, including **Barney's of New York, Diane von Furstenburg, Links of London,** and **Jimmy Choo.** The list of celebrity chefs and restaurants would make a certain food cable channel jealous. There's Wolfgang Puck's **CUT,** Charlie Trotter's **Restaurant Charlie,** Emeril Lagasse's **Table 10,** and Shimon Bokava's **SushiSamba,** to name just a few. For those who want to be sure that no one will be wearing the same outfit at the club, try **Annie Creamcheese.** This is the first high-end mall vintage store in the world. It's couture from the 1960s, 1970s, and 1980s that wasn't cheap then and isn't cheap now. Once you're tired of walking from store to store, have a seat across from the waterfall, between the escalators. Here the Living Garden relives the childhood fantasy that inanimate objects, such as statues, could move, and, if you watched a creeping vine long enough, it would look back. This isn't one of those shticks where the unsuspecting bystander is surprised when a statue suddenly jumps at them. This is imagining the statues coming to the fountain to do their daily tasks. The ambient music is relaxing and along with the waterfall the show is downright refreshing. When everything else in Las Vegas moves at an alarming pace, the Living Garden moves at a meditative one.

Town Square (702-269-5000; www.townsquarelasvegas.com; 6605 Las Vegas Boulevard South) Located south of Sunset Road on the Strip, Town Square Las Vegas embodies a shopping concept whose time has finally come in Las Vegas—it's a complex of shops and restaurants laid out like a tiny town, with a park at its center. Abundant free parking is available outside the mall itself, both covered and uncovered, and metered parking is available within Town Square, so it's possible to drive right up to the shop or restaurant of your choice. But if you choose to walk, you'll enjoy Town Square's modern Mission-style

Pick up a healthy lunch and enjoy it al fresco at Town Square Mall. Leah Koepp

architecture and the lovely seasonal flowers, palm trees, and ornamental grasses that line its flagstone paths. With over 175 shops and restaurants and an 18-screen movie theater, there's much for the intrepid shopper to explore. **Banana Republic, Ann Taylor Loft, Chico's, ALDO, Borders Book Shop, Lucky Brand Jeans, Hollister,** and **Eddie Bauer** are just a few of the stores at Town Square, and the dining choices are equally plentiful— **California Pizza Kitchen, Claim Jumper,** and **Texas de Brazil** are all here. If a simple picnic is more your speed, nip on over to Whole Foods Market for the fixings and spread your blanket out at Town Square Park and enjoy the sunshine by the pond. Concierge service is available also, which can provide strollers, umbrellas, and wheelchairs as well as restaurant reservations, show tickets, and airport transportation.

ON THE STRIP, NOT EVERYWHERE ELSE

Agent Provocateur (702-696-7174; www.agentprovocateur.com; Forum Shops) Agent Provocateur is a petite store about the size of a sexy European boudoir. This isn't the shop to be shy in. There is only one size of each item on display, so you must ask for help with sizing. The collections from this British lingerie brand are designed to fit popular themes like pirates and witches. But don't think camp like hats with feathers, think bodice-ripping from classic romantic novels. Other lingerie lines include bridal and classic. Fans of the store include Kylie Minogue, Scarlett Johansson, Heidi Klum, and Julianne Moore.

Alexander McQueen (702-770-3490; www.alexandermcqueen.com; Wynn) The sheen of the white plastic may look like what some imagine Agent 99's closet to look like, but Alexander McQueen is not a vintage or kitsch store. Those wanting to appear to be a star will make note that Sarah Jessica Parker and Brad Pitt wear McQueen clothes. Think designs made to wear forever with a British design flair.

The Manilow Store (702-732-5111; www.lvhilton.com; Las Vegas Hilton) If you're a Barry Manilow fan, then you know this store is here because you already bought your tickets to his show at the Las Vegas Hilton. But if you have someone on your souvenir list who is an immense admirer of the man who makes the whole world sing, then this shop is one to stop in. Whether it's bobble heads, sheet music, jewelry, or wine, this store has it. If you think you've got the chops (or even if you don't), there's a state-of-the-art vocal booth where you can record yourself singing "Mandy" or many other Manilow songs.

Bonanza Gift Shop (702-385-7359; www.worldslargestgiftshop.com; 2440 Las Vegas Boulevard South) If it's kitschy and has dice on it, it can be found here. If it's a slot machine cookie jar, toilet seat, or key

Why search all over for the tackiest Las Vegas souvenir when you can find them all in one place?
Charo Burke

chain, it's here. If it has the Las Vegas Welcome Sign on it, it's found here. How about a shot glass decorated with showgirls? But of course. Throughout the 40,000 square feet there is every type of souvenir imaginable—that isn't a licensed item, that is. If it's a Cirque du Soleil T-shirt you're looking for, best to go to the resort where that particular show plays. Definitely worth the visit.

C Level (702-933-6867; www.clevel-lv.com; 750 South Rampart) Dressing rooms, who needs 'em? That's up to you at this ultraposh men's and women's clothing and accessory boutique where the glass dressing rooms let you choose how much of you everyone sees. Using adjustable lighting, the customer can share the experience of trying on clothes as much or as little as wanted. Named one of the best boutiques in the nation for up-and-comers by Lucky magazine, there's even a PlayStation station to keep your kids or partner occupied. The men's level has a pool table for when shopping just becomes too much even for themselves. Owner, Edith Castillo, handpicks the clothes found here; designers include Ya-Ya, L.AMB., Voom, and 12th Street.

Champagne Suzy Boutique (702-632-9442; Mandalay Bay) Champagne Suzy is a modern-day burlesque hero, like her foremothers Gypsy Rose Lee and Blaze Starr. Suzy sees the striptease dance as an art form. Live models in the display window showcase the lingerie and sexy clothing. At her boutique is clothing and lingerie with a 1920s and 1930s style, designed for re-creating the bump and grind found at Forty Deuce, the burlesque club next door.

Chippendales Store (702-252-7777; www.chippendales.com; Rio) From the famous calendars of the infamous dancers to naughty underwear for him, the Chippendales store carries the expected trinkets. Thankfully for some, this store provides a way to purchase mugs, pens, T-shirts, and hats emblazoned with male specimens without having to actually see the show. For lovers of the all-male revue, it's an opportunity to take home a souvenir.

Davidoff of Geneva (702-737-0326; www.davidofflv.com; Mandalay Bay Place) Cigar and pipe smokers feel that their vice is a suave one. Davidoff of Geneva is a polished store with sleek wood and shiny glass cases. The cigars are on display like artifacts collected by Indiana Jones, and the staff guides you to your choice. Their knowledge and enthusiasm for cigars and pipes shows in their service. The pipe smoker or collector will be a kid in candy store when they see the hundreds of pipes available, including an array of beasts mythological and factual. The smaller kiosk store is located in the Mandalay Bay casino. The full-size store is in the Mandalay Place shops. Two other locations can be found at MGM Grand (702-933-2105) and the Venetian (702-733-5999).

FAO Schwartz (702-796-6500; www.fao.com; The Forum Shops) Claim it's for the kid(s) that had to be left at home with grandma but admit it, really a trip to FAO Schwartz is more for those who go than those who get. This one's three stories high with a 47-foot-high Trojan horse at the entrance. The famous extra-large Dance-On piano is on the second floor, which is also where dolls are located. Barbie fanatics will be drawn to a totally pink area here. Others may want to keep far from the palace of pink. Stormtroopers and Hogwarts merchandise can be found on the third floor.

Fruition (702-796-4139; wwwfruitionlv.com; 4139 South Maryland Parkway) A vintage store that specializes in urban and 1980s fashion with an emphasis on old-school hip-hop, that's Fruition. It not only takes a stylish individual to pull it off, but a store that's willing to track and hunt down the specialized items from Nike, Cross Colors, Fila, Jeremy Scott, Dr.

Romanelli, and a host of others. The shop's blog (link on the store's Web site) is an excellent way to see if they have any Instapump Reeboks in Fury from the 1997 collection or retro Adidas Olympic sweatshirts and sport suits.

The Hat Company (888-830-4287; www.thehatco.com; Las Vegas Outlet Center) The name says it all. Hats, hats, and more hats. There's some for the Red Hat Society, a nice selection for those with large craniums, and those who want to tell everyone back home they went to Mardi Gras, not Las Vegas. At the time of this writing, there were four different Indiana Jones hats that range from the collector's edition at $350 to the Stetson at $120. If you've arrived in Las Vegas during the warmer months and didn't pack a hat to keep the blistering sun off your face, here's your next stop.

Inexpensive options and a wide array of sizes may be found at the Hat Company. Charo Burke

Hermès (702-650-3116; www.hermes.com; Wynn Encore) Women in Paris and throughout Europe respect and understand a Hermès scarf. The flowing fabrics with bold patterns are a sign of class and good taste. While this may not be the case with all employees, it's said that the Las Vegas locations have the friendlier employees of all the Hermès boutiques. They'll also show you the many ways to wear a Hermès scarf, bringing you closer to looking like a Parisian woman. The men's Hermès line can also be found here, including ties and cuff links.

Indian River Gallery (702-598-3929; www.indianrivergallery.com; Miracle Mile Shops) A phenomenal gallery carrying the work of some of the finest Native American artists. The bronze collection alone is worth the trip. There's also stunning jewelry from acclaimed artisans such as Charles Loloma. The pottery is truly astounding to behold and best appreciated in person. The Acoma pots by S.L. Stevens are stunning. It takes guarded, passed-down, knowledge to create the clay, and a steady hand to use a sliver of yucca as the brush. Those interested in starting with something small shouldn't be intimidated. The staff are patient and knowledgeable. They also carry kachinas, weavings, fetishes, baskets, paintings, and knives.

Lamborghini (702-671-0025; www.lamborghinilasvegas.com; 7770 Dean Martin Drive # 301) The Lamborghini Las Vegas showroom and fashion store at the original location on Dean Martin Boulevard, and now its newest location at the Palazzo Resort and Casino, are dreams come true for car enthusiasts. The 20,000-square-foot original showroom features exotically engineered beauties including the new Lamborghini Reventon. Not in the mood for spending hundreds of thousands on a car? The Lamborghini Las Vegas has used models for those still wanting the thrill but not the hefty price tag. But, if you are one of the mere mortals who can only dream about owning a Lamborghini, don't be sullen. The location on Dean Martin also has a fashion section in its store and sells those important accessories such as hats, briefcases, swimsuits, fur-trimmed jackets, iPod carriers, and logo shirts that can only reveal your true passion for the cars. Stop by, drool, and marvel at the unique craftsmanship and elegance that can be found only in a Lamborghini.

Leor Jewelry & Timepieces (702-944-3483; The Palms) The Yerushalmi family has owned successful jewelry stores throughout Las Vegas for more than 30 years. Each of the casino locations caters to the clientele of that property. As this one is on The Palms, like those who frequent the property, the merchandise at Leor is young, edgy, hip, and cutting edge. Thos looking for watches hard to find else where, will want to stop in to look over the Tag Heuer, Chopard, and IWC lines. The jewelry here sets the bar when it comes to celebrity bling. Some of the stars buying their ice at Leor include Shaquille O'Neal, Vince Carter, Justin Timberlake, Jennifer Lopez, Jackie Chan, Barry Bonds, and Britney Spears. Rapper Ginuwine had his PlayStation controller adorned with $250K worth of diamonds here.

M&Ms World (702-736-7611; www.mymms.com; 3785 Las Vegas Boulevard) Not only are M&Ms one of America's favorite candy, but there are enough of them sold to warrant a four-story store. What do you fill up 28,000 square feet of retail space with? How about 22 colors of the candy? Whether you want them to match your team jersey or your wedding bouquet, chances are the color is here. In fact, those which do not melt in your hand are movie stars as well. The free 3D movie "I Lost My M In Las Vegas," starring Red and Yellow from the commercials, is surprisingly worth it.

Mikimoto (702-414-3900; www.mikimoto.com; The Venetian) The cultured pearl has been a sign of class since Kokichi Mikomoto created the first in 1893. So revered and respected are Mikomoto pearls that only the top 5 percent of Japan's harvest is good enough for the name. The Tournament of Roses has had the crown designed and produced by them and when they are not being worn by the Rose Queen and Rose Princesses, they can be seen on display here. They have also provided the Miss Universe Crown and Carrie's necklace in the Sex and the City movie.

New Rock, Boots and Shoes (702-614-9464; www.newrockstore.com; 804 Las Vegas Boulevard South) These are serious boots made for serious stomping. Imagine Marilyn Manson mixed with Mad Max and a bad-ass comic-book hero. Apparently they are very comfy to wear, which is humorous, since they are pretty intimidating to look at. This is one of the few stores carrying this Spanish brand exclusively.

Plant World (702-878-9485; www.plantworldnursery.com; 5311 West Charleston Boulevard) Just because Las Vegas is in the Mojave Desert does not mean that the city is arid and barren. Plant World, since its opening in 1976, has carried the largest selection of trees, shrubs, and other plants and plant accessories in the Las Vegas Valley. It has an incredible selection of tropical varieties and exotics that are surprisingly desert friendly, as well as plants that are native to the region. The selection is vast and broken up into sections of shrubs, roses, sod, vines, perennials, vegetables, bonsais and topiaries, cacti, palm trees, ground cover, and even drought-tolerant plants. Pick up a grapevine, a magnolia tree, or even a fern for your bathroom. While there, make sure to stop at the houseplant greenhouse for blast of jungle atmosphere, dripping with large leaves and vines from every corner. Then, stop by the large outdoor birdcage with dozens of parrots, macaws, and parakeets as they relish life in the warm Las Vegas sunshine.

Punishment MMA (www.punishmentathletics.com; Hooters Casino; 115 East Tropicana) Tito Oritz, champion mixed-martial-arts fighter, now has a clothing store featuring his own clothing line called Punishment, along with other top MMA clothing lines such as TapOut, Sinister, DeathClutch, Throwdown, Hitman, and Warrior.

Reading Room (702-632-9374; Mandalay Bay)
There are rare bookstores in Las Vegas, as in many other cities. However, the Reading Room is a bookstore in a casino, which is exceedingly rare. There was a time when rumors of their untimely closing were exaggerated but the store is open and succeeding. Here's the only traditional bookstore on the Strip and it's stocked with all types of titles, not just those written to read by the pool. Join in on the lively discussion each Tuesday night when the Socrates Café Discussion group holds an open meeting. All are welcome.

Sephora (702-737-0550; www.sephora.com; Miracle Mile) Europe's leading beauty chain, they're not in this book because this is their only U.S. location. There are plenty of them around the nation. But, should you get to Las Vegas and realize that you didn't bring the nail polish that matches the dress you brought or that your mascara is almost out and you are loyal to a specific brand, you can rest assured, it's most likely on their shelves. Check their Web site for store events, complimentary swag, and consultations. Two more locations can be found at the Venetian (702-735-3896) and Town Square (702-361-3727) at 6671 Las Vegas Boulevard, Space A-131.

The Reading Room is the only bookstore on the Strip. Charo Burke

St Andrews Golf Shop (702-897-9500; www.cgclv.com; 6730 Las Vegas Boulevard South) Like to try before you buy? St Andrews is part of the Callaway Golf Center, making the store more like part of a golf amusement park. This retail shop is 5,000 square feet and boasts 13,000 golf-related items on-site. There's selection, a par-27, nine-hole course, and Bistro 101 to grab a bite to eat. For golfers is there much more? Suite 160.

Outlet Malls

Fashion Outlets of Las Vegas (702-874-1400; I-15 at Exit 1, Primm) Las Vegas in the name is a bit misleading. It's more like 30 minutes outside Las Vegas on the Nevada/California border. But, for serious deal seekers, there are serious deals, up to 75 percent off, to be found here. Stop by any of the 100 or more name-brand retailers such as the **Williams-Sonoma** outlet for bargains on home and cooking accessories; the **Old Navy** outlet store for fun, casual apparel; **Nine West** outlet for some dazzling shoes; **Zales** outlet for sparking diamonds, the **Hugo Boss** men's clothier, **Kenneth Cole,** and Neiman **Marcus's Last Call** on a variety of goods. If you think it's too far from Las Vegas, think again. The mall offers $15 round-trip Shoppers Shuttle trips from MGM Grand Hotel and Casino, Miracle Mile Shops at Planet Hollywood Resort & Casino, and the Fashion Show Mall, as well as return trip times throughout the day, seven days per week. Shopping packages are also available with casinos as well as the nearby Primm Valley Resort & Casino that can offer discounted hotel rooms, dining deals, and even Desperado roller coaster passes for your overnight shopping extravaganza.

Las Vegas Outlet Center (702-896-5599; www.premiumoutlets.com; 7400 Las Vegas Boulevard South) Though the Las Vegas Outlet Center is located on the Strip, it's at the southern end and is not a pleasant walk from the nearest resort, Mandalay Bay. It is best to drive, take a cab, or ride the Deuce bus. It isn't the fanciest mall in Las Vegas, but maybe it shouldn't be. A glitzy outlet mall may defeat the purpose of shopping there, deals. Of the three outlet malls, this is the most accessible when it comes to cost. The stores are mainstream, few are posh, and most are casual. The stores here are easily recognizable like **Adidas, Coach, Reebok** and **Tommy Hilfiger.** The 130 shops are not surrounded by themed décor or dancing topiaries. Here, it's purely about the shopping. There is an annex located at the south end of the parking lot. This is where **Nine West** and **Saks Fifth Avenue's Off 5th** are and they can be easily missed. If these stores are of interest, start here. The mall is laid out in a linear fashion and once you get to the end, getting back is fatiguing. Don't expect fine dining at this mall. There is sustenance to be found at the two food courts. Separate from the mall but in the parking lot are national chain restaurants.

The best outlet store selection is at Premium Outlets.
Leah Koepp

Las Vegas Premium Outlets (702-474-7500; www.premiumoutlets.com; 875 South Grand Central Parkway) Located in downtown Las Vegas adjacent to the World Market Center, Las Vegas Premium Outlets is the place locals and tourists alike go for deals on high-end clothes, shoes, and accessories. You'll find an outlet here for many major name brands: **Kenneth Cole, Lacoste, Nautica, Brooks Brothers, Tommy Hilfiger, Nine West, Coach, Salvatore Ferragamo**, and **Benetton** are all here. Even children's brands like **Gymboree, Polo Ralph Lauren Children**, and **Kids & Baby Gap** are here. Stroll this open-air mall's sidewalks and you'll also find Dooney & Burke, Guess, and Ed Hardy. There is only one sit-down restaurant in the Premium Outlets, a seafood and sushi buffet called Makino, a local favorite, and all other dining is food-court style. The fare available, however, is reasonably varied; there is a Dairy Queen and a Subway, but also Chinese, Italian, and Japanese fast food. Easy access from here to downtown and the Strip via West Charleston Boulevard.

Throughout Las Vegas

Academy Fine Books and Antiques (702-471-6500; 2026 East Charleston) The quintessential used bookstore with quasi-organization, including stacks of books on the floor and the smell of paper and dust: think "old library." The subject matter runs the gamut from history to new age to vintage comic books. Owner Gary is conversational and erudite, ready to share his personal story about that famous L.A. poet whose book you're looking for.

The Attic (702-388-4088; www.atticvintage.com; 1018 South Main Street) Claims to be the largest vintage clothing store in the world. And while that can't be confirmed, it is one of the most fun. From wigs to chairs, this store has it all. The best-made souvenir in town in one of the Attic's Las Vegas welcome sign bowling shirts. This is for someone who's looking for quality and not something to be shoved in the back of the closet. Lovers of vintage clothing relish the opportunity to wear an ensemble not found at the mall. The Attic is the anti-mall.

Bass Pro Shop (702-730-5200; www.basspro.com; 8200 Dean Martin Drive) While there are not any bass to be caught anywhere in the vicinity of the Las Vegas metro area, Bass Pro Shop opened their first West Coast store here. Like the others, it is massive and stocked with everything an outdoor enthusiast needs or desires. There's streams, waterfalls, stocked aquariums and ponds, dioramas, bass-fishing demos, and old-timey shooting gallery, so it's a nice side trip for little ones. For the bigger folks there's an archery range, rock wall, golf simulator, and rifle range that are available for a small fee. Should everyone traveling on this trip to Las Vegas not feel the same way about the outdoors, the Silverton Lodge and Casino is attached.

Bell Book and Candle (702-386-2950; www.lasvegasbbc.com; 1725 East Charleston Street) Bell Book and Candle has been around over 30 years, longer than any other occult store in Las Vegas. Like the name implies, the store carries books on all matters of subjects that by definition are considered occult. And candles, of course, both the ones for decoration and those that have specific purposes. The store is the only carrier in Las Vegas of Egyptian Uttati oils. If you're looking for Wicca classes and plan on staying in Las Vegas for a while, classes start every six to eight weeks. This is a good stop for an authentic tarot reading or astrology chart.

Cigar Box (702-405-5755; www.cigarbox.com; 1900 Western Avenue) While this book was being written, Cigar Box moved to a new and better store. What they had at the old location was more than 200,000 cigars from 30 brands. In the new spot the humidor is even grander than it used to be. The staff is very helpful and happy to show you how to choose the best cigar for you. There's a lounge for smoking them without getting an evil eye or suggestive cough.

Dead Poet Books (702-227-4070; 937 South Rainbow) Bless the locally owned bookstore with staff who are genial and not hipsters who can't believe you actually read that author, genre, or title. There's comfy seating and fair prices, too, making for a literary jackpot. There's a small LP section and an eclectic mix of new Tarot card collections.

D'Loe House of Style Then and Now (702-382-5688; 220 East Charleston) Vintage fabulousness can be found past the doors of this hot pink and blue façade. Owned by Mario D'Loe, a Cirque du Soleil costume designer, celebrities like Brad Pitt and The Killers have been seen sporting über-cool shirts of eras gone by from these very same racks. The finds here are mostly menswear from the 1950s to the 1970s.

Unlike other Las Vegas shops, Funk House is not about couture and labels. Charo Burke

Funk House (702-678-6278; www.thefunkhouselasvegas.com; 1228 South Casino Center Boulevard) The objects of the 1950s and 1960s are a draw for lovers of design aesthetic, especially glass, toys, and jewelry. The Funk House has a strong collection of these, plus really off-the-wall items, the most attention-grabbing of which are the snappily decorated coffins for sale. Use one as a coffee table or to say good-bye to a loved one.

Gambler's Book Shop (702-382-7555; www.gamblersbook.com; 1550 East Tropicana Avenue #4) If you believe the casinos can be beat at their own game, this store carries the book on it. From poker to roulette to sports betting, there are over 4,000 titles here, including out-of-print books. There are also books on luck, the history of the con artist, and professional poker player bobble heads. Since 1964, Howard Schwartz—a.k.a. "the gamblers' librarian"—has personally reviewed more than 1,000 gambling books in 30 subcategories. He and the staff believe in moderation and preach "money management."

Gambler's General Store (702-382-9903; www.gamblersgeneralstore.com; 800 South Main Street) Wish you had a vintage slot machine that resembled a one-armed bandit for the den? This is the place to find one. Calling themselves the world's largest gambling superstore may not be that far off. It's hard to imagine a bigger one anywhere else in the world. From chips from casinos long gone to personalized chips for the weekly game back home, this store has what every gambler, novice to professional, might want.

If it's a book, DVD, or pamphlet about gambling, it's probably in stock at Gambler's General Store. Charo Burke

Gem and Bead Mall (702-616-6809; 1335 East Sunset Road, Suite D) For anyone who makes jewelry for fun or for a living and for those who are just plain crafty, the Gem and Bead Mall is a must stop. The walls of this 5,000-square-foot warehouse are lined with beads and gemstones. In between the walls are tables filled to the hilt with more beads and gemstones. The glass cases contain the more valuable items such as turquoise, amber, zoisite, coral, jade, and Swarovski crystals. For the beading enthusiast, they also carry books, tools, a large selection of wires, displays, and findings. The décor inside is what it is. The only color in the place comes from the beads themselves. But because it is very clean and well lit, perusing is fun. The employees are very warm and helpful, even to novices. There is a comfortable seating area for the non–bead lover and they offer magazines and bottled water. This is one of only two locations in the country. The original store is in San Diego, California.

Gypsy Caravan Antiques (702-868-3302; 1302 South 3rd Street) Not a storefront in the traditional sense, Gypsy Caravan Antiques is comprised of a few historic cottage homes. In the courtyard are architectural, garden, and patio items that, while too big to pack in a suitcase, are fun to peruse. There are so many treasures throughout the cottages that it can be a bit overwhelming. When this happens, head back to the courtyard for a rest stop.

The Gem & Bead Mall has items for the bead enthusiasts and comfy couches for the non-enthusiasts. Crystal Wood

Main Street Antiques, Art & Collectibles
(702-382-1882;
www.mainstreetantiqueslv.com; 500 South
Main Street) If you can't find something to
smile at in this 15,000-square-foot, two-
story store, then maybe collectibles shopping isn't for you. To help in finding the
right genre of collectible, there's the Tiki
room for the island-inspired items, the
Silver Slipper room features accent furniture made of chrome and glass, and a room
dedicated to Route 66 and Sunset Highway.
There are of course rooms that favor vintage Vegas and Elvis. They offer gift wrap-
ping and worldwide shipping.

Rainbow Feather Dyeing Company (702-
598-0988; www.rainbowfeatherco.com;
1036 South Main Street) This is a feather
extravaganza. There's goose, duck,
chicken, peacock, turkey, pheasant, and
ostrich by the pound and they can be custom dyed or come in the standard rainbow of colors. There are boas of every

Main St. Antiques is fun even for those not interested in buying. Charo Burke

type of feather and color ranging from $3.50 to $115. There are earrings of beaded peacock
feathers and superb fans that unfold to almost 180 degrees. And some of the best angels'
wings (children's and adult sizes) that you are likely to see—at a perfectly reasonable price.

Ralph Jones Display (702-382-4398; www.ralphjones.com; 2576 East Charleston) Some
may consider it an odd choice for a shopping listing in a travel book, but this store is
important to know about. If you own or manage a company or are one of the 5.9 million
conventioneers attending one of the 22,000 conventions and meetings in Las Vegas, Ralph
Jones Display may come in handy. The company sells a variety of hardware and shelving,
racks, cases, furniture, fixtures, mannequins, counters, and counter display items that can
complete any products in a sales booth or retail outlet. And when it comes to holiday sales,
Ralph Jones Display takes "it's the season" merriment very seriously. Customers can buy
decorated trees, ribbons, ornaments, floral arrangements, lights, and garlands that are
elegant and befitting your organization. Ask for design assistance from one of their
Christmas experts.

Record City (702-735-1126; www.recordcityonline.com; 300 East Sahara Avenue) Vintage
vinyl fans rejoice! Located two blocks east of the Strip and in a no-frills building that is easy
to miss, this is the first of three near-the-action locations in Las Vegas. (Go to 553 East
Sahara Avenue or 4555 East Charleston Boulevard locations for additional selections.)
Record City, with its thousands of items in inventory, has been a source of rare and hard-to-
find music, movies, and collectibles for over twenty years. A visit to Record City will allow
you to consult with a knowledgeable staff and find copies of those missing records from
days gone by. This place can easily accommodate the casual browser to serious collector.

Red Rock Running Company (702-870-4786; 7350 West Cheyenne) Looking for the flashiest or hottest running shoe? Then this isn't the store for you. But if you are looking for the best running shoe for your run, have questions, and want to trust the person helping you choose, then a stop here is recommended. Along with the best selection of shoes, they also carry apparel, accessories, and, of course, socks. For a detailed fitting, call ahead for an appointment. This includes: treadmill shoe analysis, foot evaluation, current shoe review and inspection, goals, past injuries, and history. All before even trying on a shoe.

Sedona Style (702-732-4002; www.sedonastyle.net; 7850 Dean Martin Drive) Fight the overpriced, snobby home stores and stop by the locally owned Sedona Style. Here are imports from Italy, Spain, Mexico, and other locales with a rustic style with an acceptable price tag. The furnishings here include chairs, tables, lamps, and mirrors. The choice of accessories ranges from masks to ceramic pots. All are artfully stuffed into a rather diminutive storefront, but that's also part of the fun.

Serge's Showgirl Wigs (www.showgirlwigs.com; 953 East Sahara Avenue A-2) The female locks and tresses on the stages of Las Vegas are often supplemented. From showgirl to lounge singer, the facade of a flowing, perfectly coiffed mane is as important to a Las Vegas image as any logo. For more than 30 years, Serge's Showgirl Wigs has been here to assist the women of Las Vegas keep up that image and maybe save them some time getting ready for work. With the largest wig showroom in the country, carrying 2,000 wigs and stylists on duty full time, there's something here for every wig wearer and wannabe wig wearer. Prices range from $200 to $1,700.

Sharmark (702-362-8621; www.sharmark.com; 3320 Wynn Road) For 25 years Sharmark has helped accessorize brides, rodeo queens, and lovers of beaded crochet. Their handcrafted crochet vests were showcased in a *Sports Illustrated* swimsuit issue set in Rio. The caplets, shawls, handbags, vests, capes, and ponchos have a distinct romantic look; some are heavily beaded and others let the stitch pattern come through. Though you may have seen their Sharmark or Knot-Knots label carried at stores around the nation, the prices here are far more reasonable.

St. Aubin for Trains (702-644-4799; www.staubinonline.com; 1335 East Sunset Road) Serious collectors of large-scale garden trains know what it means to have a St. Aubin's store nearby. The only other one is located in Woodstock, Illinois, and it is mighty famous. For those who are curious about this hobby or just want to look around, the owners and employees are friendly and outgoing. Questions are treated with respect, not snickering. The store is not as dressed up as the Illinois location—it has more of a warehouse look. Each month the Las Vegas Garden Railway Society take monthly outings. Anyone is welcome to join the club. Dues are $20 per year and the application form can be found at the register.

Model train collecting is alive and well in Las Vegas. Crystal Wood

T&T Ginseng is the real thing for Chinese herbs and medicine. Charo Burke

T&T Ginseng (702-368-3898; 4115 Spring Mountain Road E103) Tea lovers and those interested in Chinese herbal medicine should take the short trek to Las Vegas's Chinatown to check out their interesting wares. The selection is overwhelming and fascinating at the same time. There is ginseng in barrels and scores of herbs and teas, and an herbalist on site.

Valentino's Zoot Suit Connection (702-383-9555; www.valentinoszootsuitconnection.com; 906 South Sixth Street #103) Those Carmen Miranda chunky high heels of the 1940s are back in style because, as everyone knows, what's old is new again. The looks of the 1920s through the 1950s are in style again because the clothes had exactly that: style. Why wear just any cocktail dress to the party? Go with the one that shows class and originality. Valentino's has options for men, too, like Hawaiian broadcloth shirts, hand-painted ties, and, of course, zoot suits. No man should leave Las Vegas without a powder-blue felt fedora. Like their slogan says, "for the cool in you." The only drawback is that the store doesn't have any choices in the larger sizes.

The upcoming City Center will have a 4,000-room resort, four more hotels, and an Elvis-themed Cirque du Soleil show. CityCenter Land LLC

10

INFORMATION

Simple and Handy Help

Vacations should be fun, not stressful. We've included this chapter to help you prepare for your trip and provide you with basic information you may need while in Las Vegas and the surrounding areas. Use this list to quickly find the information you need:

AMBULANCE, FIRE, AND POLICE

Dial 911 in the Las Vegas area to reach all emergency services. For nonemergency police matters, dial 311.

AREA CODE

Calling between Las Vegas, Henderson, and Green Valley is free of charge; the area code is 702 for all of Clark County.

BIBLIOGRAPHY

Architecture

Barnard, Charles F. *The Magic Sign: Electric Art—Architecture of Las Vegas.* Cincinnati: ST
    Publications, 1993.
Hess, Alan, and Robert Venturi. *Viva Las Vegas: After-Hours Architecture.* San Francisco:
    Chronicle, 1993.
Highsmith, Carol, and Ted Landphair. *Las Vegas: A Photographic Tour.* Hills, MN: Crescent
    Publishing, 2003.

Reynolds, Deon. *Las Vegas: Portrait of a City*. Portland, OR: Graphic Arts Center Publishing Company, 2006.

Fiction
Goldman, William. *Heat*. New York: Warner Books, 1985.
King, Stephen. *The Stand*. New York: Doubleday, 1990.
O'Brien, John. *Leaving Las Vegas*. Wichita, KS: Watermark Press, 1991.
Ventura, Michael. *The Death of Frank Sinatra*. New York: Henry Holt, 1996.

Gaming
Alvarez, A. *The Biggest Game in Town*. Boston: Houghton Mifflin, 1983.
Craig, Michael. *The Professor, The Banker, and The Suicide King: Inside the Richest Poker Game of All Time*. New York: Warner Books, 2005.
Holden, Anthony. *Big Deal: A Year as a Professional Poker Player*. New York: Viking, 1990.
McManus, James. *Positively Fifth Street: Murderers, Cheetahs, and Binion's World Series of Poker*. New York: Farrar, Straus, and Giroux, 2003.
Mezrich, Ben. *Bringing Down the House: The Inside Story of Six M.I.T. Students Who Took Las Vegas For Millions*. New York: Free Press, 2002.

History and Culture
Ainlay, Jr., Thomas "Taj," and Judy Dixon Gabaldon. *Las Vegas: The Fabulous First Century*. Mount Pleasant, SC: Arcadia Publishing, 2003.
Burbank, Jeff. *Las Vegas Babylon: True Tales of Glitter, Glamour, and Greed*. New York: M. Evans and Company, Inc., 2005.
Chung, Su Kim. *Las Vegas Then & Now*. Berkeley: Thunder Bay Press, 2002.
Ferrari, Michelle, and Stephen Ives. *Las Vegas: An Unconventional History*. New York: Bulfinch Press, 2005.
Pileggi, Nicholas. *Casino:* Love and Honor in Las Vegas. New York: Simon & Schuster, 1995.
Schumacher, Geoff. *Sun, Sin and Suburbia: An Essential History of Las Vegas*. Las Vegas: Stephens Press, 2004.
Thompson, Hunter S. *Fear and Loathing in Las Vegas: A Savage Journey to the Heart of the American Dream*. New York: Random House, 1976.

Films
21 (2008)
Con Air (1997)
Corvette Summer (1978)
Damnation Alley (1977)
Diamonds Are Forever (1971)
Domino (2005)
Fear and Loathing in Las Vegas (1998)
Honeymoon In Vegas (1992)
Leaving Las Vegas (1995)
National Lampoon's Vegas Vacation (1997)
Ocean's Eleven (1960, 2001)
Resident Evil: Extinction (2007)
Swingers (1996)

Very Bad Things (1998)
Viva Las Vegas (1964)
What Happens In Vegas (2008)
The Hangover (2009)

CHILD CARE

Las Vegas was touted as a family destination in the 1990s, but here in the 21st century, it seems the pendulum is swinging back the other way. There are many places you can take kids, but at those times when it isn't convenient to include the kids, here's a short list of licensed child care centers and providers. Parents can contact the Nevada Division of Child and Family Services, Bureau of Services for Child Care at 775-684-4463 for more information about child care providers and to view their licensing information.

Some available options include:

Kids Quest (hourly rate applies; located inside all Station Casino properties and inside the Palms Hotel-Casino; five hours maximum and parents must remain on the property)

Around The Clock Child Care (702-365-1040; located at 2692 Redrock Street Suite 2, Las Vegas, 89146; four-hour minimum of $48 per child and $10 each additional hour)

Nannies and Grannies (702-364-4700; www.nanny4u.com; providers come to you; $60 minimum, first four hours for one child)

CLIMATE AND WEATHER

Since the Las Vegas valley is a desert, one might assume that it's always hot, or at least warm year-round, but this is not the case. Even though the seasonal changes aren't outwardly apparent, make sure to prepare for both heat and cold, and the pesky winds that plague the area especially during the spring and fall.

Spring: Ah, spring! In Vegas it is the absolute best time of year, weather-wise. Stunning sunny days and clear, cool nights are the norm. Daytime temperatures in the 70s and 80s are not uncommon as early as mid-March. Spring also brings wind, however, and that wind can still have a little winter (and a lot of dust) in it. In early spring (mid-March to mid-May) have a jacket or sweater and pants along, just in case. By mid- to late-May, temperatures have warmed considerably and may even be hitting the 100s.

Summer: No two ways about it—in Vegas, the only thing hotter than the slots is summer. The heat is no joke, either. During the day, temperatures routinely rise into the 100s, and may rise into the 110s; evening temperatures will still hover in the upper 80s. Wearing sunscreen is imperative, as is drinking plenty of water, and a hat can be your best friend. Light clothing is a must while outdoors during the day, and the only time a jacket or sweater is necessary is in the case of extreme air conditioning. Afternoon pop-up thunderstorms are not uncommon from July through late August.

Autumn: Another wonderful time of year to be in Vegas. Late September can still be hot, but once October begins and the nights lengthen a bit, the daytime temperatures once again dip into the 80s and low 90s, making for some gorgeous weather. Even into November, daytime temps usually stay in the 60s and 70s, with evenings getting down into the 50s. However, as with spring, as autumn progresses winds can manifest and be quite chilly at times. It's not a bad idea to have a jacket and long pants handy, especially later in autumn when those winds herald winter's approach.

Winter: It can get surprisingly cold in the desert, and here in Vegas we definitely feel the chill during the winter months. Daytime temps usually run in the 50s in December and January, but can dip into the 40s when a weather system blows in from the west. Nights get cold, and temps in the 30s are possible, especially when it's windy, which is often the case in winter. In most years precious little rain actually falls, but winter is Vegas's rainy season, so at times an umbrella or raincoat may be necessary.

Avg. Temperatures (degrees Fahrenheit)/Precipitation: January 58/.50, February 63/.45, March 69/.40, April 78/.20, May 88/.20, June 100/.20, July 106/.45, August 103/.55, September 95/.30, October 82/.25, November 67/.45, December 58/.30

SPECIAL-NEEDS SERVICES

Visitors with special needs will find Las Vegas easy to navigate. Accessibility is the rule at all Vegas properties; contact hotel concierges or front desks with special requests or questions. Most showrooms, casinos, attractions, restaurants and swimming pools all offer special-needs access, and the elevated crosswalks are equipped with elevators for use by wheelchairs and scooters. Both the Las Vegas Deuce bus and the Monorail are accessible to wheelchairs. Local companies from which wheelchairs and scooters can be rented include **Ability Center** (702-434-3030), **Active Mobility** (702-736-4399), and **Better Life Mobility Center** (702-876-9606) and many Strip and downtown properties have scooters available for rental on-site. Transportation for special-needs visitors can be arranged through **Nevada Medi-Car** (702-382-5820) or **Las Vegas Transportation** (702-248-2631), which also offers a service called **Scooter Moves** (800-621-1535) that caters to the luxury scooter set, featuring Lincoln limousines and Town Cars equipped with state-of-the-art lift systems.

INSIDER TIP: If a wheelchair would be helpful due to all the walking in Las Vegas, check with the front or bell desks of your hotel, or even the one you're just sightseeing in. Many have wheelchairs available at no charge, though a credit card is needed for a deposit.

HOSPITALS

Centennial Hills Hospital
702-835-9700
6900 North Durango Drive, Las Vegas

Desert Springs Hospital
702-733-8800
2075 East Flamingo Road, Las Vegas

Southern Hills Hospital and Medical Center
702-880-2100
9300 West Sunset Road, Las Vegas

Spring Valley Hospital Medical Center
702-853-3000
5400 South Rainbow Boulevard, Las Vegas

St. Rose Dominican Hospital
702-564-2622
102 East Lake Mead Parkway, Henderson

St. Rose Dominican Hospital—San Martin Campus
702-492-8000
8280 West Warm Springs Road, Las Vegas

St. Rose Dominican Hospital—Siena Campus
702-616-5000
3001 St. Rose Parkway, Henderson

Summerlin Hospital and Medical Center
702-233-7000
657 Town Center Drive, Las Vegas

Sunrise Hospital and Medical Center
702-731-8000
3186 South Maryland Parkway, Las Vegas

Valley Hospital Medical Center
702-388-4000
620 Shadow Lane, Las Vegas

LOCAL MEDIA

Newspapers
Las Vegas CityLife
Las Vegas Review-Journal
Las Vegas Sun
Las Vegas Weekly

Magazines
Las Vegas Life
Las Vegas Magazine
Vegas Magazine

Television
KVBC Channel 3 (NBC)
KLAS Channel 8 (CBS)
KTNV Channel 13 (ABC)
KVVU Channel 5 (Fox)
KLVX Channel 10 (PBS)
KVCW Channel 33, Cable 6 (Independent; The CW)
KINC Channel 15 (Spanish Language; Univision)

Getting Hitched Sin City Style

What's the most popular thing to do in Las Vegas besides gamble? Get married! More than 100,000 couples per year get married in Vegas, making it the number-one wedding destination in the world. Why Vegas? Partly because, well, who doesn't want to tell their friends they had a Vegas wedding? Also, the options available to couples planning weddings are practically limitless—you can get married by Elvis, James Bond, or Liberace if you desire. You and your betrothed can be driven to the altar by Elvis (or a reasonable facsimile thereof, wink wink). You can drive yourself to the altar, on a Harley, and get married astride your hog. You can even

Not all Las Vegas weddings are on the Strip.
Courtesy Loews Lake Las Vegas Resort

(and we know this sounds crazy) have a totally traditional wedding with all the trimmings, the white wedding gown, the tux, and everything, and totally forget that you're getting married mere steps from the Strip. But probably the number one reason to get married in Las Vegas: it's so damn easy. Read carefully, because here's the legal skinny on marriage in Nevada:

- The bride and groom both need to appear in person to apply for the marriage license.

- The charge for a marriage license is $55.00, cash only (it IS Vegas, after all).

- You'll need to show a government-issued photo ID—a valid driver's license, passport, birth certificate, or valid military ID are all acceptable.

- If you have been previously divorced, you don't need to produce your divorce decree when applying for a marriage license. The state of Nevada will take your word for it when you sign on your license application that you are legally divorced.

- Nevada doesn't require a waiting period or blood test to process your application. Upon providing the correct documents and paying your money, your license is issued on the spot.

- More in-depth information (including information for visitors from abroad) can be found at www.accessclarkcounty.com/depts/clerk/pages/marriage_information.aspx.

You can apply for a license at any of these marriage bureau locations:

IN LAS VEGAS:

Regional Justice Center
201 East Clark Avenue
Las Vegas, NV 89155
Phone: 702-671-0600
Fax: 702-385-8911
Hours: 8:00 AM–12:00 midnight daily, including holidays.

IN HENDERSON:
240 South Water Street
Henderson, NV 89015
Phone: 702-455-1055

Fax: 702-455-1056

Hours: Thurs. and Fri. 7:30 AM–6:00 PM (closed for lunch from noon to 12:30 PM). Closed all legal holidays.

IN MESQUITE:

500 Hillside Drive

Mesquite, NV 89027

Phone: 702-346-1867

Fax: 702-346-1513

Hours: Wed. 8:30 AM–3:30 PM (closed for lunch 11:30 AM–noon), Fri. 3:00 PM–9:00 PM, and Sat. 9:00 AM–3:00 PM. Closed all legal holidays.

IN LAUGHLIN:

101 Civic Way

Laughlin, NV 89029

Phone: 702-298-1097

Fax: 702-298-5385

Hours: Sat. thru Thurs. 8:00 am–5:00 pm, Fri. 8:00 am–8:00 pm (closed for lunch noon–1:00 pm). Closed all legal holidays.

Now that you're legal, it's time to decide where to tie the knot. Here's just a sampling of chapels, to get you started:

Vegas Weddings (800-823-4095; www.702wedding.com; 320 South Third Street and 555 South Third Street) Vegas Weddings has two locations, both in downtown Las Vegas—their original location, at 320 South Third Street, known as their Garden Chapel, and their newest chapel at 555 South Third Street. Both sites feature beautiful, intimate wedding chapels as well as reception rooms, but the newer location, opened in summer 2008, boasts The Wedding Chapel, which can accommodate up to 100 guests, and is adorned with stained-glass windows, a grand piano, and crystal chandeliers hanging from a high, dramatic ceiling. Automated doors are opened at the beginning of each ceremony, for that "Aaaaaaah" moment as the bride enters the chapel. There are two other, smaller chapels on-site, as well as a warm and inviting reception area that can accommodate up to 80 guests. The most unique feature of the 555 South Third Street location, besides its charming appearance (it has the look of a country church, complete with stone exterior and white steeple), is "The Fast Lane," a drive-through tunnel that not only protects the wedding parties from the wind and weather as they arrive but also houses the world's only walk-up wedding window. As for services, Vegas Weddings employs its own florists and photographers, so they can handle every detail of that special day and offer wedding and vow renewal packages at many different price points; they also coordinate off-site weddings in places like the Grand Canyon, Valley of Fire, and Lake Mead. And yes, they do Elvis weddings!

Chapel of the Flowers (800-843-2410; www.littlechapel.com; 1717 Las Vegas Boulevard South) Located right on Las Vegas Boulevard just south of downtown, Chapel of the Flowers is an oasis of tranquility in the midst of the excitement of the Strip. You won't find any madcap matrimony action here: Elvis hasn't just left the building—he's never been anywhere near the building. Chapel of the Flowers offers a traditional, intimate wedding experience; each of their three chapels, the Victorian, the Magnolia, and the La Capella, is tastefully decorated with romance in mind. Also on the grounds are the Gazebo and the Gardens, each a great setting for al fresco weddings. The Gazebo accommodates eight guests, perfect for those very intimate outdoor ceremonies. The Gardens can be utilized for both weddings and receptions, and accommodates weddings of up to 100 guests and receptions of up to 60. And although it's an outdoor setting, it can be completely enclosed to keep out the elements if need be. Chapel of the Flowers provides each client with their own wedding coordinator and handles all the floral, photography, and videography details on-site so that special day can be as worry-free as possible.

Viva Las Vegas Theme Weddings (800-574-4450; www.vivalasvegasweddings.com; 1205 Las Vegas Boulevard South) If you're planning the quintessential Vegas wedding, this is place for you. Viva Las Vegas Theme Weddings is family-owned and operated; owner Ron Decar, along with his staff, brings his years of experience as a performer on the Las Vegas Strip to create ceremonies that aren't simply weddings, they're events. A host of themes are available, anything from Phantom of the Opera, to James Bond, to Intergalactic—you can even be driven to the altar by Elvis in his pink Cadillac! And if you dream up something for your special day that Viva Las Vegas doesn't offer, they will help you bring that dream to life. Of course, traditional wedding ceremonies are available as well, and can be performed in either their breathtaking indoor chapel or their intimate garden gazebo.

ROAD SERVICE

Having vehicle trouble is never pleasant, but a breakdown while on vacation can feel like a disaster. AAA members can call for emergency road service at 1-800-222-4357 (1-800-AAA-HELP) anytime, day or night. The Nevada Department of Transportation, or NDOT, offers the Freeway Service Patrol Program, which provides free roadside assistance to lost or stranded motorists. They don't work on an on-call basis, but Freeway Service Patrol vehicles regularly patrol the 215 beltway and I-15 corridor from the Las Vegas valley south to the Nevada/California state line. They patrol Monday through Friday from roughly 6:00 AM to 7:00 PM within the valley, and from Russell Road down to the state line on Saturday and Sunday from 10 AM to 6 PM. Call 775-888-7000 for more information.

SEASONAL EVENTS

It goes without saying that there's always something interesting and fun going on in Las Vegas, otherwise it just wouldn't be Vegas! However, not all the fun is always on the Strip or Fremont Street. There are many different events happening all year round, both in and around town, and most of them draw large crowds. We in Vegas are spoiled; parking is usually free, but be forewarned that at some events a fee may be imposed. Always bring plenty of water and sunscreen to outside events, and at some gatherings it may be advisable to bring along your own shade as well. Hats are de rigueur when enjoying the outdoors!

January

Celebrate Martin Luther King Jr.'s birthday by turning out for the annual **Martin Luther King Jr. Day Parade** in downtown Las Vegas. As the parade makes its way down 4th Street, cheer on the procession of cheerleaders, baton twirlers, fire trucks, local officials waving from the backseats of convertibles, high school marching bands, and the Las Vegas Buffalo Soldiers riding horseback in the brisk January sunshine. Check out a **UNLV Rebels basketball game** (www.unlv.edu) at the Thomas & Mack Center on the campus of UNLV, and don't forget to wear your Rebel red!

February

Even though Las Vegas never hosts the big game itself, **Super Bowl parties and celebrations** of all kinds are legion on Super Bowl weekend each year. Every Strip property, bar, and club in town has its own shindig, usually with food and drink specials and multiple massive screens televising the game; special cover charges are usually in effect. Hockey fans, cheer on the Las **Vegas Wranglers Hockey Club** (702-471-7825; www.lasvegaswranglers.com) of the ECHL AA Hockey League when they hit the ice for scheduled home games in the O-Rena at the Orleans Hotel and Casino you'll experience all the fun and excitement of big-league hockey, but in a more intimate venue and at a lower cost. Venture 45 minutes south on US 95 to Boulder City for the **Dam Short Film Festival** (702-293-4848; www.damshortfilm.org), a four-day-long annual film festival held at the historic 400-seat Boulder Theatre. Featuring over 100 short films and growing each year, the festival showcases the talents of independent short filmmakers from around the world, spanning all genres, including documentary, sci-fi, drama, comedy, and animation.

March

March is a big sports month in Las Vegas. The **Mountain West Conference College Basketball Championships** (866-388-FANS; www.unlvtickets.com) are held at the Thomas & Mack Center during the second week of March each year; the performance of teams playing in this tournament often determines who will make it to the NCAA Tournament. **NASCAR Weekend** at the Las Vegas Motor Speedway draws massive crowds every year with multiple races and events around town for fans; consult the Las Vegas Motor Speedway Web site (www.lvms.com) for dates, tickets and information. **Big League Weekend** takes place at Cashman Field (702-386-7200; www.lv51.com) in March of each year, although the name is a bit of a misnomer—over the years the event has been so popular that it's actually now comprised of two weekends, and often one of the weekends is in April. The Chicago Cubs, Seattle Mariners, and Colorado Rockies usually participate, and it's a great way to see some of your favorite teams in an intimate setting; Cashman Field seats about 15,000, and the smaller size of the stadium gives big league baseball a homey, minor-league feel.

Mirrored Bentleys on display at the Liberace Museum Courtesy Liberace Museum

April

Community events start to ramp up in April, and there are a few very popular happenings that take place this month. Take a sip for a scholarship at **UNLVino** (www.unlvino.com), Las Vegas's premier wine-tasting event presented by Southern Wine and Spirits of Nevada. It is a fund-raiser, all of the net proceeds of which benefit the William F. Harrah College of Hotel Administration. A Las Vegas institution for almost 40 years, UNLVino is comprised of three events, each priced and ticketed separately. Festivities kick off with Bubble-Licious, a champagne and sparkling wine tasting held on Thursday night; on Friday, Auss-Some and Then Some is an evening affair highlighting wines from the Southern Hemisphere. On Saturday afternoon, the Grand Tasting is held. The most popular event of the three, the Grand Tasting features hundreds of wines from about 750 wineries and is a must-attend for wine fans. Logandale, Nevada, a small farming town about an hour's drive north of Las Vegas, hosts the annual **Clark County Fair and Rodeo** at the Clark County Fairgrounds (888-876-FAIR; www.ccfair.com; 1301 Whipple Avenue, Logandale). The usual county fair elements are all here—four days of livestock and pet shows, art and craft exhibits, lots of down-home cookin', live music, magicians, jugglers, carnival games and rides, of course, the rodeo. The fair culminates on Sunday with the crowning of Miss Clark County Rodeo and the Professional Rodeo Cowboys Association rodeo finals. Chill out to hot sounds at the **Las Vegas City of Lights Jazz and Rhythm & Blues Festival** (800-969-VEGAS; www.yourjazz.com; 500 Grand Central Parkway) at the Clark County Government Building amphitheater. This venue, on the grounds of the new Clark County government headquarters, is a lovely oasis adjacent to the World Market Center in the middle of downtown Vegas. Each year the 10-hour City of Lights Festival features some of the biggest names in jazz and R&B performing in the awesome April sunshine. Although there is some shade available, it is advisable to bring along a hat and sunscreen, in case you can't find a spot in the shade. Food and merchandise vendors are on hand to provide refreshments and goodies.

May

In May, the temperatures heat up and so does the event calendar. **Las Vegas Helldorado Days** (www.elkshelldorado.com) is a Las Vegas tradition dating back to 1934, celebrating the characters that first settled in what was then a just another dusty desert mining town and the lifestyle of those early Las Vegans. The four-day festival's multiple events take place on the third weekend of May each year. There's a carnival, a poker tournament, a fireworks show, and a rodeo, and all events take place downtown. An event celebrating the more contemporary characters that make Las Vegas unique begins each May at the Rio Hotel and Casino: the **World Series of Poker** (www.wsop.com) deals its first hand during Memorial Day weekend each year. The tournament is open to the public, and with almost 60 separate events, and pots totaling thousands of dollars up for grabs in each one, both amateur and professional poker players go all-in vying for the big money. The tournament stretches through until July, when the 13-day World Championship No-Limit Texas Hold 'Em event takes place—the winner isn't determined until November, when the final table is played. If outdoor family-friendly fun is more your speed, take a ride 45 minutes southeast of Vegas to enjoy food, drink, fantastic weather, and the small-town charm of Boulder City at the **Spring Jamboree** (www.springjamboree.com), a yearly two-day celebration taking place on the first weekend of May at Escalante Park. Featured events are a 5K run, live music, belly dancers, and the Spring Jamboree car show, which spans both days.

June

Duck out of the desert heat and into a cool movie theatre for one of the many films featured in the **Cinevegas Film Festival** (www.cinevegas.com; www.palms.com) held in the second week of June at the Brenden Theatres inside the Palms Hotel and Casino. Cinevegas' popularity has skyrocketed in the last few years thanks to its ability to draw edgy young movie stars to its events, but it's more than just a party for celebrities, it's a serious film festival featuring submissions in all categories: drama, documentary, shorts, and animation, to name a few. Grab your sunscreen and your tie-dye T-shirt and head out to the Clark County Government Building amphitheatre for **Reggae in the Desert** (702-474-4000; www.reggaeinthedesert.com), which takes place the second weekend in June. Rock to the classic sounds of some reggae greats, snack on some authentic Caribbean fare, and feel "irie" with a few thousand of your best friends. All ages are welcome, and food vendors are on hand to keep you refreshed.

July

Most of July's annual events center around Fourth of July celebrations, parades, and fireworks. The **Las Vegas 51s Baseball Team**, the AAA affiliate of the Toronto Blue Jays, (702-386-7200; www.lv51.com; 850 Las Vegas Boulevard North) hosts two very popular back-to-back **Fireworks Nights** during the first weekend of July each year. Come out to Cashman Field, cheer on our 51s, and stay after the game for some fantastic fireworks. The beauty of AAA baseball is that you can have a full night of fun at the ballpark without draining your bank account, and the smaller minor-league parks give you an up-close view of the game you can't get at big-league parks. These games always sell out, so get your tickets early! For Independence Day celebration of a more cultural kind, join the **Las Vegas Philharmonic** at Hills Park in Summerlin (702-631-1000; www.lasvegasphilharmonic.com; 9100 Hillpointe Road) for an evening of marches and patriotic music performed under the stars. The finale, a full fireworks show staged by pyrotechnics wizards the Zambellis, is set to the "1812 Overture"; bring your picnic baskets and enjoy the show! Many of the Strip resorts host their own fireworks shows on the Fourth. **Station Casinos hosts "Lights Over Vegas,"** a multiproperty fireworks show with displays at their six properties: Red Rock Resort, Green Valley Ranch, Texas Station, Santa Fe Station, Fiesta Rancho, and Sunset Station and the **California Hotel** downtown hosts its very popular annual fireworks display. Check with the concierge or bell desk for details about your hotel's Independence Day festivities. The Summerlin Council coordinates its annual **Summerlin Patriotic Parade** each year on the Fourth, one of Las Vegas's largest parades each year. Tens of thousands of spectators line the parade route to take in the marching bands, floats, and helium balloons. The parade starts at 9 AM on Hillpointe Road in Summerlin and makes its way down Hills Center to Trailwood Drive. For more information, call the Summerlin Council at 702-341-5500.

August

The extreme Vegas heat keeps a damper on activities during the height of summer—it's a slow time of year, event-wise, and due to the heat, the off-season for tourists. That's why it's a great time to head up to the mountain cool of Cedar City, Utah (about a three-hour drive north from Las Vegas) and catch a play at the **Utah Shakespearean Festival** (1-800-PLAYTIX; www.bard.org). This extremely popular event showcases works of the Bard in both indoor and outdoor theaters, the latter modeled closely after the Globe Theatre, the

British theater where Shakespeare's plays originally ran. The festival calendar stretches from June through October, but July and August are the busiest months, with multiple venues hosting productions each day. And it's not only plays; there are literary seminars and symposia, play orientations that give you some background and perspective on the productions before you see them, and special non-Shakespearean productions. Cashman Field Center hosts the annual **Harvest Festival, the Original Art & Craft Show** (www.harvestfestival.com; 850 Las Vegas Boulevard North) during the final weekend of August. The festival features over 300 artisans showing and selling their unique handmade pottery, jewelry, clothing, accessories, home décor, and edible treats in the air-conditioned comfort of the big exhibit hall and a portion of the proceeds are donated to charity.

September

In many areas, September is the beginning of autumn, but in Vegas, it's just the end of the summer. Temperatures routinely get into the upper 90s and lower 100s, so folks still keep a low profile, but that doesn't mean that there's nothing at all to do. The **Las Vegas Greek Food Festival** (702-248-3896; www.vegasgreekorthodox.com) is four days of nonstop Greek food, music, dancing, and culture. All the authentic Greek faves are prepared while you wait—baklava, souvlaki, loukoumades, dolmathes, and saganaki, with retsina to wash them down. The courtyard is filled with vendors selling souvenirs and mementos, and the live entertainment is constant and raucous. St. John the Baptist Greek Orthodox Church hosts the Festival every year, and it's consistently one of the most popular events in town, which means parking is at a premium, and you should prepared to park a ways away from the festival and walk in. Cruise out to Water Street in downtown Henderson, just southeast of Las Vegas, for the **Super Run Car Show** (702-643-0000; www.superrun.com), taking place in late September. Classic cars, live entertainment, food, a variety of car- and racing-themed events, and hourly prize drawings are all part of this free three-day event. Proceeds from sales of food and concessions benefit local schools and sports teams, as well the Henderson Boys & Girls Club. **The San Gennaro Feast** (702-286-4944; sangennarofeast.com) is held twice annually in Las Vegas, once in May, and once again in mid-September. You'll partake of wonderful Italian food such as ravioli, gnocchi, spaghetti, and pizza, and delectable sweets like cannoli prepared before your eyes, and then maybe take a stroll through the fairground and play a few carnival games while enjoying some live entertainment. At San Gennaro, everyone's Italian for a night!

October

Hark back to days of old at the **Age of Chivalry Renaissance Festival** (702-455-8200; www.lvrenfair.com; 2601 East Sunset Road), presented by Clark County Parks and Recreation at Sunset Park. It's a three-day event in which you can get a glimpse of what life may have been like in the middle ages; methods of ancient warfare and craft are demonstrated, as well as styles of dress and everyday life. Grub and grog are on hand, too, and wenches to serve it. Keeping with the "Renaissance" theme, **Shakespeare in the Park** (www.hendersonlive.com) is presented the first weekend of October by the City of Henderson Cultural Arts and Tourism Department, and each performance is preceded by an Elizabethan Festival. Enjoy classic works by the Bard, presented by acclaimed theatre companies from around the nation, free of charge and under the stars at a beautiful suburban park in the Henderson/Green Valley Area. A little farther southeast in Boulder City is the annual **Art in the Park** (www.bouldercityhospital.org/art-in-the-park) event benefiting the Boulder City Hospital

The desert's beauty surrounds Las Vegas. Las Vegas News Bureau

Foundation. One of the largest juried outdoor art festivals in the southwest, this free two-day event is open to the public and routinely draws more than 100,000 visitors each year. It's so large they need three parks to pull it off—it's held in Escalante, Wilbur, and Bicentennial parks, and each of the event's two days feature live entertainment, food, art demonstrations, and raffles. The **World Finals of Professional Bull Riding (PBR)** (1-866-388-FANS; www.pbrnow.com; www.unlvtickets.com; 4505 South Maryland Parkway) hit Vegas in late October into early November; bronco busters from all over the world compete for big money and bragging rights at the Thomas & Mack Center.

November

Las Vegas observes Veterans Day with the largest **Veterans Day Parade** in the country, beginning downtown on Gass Avenue and making its way up Fourth Street to the Fremont Street Experience. Veterans past and present who have fought for our freedom are honored by the Mayor and other local officials, and marching bands demonstrate their skills while playing marches and patriotic music. The parade is free and the public is welcome. Patriotic goings-on continue Veterans Day weekend with the **Aviation Nation Air Show** (www.aviationnation.org) taking place out at Nellis Air Force Base. Aviation Nation is among the largest air shows in North America; it is two days of astounding aerial demonstrations of a wide variety of military aircraft and hardware, culminating each of the two days in an almost hour-long show featuring the USAF Thunderbirds. It is also free and open to the public, and there is no charge for parking. However, this is a very popular show and draws huge crowds each year, and Nellis AFB does not allow public parking on base. Free shuttle buses provide transportation onto the base, so consult the Aviation Nation Web site for information on where to park and where to catch the shuttle.

December

December is loaded with great things to do, both holiday-themed and otherwise. The **National Finals Rodeo** (www.nfrexperience.com) is one of the biggest events to hit Vegas all year; thousands of rodeo fans descend on Vegas to whoop and holler and cheer on their favorite rodeo stars at the Thomas & Mack Center. For the nine days that NFR is in town, rodeo fans are the belles of the ball; Strip and downtown resorts pull out all the stops catering to the cowboy crowd. Concurrent with the NFR is the **Cowboy Christmas Gift Show,** held each year at the Las Vegas Convention Center (702-892-0711; 3150 Paradise Road). Hundreds of vendors from all over North America are on hand showcasing their unique western-themed gifts, crafts, accessories, and pottery. Winter holidays in Vegas just wouldn't be complete without a trip through the **Magical Forest** at Opportunity Village (www.opportunityvillage.org; 6300 West Oakey), a winter wonderland for all ages featuring lots of holiday displays, photos with Santa, a train ride through the forest, and most importantly, hot chocolate and funnel cake. The Magical Forest is open nightly each year from just before Thanksgiving through New Year's Day. The **Conservatory and Botanical Gardens at Bellagio Las Vegas** (www.bellagio.com; 3600 Las Vegas Boulevard South) decks its halls with boughs of holly and other trappings of the season each year; stunning holiday displays are on view beginning directly after Thanksgiving through the entire month of December 7 days a week, 24 hours a day. Once the holidays are past, it's time to focus on **New Year's Eve;** many Strip properties host parties and fantastic fireworks shows each year, and the Strip itself is closed so that revelers can turn out by the thousands between the Sahara Hotel and the Mandalay Bay Hotel and ring in the New Year. The Downtown area also hosts many parties and fireworks displays; concerts rock the **Fremont Street Experience** up to midnight and beyond.

SMOKING AND THE NEVADA CLEAN INDOOR AIR ACT

In December of 2006, Nevada's smoking laws changed. For many, this may have marked an enormous turning point for Las Vegas. It's much simpler to list where you can smoke than where you can't. You can smoke in all casino gaming areas. This means you can't smoke in the restaurants, showrooms, bathrooms, elevators, or anywhere else in the casino. Smoking is permitted in stand-alone bars without a kitchen or food license. And you can still smoke in strip clubs and tobacco stores. Some casinos provide no-smoking gaming tables and poker rooms, but they are not required to.

General Index

Lodging by Price

Inexpensive	Under $50 per night
Moderate	$50 to $100 per night
Expensive	$100 to $150 per night
Very Expensive	$150 and above per night.

Inexpensive

Moderate

Expensive

Very Expensive

Dining by Price

Inexpensive	Up to $20
Moderate	$20 to $35
Expensive	$35 to $75
Very Expensive	$75 and up

Dining by Cuisine